The
Kosher
Baker

The Kosher Baker

Paula Shoyer

Over 160 Dairy-free Recipes from Traditional to Trendy

Brandeis University Press

WALTHAM, MASSACHUSETTS

PUBLISHED BY UNIVERSITY PRESS OF NEW ENGLAND

HANOVER AND LONDON

HBI SERIES ON JEWISH WOMEN
The HBI Series on Jewish Women is supported by a generous gift from Dr. Laura S. Schor.

BRANDEIS UNIVERSITY PRESS
Published by University Press of New England
One Court Street, Lebanon NH 03766
www.upne.com

Manufactured in China
Designed and typeset in Whitman and
Fresco Sans by Eric M. Brooks

For permission to reproduce any of the
material in this book, contact Permissions,
University Press of New England,
One Court Street, Lebanon NH 03766;
or visit www.upne.com

Library of Congress
Cataloging-in-Publication Data
Shoyer, Paula.
The kosher baker: over 160 dairy-free desserts
from traditional to trendy / Paula Shoyer.
    p. cm.—(HBI series on Jewish women)
Includes bibliographical references and index.
ISBN 978-1-58465-835-1 (cloth: alk. paper)
1. Jewish cookery. 2. Baking. 3. Desserts.
4. Milk-free diet—Recipes. I. Title.
TX724.S535   2010
641.5'676—dc22   2010011134

5 4 3 2 1

To GG,
my grandmother,
Sylvia Altman (z"l),
a baker extraordinaire,
famous for saying
"Isn't that the best?
You never had a cake
so good."

Contents

Throughout this book, the symbol ◇ indicates a recipe that is appropriate for Passover use.

2 : *Two-Step Desserts*

3 : *Multiple-Step Desserts & Breads*

Preface

In the beginning . . . my mother baked once a year with cake mixes during Passover.

My universe of homemade desserts was dark until a wind blew over from Brooklyn bringing the smell of yeast cake and rugelach baked by my grandmother, Sylvia Altman. Back in Long Beach, I had to fend for myself and bake desserts in my Easy Bake Oven, lamenting the choice of flavors, but grateful for the smell of my "kitchen."

Later, in high school, my best friend Limor invited me to her home for her mother Aliza's homemade chocolate babka. It was my first glimpse at the potential for great parve (dairy-free) desserts.

After thirty years of eating parve desserts that were the equivalent of sugar-covered cardboard at countless kiddushes *and* in people's homes, my husband's work led us to Geneva, Switzerland, where heavenly pastry shops were on every corner and kosher caterers baked delicious parve desserts.

In Geneva, I worked as a legal advisor and speechwriter for a Jewish organization for two years. After I gave birth to our lovely Emily, I returned to work and found my office less family-friendly than I had hoped. I decided it was time to take advantage of the culinary opportunities in Europe. I had always been happiest baking and I thought that cooking school would teach me how to bake better desserts for my family and friends; I was not seeking a new career. I enrolled in the Ritz Escoffier École de Gastronomie Française in Paris, France. There I learned to bake delicious buttery French desserts, but none I could eat after a meat meal. So I worked slowly and scientifically to convert every dessert I learned in school, plus those I tasted on my travels, into a kosher, parve dessert. Someone begged me to bake them a pear tart for a party. The next thing I knew, I was filling seven dessert orders a week for celebrations and dinner parties.

One day, someone asked me to teach a cooking class as a fundraiser for a Jewish organization—in French—and I enjoyed it so much that when I returned to the United States, I started the Paula's Parisian Pastries Cooking School. Though based in the Washington, D.C., area, I now teach cooking classes all over the country to satisfy the demand for great kosher food and desserts. After gaining some recipe testing and editing experience for two books in the Kosher by Design series, I realized that it was time to write my own book and share my recipes with everyone. To accomplish this, I needed one more ingredient—a publisher. At a Jewish food history conference in Washington, D.C., I had the pleasure of walking with Shulamit Reinharz to lunch. Shula is an author and professor at Brandeis University, of which I am an alum. Shula was happy to put me in touch with University Press of New England, who publishes for Brandeis, and the recipe was complete.

After having exhausted the few parve recipes in their favorite kosher cookbooks, kosher bakers are always looking for new parve dessert recipes. And they want more contemporary choices, too. Kosher bakeries are selling the same cookies and cakes I have eaten since I was a child!

The Kosher Baker brings you over 160 dairy-free desserts for every occasion and holiday—no matter who you are baking for. I've included updated classics, parve versions of your favorite dairy desserts, and some unique creations. There are cookies, cakes, plated desserts, tarts and pies, French pastries, and Passover, gluten-free, and no-sugar-added desserts. There is something for everyone.

I am an avid entertainer, often cooking for large groups, and I have found that what drives my dessert choice for each meal is the amount of time I have. Too often, I've left desserts for the last minute. To help you choose a dessert according to the time you have, I've organized the first three parts of the book (a fourth part is devoted to Passover and no-sugar-added desserts) according to approximate preparation time: part 1, under fifteen minutes; part 2, fifteen to thirty minutes; part 3, thirty minutes plus. Within each of these parts, there are chapters devoted to traditional categories of desserts.

In *The Kosher Baker*, you will find over forty-five desserts that can be mixed in one bowl and ready for the oven in less than fifteen minutes. If you have extra time, you may choose a dessert based on the nature of the event, who you are baking for, how motivated you are that day, or what fruit or other ingredients you have on hand. The organization of this book enables you to choose a dessert based on time, degree of challenge, category, or flavor. It is up to you.

Parve desserts are no longer something less than their dairy counterparts. The age of the kichel and that rainbow-colored sponge cake is officially over. I am declaring a new era in parve desserts. Kosher people are entitled to the same fabulous desserts everyone else is eating. Now you can fool everyone—though the skeptics will always want to be reassured that the delicious dessert you've just served them is really parve. And I say, let them ask!

Paula

Acknowledgments

Thanks to my skinny kids, Emily, Sam, Jake, and Joey, who can eat endless amounts of desserts and comment expertly. I love you. Andy, the greatest husband, father, and person I know, who this book sent to Weight Watchers, thank you for all of your love and unwavering belief that I could do this. To my parents and in-laws, brothers and their families, your love and confidence in me nourishes my soul.

Special thanks go out to my fan club: Limor Decter, Laurie Strongin, Suzin Glickman, Karina Schumer, Elena Neuman Lefkowitz, Nechama Shemtov, Judith Gold and Lisa Flaxman (z"l), for your love and for cheering me on through these many years, making sure I never gave up. I always appreciate the students of the Paula's Parisian Pastries Cooking School for the excitement they demonstrate each time we bake together and for begging me to write this book.

I could not have perfected these recipes without my international group of recipe testers: Rhonda Alexander-Abt, Limor Decter, Elena Neuman Lefkowitz, Maria Sloan, Lisa Silverman, Suzin Glickman, Aaron Bobeck, Trudy and Shira Jacobson, Marla Satinsky, Steve Shoyer, Andrea Neusner, Beth Heifetz, Evie Wolfson, Rachel Englender, Sarah Smith, and Selma Stern. Thank you for your time and attention to detail. All of my long hours in the kitchen were made so much more pleasant and easier by Betty Supo. Thank you for all your help in the kitchen and your advice on so many desserts.

The stunning photos are the work of Michael Bennett Kress, who is incredibly talented and a real mensch to work with. The design of the photos was done by Gina Okon, food stylist, who is so creative and approached each dessert, from simple to fancy, as a work of art to enhance even further. Another thank you goes out to my friend Barb Freda who consulted on the styling of the photos.

I am grateful to Lily Starr for lending me so many beautiful platters and dishes for the photo shoots. The pictures reflect her elegance and amazing aesthetic.

A round of applause to my creative team at the University Press of New England: Phyllis Deutsch, Eric Brooks, Richard Pult, David Corey, Amanda Dupuis, and Lys Ann Weiss. All of you provided amazing support and energy from the beginning and reassured me that I was in great hands. All of you really understood what I was trying to create. I cannot imagine a nicer, smarter, or more committed family of people to create this book with me. This book owes its polish to my editor Holly Jennings, who worked hard to keep improving the language and organization of the book. Finally, an extra thank you to Lisa Silverman for proofreading.

An Introduction to Kosher Baking

One of the key aspects of kosher laws is the separation between dairy and meat. Separate utensils are used for each, and a waiting period is observed between eating them. The kosher lifestyle often revolves around meat-based meals for Shabbat and holidays and kosher Jews are not permitted to eat dairy desserts after consuming a meat meal. For baking purposes, this means that any dessert following a meat meal must be "parve"—neither meat nor dairy.

A baker of parve desserts cannot use butter, milk, cream, or any ingredients containing any dairy component. What makes kosher baking unique is the ability to work around these restrictions and find dairy-free substitutes to prepare our favorite desserts. In some cases, dairy-free ingredients can be evenly substituted for their dairy equivalents but often the recipes require adjustments as some ingredients do not behave the same as the dairy ones. There are also some ingredients, such as condensed milk, which have no dairy-free equivalent—so you have to get very creative. The challenge for the kosher baker is to find successful substitutions or use techniques to create your own to give desserts the consistency and flavor required to mimic the dairy equivalent.

In 2010, we are spoiled with the availability of so many great dairy-free products for use in baking parve desserts. Kosher bakers did not always have so many dairy substitutions available to them. Our ancestors in biblical times were probably limited to using olive oil in desserts. Our Eastern European Ashkenazi great-great grandmothers living in the nineteenth century could only use fats rendered from meat and poultry to use in cakes—not a particularly healthy option. American cookbooks from the earlier part of the twentieth century all have vegetable oils in their dessert recipes, which work well in cakes and some cookies.

Things improved greatly during the twentieth century with the introduction of Crisco shortening in 1911, Rich Whip whipping cream in 1946, and Coffee Rich non-dairy creamer in 1961. Bakers could create flakier crusts with Crisco and use the parve creams to copy fancier American pies and French desserts. Although margarine was invented in France and introduced in the United States in the 1870s, it contained dairy products until sometime in the late 1960s or early 1970s.

Today, there are so many parve margarines to choose from to substitute for butter. We can also use soy milk, soy-based cream cheese and sour cream as well as high quality dairy-free chocolates to prepare great dairy-free desserts. All of these products are often available in regular supermarkets and have allowed me to create delicious desserts, in particular French pastries, which my ancestors never could.

In addition to greatly aiding the kosher community, these products are welcomed by the large non-kosher lactose-intolerant community, which also deserves tasty sweets. Most lactose-intolerant people were diagnosed soon after birth and have missed out on flavorful desserts their whole lives. There are also many people who choose to eat dairy-free diets as many studies link milk consumption with various medical symptoms and diseases. This book is my gift to anyone searching for dairy-free desserts that no one can tell contain no dairy.

How to Use This Book

I made it easy for you to choose a recipe because I have organized the book in a new way: Part 1 presents the fundamentals of kosher baking in the form of quick, easy and elegant desserts. All of the desserts are ready for the oven in approximately fifteen minutes or less and often require the use of only one bowl. Any secondary steps take moments. This section is for you if you are (1) a novice baker, (2) baking multiple desserts for one occasion, or (3) running out of time but still need a great dessert. This section includes one-bowl cakes and bar cookies, quick cookies, pastries made with frozen puff pastry, and easy tarts and pies.

Part 2 is for you if you (1) have more time on your hands or (2) are ready for two-step desserts or (3) are already are an experienced baker. This section consists of recipes that often require two steps and usually demand between fifteen and thirty minutes of prepa-ration time. Recipes include fancier cookies, layer cakes, pies, and pastries with fillings.

Part 3 contains desserts that require multiple steps, though each is manageable with good planning. These are often challenging desserts that require thirty minutes or more, and may include chilling part or all of the dessert for several hours or overnight. But even if you're not a master baker, you can find recipes for your skill level in this part—it includes some desserts that are actually easy to prepare, but do require more time to make than the recipes in parts 1 and 2. Some kosher cooks spend a lot of time design-ing creative meals and arranging beautiful tables; they really want to dazzle their guests with special desserts. If you are one of those cooks, you will enjoy making and serving the recipes in this part. It includes what I call the "designer collection": yeast breads and fancy cakes, petit fours, elegant French tarts, mousses, and plated desserts. Part 3 is also for the baker who plans well before Shabbat or a holiday. For example, you can make a dough one day and chill it, prepare a filling a few days later, and then assemble the final dessert after that. Each step is brief, but you can divide your work up over a few days.

Part 3 also contains a variety of challah recipes as well as unique ways to shape and flavor challahs for special occasions. Everyone has their favorite, but it's fun to try some new ones or experiment with new shapes and flavors.

Part 4 contains desserts that you need in your arsenal, even if you make them infrequently. It includes Passover desserts and no-sugar-added desserts. The Passover desserts are generally those recipes that have uniquely Passover ingredients. Additional desserts that are naturally gluten free and may be served on Passover are scattered throughout the book. These are indicated with a special "◊" icon, and also listed in the Passover section. There are even some year-round desserts in the book that can be easily modified for Passover with just one or two changes. All Passover desserts, including those that are variations on year-round desserts, are listed in the index to help you quickly find them.

I have included desserts with no added sugar because diabetes affects so many people in the Jewish community. No longer do your diabetic guests have to eat fruit while you eat pastries. These recipes are good enough for anyone.

Finally, there is a separate appendix of icings and sauces that you can mix and match with your desserts, as well as appendixes about resources and metric conversions.

Remember to read every recipe through before you start and make sure you have all the ingredients and equipment you need. Always double-check the oven temperature to make sure you set it right. Use the freshest ingredients. Don't rush. Be safe. And finally, make sure you share your desserts with others.

Bakeware, Tools, & Equipment

Kosher bakers either have separate parve baking equipment and utensils, or use meat equipment as dessert tends to follow meat-based meals. Any cook only wants to store what he or she actually needs. The following is a list of basic equipment you need to set up your kosher baking kitchen and bake the easier desserts of the book:

CAKE PANS

9 x 13-inch pan

11 x 14-inch glass pan

8-inch square pan

Two 8- or 9-inch round baking pans

9-inch loaf pan with non-stick coating

12-inch loaf pan with non-stick coating

8- to 12-cup capacity Bundt or tube pan—I like the silicone ones

9- to 10-inch springform pan

Muffin pans to hold 18 muffins/cupcakes—typically 2 muffin pans, each with 12 cups

Mini muffin pans

COOKIE SHEETS

Two large cookie sheets—Cookie sheets are rimless, though some may have a rim on one side to make it easier to remove from the oven. I prefer the lighter-colored ones as the darker metals retain more heat and can burn your desserts.

Jelly roll pan—a cookie sheet with about 1 inch sides. It is sometimes also called a "sheet pan."

PIE AND TART PANS

8- or 9-inch tart pan, either a ring with no bottom or one with a removable bottom

8- or 9-inch pie pan

SAUCEPANS

Double boiler or heatproof bowl that fits snugly over a
medium saucepan

Small heavy-bottomed saucepan

10- or 12-inch saucepan that is deep and has a heatproof handle
for use in the oven

UTENSILS AND EQUIPMENT

Stand or hand-held mixer with whisk, hook, and paddle attachments

Food processor

Dry measuring cups—include a 2-cup measuring cup, which makes
measuring go faster

Measuring spoons

2-cup liquid measuring cup, made of glass or clear plastic

2 to 3 silicone spatulas, different sizes

One wooden spoon

Large wire whisk

Small cookie cutters to decorate the tops of pies

Small, medium, and large stainless steel mixing bowls

Large microwave-safe glass bowl

Zester—either box grater or microplane

Silicone pastry brush

Cookie cutters—metal or plastic, different shapes, including several
sizes of round cutters

Large metal flat-blade spatula

Rolling pin—I like the long French ones—you can roll more dough
at a time

Fine-mesh strainer or sieve—for straining and sifting

Melon baller

Vegetable peeler

Juicer—either hand or electric

Scissors—designated for kitchen use only

Paper cupcake baking cups

Parchment paper or two Silpat silicone mats to fit your cookie sheets
and jelly roll pans

Parchment paper for rolling out dough

Waxed paper

Wooden or metal skewers or long toothpicks and regular-length
toothpicks to check cakes for doneness

Cooling racks

Long serrated knife to slice cake layers

SPECIALTY PANS AND TOOLS

(The pans and tools in this list are used for the fancier desserts in the book.)

Madeleine pans

Twelve 3- or 4-inch ramekins

Sixty 1½-inch mini tart pans

8- or 9-inch soufflé dish

Twelve 3-inch fluted molds—for chocolate molten cakes

Pastry bags with couplers and ¼-inch round and star tips. Additional tips will be useful but not necessary.

8-inch frying pan or crêpe pan

8-inch dessert ring with no bottom

8-inch cardboard circles

Pie weights—you can buy a jar of weights or use dried beans to bake a tart shell with no filling

Candy thermometer

Baking Ingredients

As in all aspects of keeping kosher, all packaged ingredients used in kosher baking must bear kosher certification. The individual brands that I recommend below all have kosher certification as of the writing of this book. You should always check the package to make sure that status has not changed. In addition, you may find baking products that are labeled "non-dairy." Do not assume they are parve unless they say so on the package. Any product labeled "non-dairy" without the parve label may contain traces of dairy and cannot be used in baking kosher parve desserts.

Flour—I prefer King Arthur flour

Granulated sugar

Confectioners' sugar

Brown sugar—light and dark

Baking powder

Baking soda

Pure vanilla extract—not imitation vanilla extract (except on Passover)

Apricot jam

Envelopes of active dry yeast—keep in the fridge

Unsweetened cocoa—everyone has their favorite, but Hershey's always works great

Unflavored kosher gelatin powder

Spray oil with flour

Spray oil

Margarine—Fleischmann's, Earth's Best. Keep some in the freezer.

Vegetable shortening—Crisco. Keep some in the freezer and some in the pantry.

Canola or vegetable oil

Eggs—all recipes are calibrated for large eggs. Please do not substitute any other size. Crack into a separate bowl and discard if there is a blood spot.

Parve plain soy milk—not vanilla-flavored

Parve whipping cream—Rich Whip

Parve coffee creamer—Coffee Rich

Parve cream cheese—Tofutti brand

Parve sour cream—Tofutti Sour Supreme

Frozen puff pastry sheets—Pepperidge Farm

Frozen puff pastry squares—I prefer Mazors, but Kinneret is fine too

Filo dough

Parve bittersweet or semisweet chocolate— my favorite is Alprose, a Swiss brand

Parve chocolate chips—Trader Joe's has great chips that are also completely nut-free

PASSOVER INGREDIENTS

Matzoh cake meal

Potato starch

Matzoh farfel

Kosher for Passover baking powder

Kosher for Passover imitation vanilla extract

Almond flour

Ground hazelnuts

Foolproof Tips & Techniques

The following are techniques that you will use throughout this book as well as in all your baking. Many are the tips I have taught my cooking school students over the years.

CRACKING EGGS

Crack into a separate bowl and discard if there is a blood spot. A blood spot renders an egg unkosher.

GREASE AND FLOUR BAKING PAN

To grease and flour a baking pan, use spray oil containing flour and spray all around the bottom and sides of the pan. You can also spray oil or rub margarine all around the pan, add 2 tablespoons flour and shake all around to cover the bottom and sides well, tapping out the excess into the sink or trash.

TESTING CAKE DONENESS

It always seems strange to me to stick a short toothpick into a cake to see if it is done. I like to use wooden or metal kebab skewers so you can check what is happening in the middle of the cake. When the skewer comes out clean, the cake is done. Remove the cake from the oven and place the pan on a wire rack to cool for ten minutes. Turn the cake out of the pan onto the wire rack and let cool completely.

QUICK THAW METHOD FOR PUFF PASTRY

To thaw a stack of puff pastry squares, remove the stack of squares from the package, wrap in a clean dish towel, and use the defrost function (not cook) in the microwave for 1 to 1½ minutes. You just want to be able to bend the stack slightly. As you peel off individual squares, the ones below will defrost. If the dough gets too soft, place back in the freezer for a few minutes.

To thaw a package of puff pastry sheets, remove from the box. Without opening the inner paper wrapping, place in a microwave and use the defrost function for 1 minute. Turn the package over and defrost for another minute. Open up the package, separate the sheets, and place them on a clean towel to continue thawing until soft enough to roll.

To thaw one sheet, remove one sheet from the box, wrap in a dish towel and place in the microwave. Using the defrost setting, defrost for 45 seconds. Turn the pastry over and defrost another 45 seconds. Remove from microwave, unroll the puff pastry sheet, and let it sit on the towel while you prepare the other ingredients.

ROLLING OUT PIE AND COOKIE DOUGH

Remove dough from freezer and let thaw on your counter until you can press it a little. Place a piece of parchment paper or plastic wrap on your counter and sprinkle with flour. Place the dough on top. Sprinkle the top of the dough with a little more flour and cover with a piece of parchment paper. Roll on top of the parchment to roll out the dough into desired size and thickness. You will want to peel back the top parchment and sprinkle some more flour on the dough as you roll.

SLICING CAKE LAYERS

With a long serrated knife, mark all around the side of the cake where you will slice into it so that you will have even layers. For a four-layer cake made with two cakes, you will be cutting each cake in half; for a three-layer cake made from one cake or a six-layer cake made from two, you will be cutting each cake into thirds. Place the knife in one hand and place the other hand on top of the cake. Slice about 2 to 3 inches into the cake while turning the cake with the other hand. Keep turning until you have sliced 2 to 3 inches in all the way around. After you have cut all around, place the knife into one cut part and gently slice straight across by joining the cuts. Repeat with the next slice. Do not fret if your slices are not perfect, or even if one is a little shredded—they will be hidden in the cake and no one will know.

FILLING AND USING A PASTRY BAG

Place the coupler inside the pastry bag, place the tip over the end of the bag and twist on the ring to secure the tip. Fold down the top of the pastry bag about 3 inches. Place your hand under the folded part to hold the bag open. Use a large spoon or silicone spatula to fill the bag three-fourths of the way. Pull the sides up, trying to keep the filling in the bag. Bring the ends together and squeeze the filling down toward the tip. Twist a few times and hold your hand around the bag so that the twisted part stays twisted. You are now ready to use the bag. The hand holding the bag is the only hand that will squeeze out the filling; use your other hand to guide the tip. Each time you pick up the bag to use, squeeze the filling down and twist.

MELTING CHOCOLATE IN THE MICROWAVE

Place the chopped chocolate in a microwave-safe bowl, such as a heatproof glass bowl. Heat for 1 minute at high power (or 45 seconds to start if you have less than

10 ounces chocolate), stir well, mixing the melted pieces into the unmelted ones. Heat in the microwave another 45 seconds and stir well again, and then finally heat another 30 seconds and stir. Remove from the microwave when the chocolate is almost all melted and stir until it is completely melted. Be sure to have oven mitts on hand to hold the bowl when you stir it.

MELTING CHOCOLATE ON THE STOVETOP

Place the chopped chocolate in the top of a double boiler—a specially designed two-part pot that allows simmering water in the lower pot to gently heat the contents in the upper pot. If you don't have a double boiler, you can create your own by placing a metal or other heatproof bowl over a medium saucepan. The bowl must be able to sit on top of the saucepan without falling into the pan. Place enough water in the saucepan so that it just touches the bottom of the bowl, usually about 2 inches. Make sure that when the bowl sits over the water it does not float. If it does, pour out a little water from the saucepan so the bowl sits securely on the rim of the saucepan. Bring the water to a boil and then turn down to a simmer. Stir the chocolate until it is melted.

MELTING MARGARINE

This can be done either at low heat on the stovetop or in the microwave. To melt the margarine in the microwave, place it in a heatproof bowl. If you are melting four tablespoons or less, microwave for 30 to 45 seconds. A full stick may take one minute or longer—start with 45 seconds and then add fifteen seconds until the margarine is melted.

BAKING IN A WATER BATH

Place the pan or pans into a larger roasting pan. Place the roasting pan inside the oven on the middle rack. Bring boiling water over to the oven and pour into the roasting pan around the pan or pans until you reach one-third to one-half of the way up the pan/pans. After baking time, carefully remove the pan/pans from the water bath (leaving the roasting pan with water in the oven to cool enough to remove it safely) and let cool.

MAKING ALMOND FLOUR

You can buy almond flour at the supermarket, but I always find it costly. I buy blanched slivered almonds and grind them in a coffee grinder that I dedicate for nuts. You can also use your food processor, but the coffee grinder yields a finer, powdered texture. Be careful not to turn your nuts into nut butter; stop grinding as soon as you see a powder. Store in a freezer bag or airtight container at room temperature for up to four months. One cup or 8 ounces of slivered almonds will make 2 cups of almond flour; ¾ cup or 6 ounces of slivered almonds will make 1½ cups of almond flour.

MAKING GROUND ALMONDS

Ground almonds are a coarser grind than almond flour. You can buy it in the supermarket, or make it yourself by grinding whole or slivered nuts in the food processor until the nuts are in very small pieces, before they turn into a powder. They can be stored as indicated in "Making almond flour," above.

MAKING GROUND WALNUTS

Several recipes call for "ground walnuts," which I generally buy already ground at stores. Ground walnuts typically have some texture and are not ground superfine to the consistency of flour. You can make ground walnuts yourself by grinding the nuts in a food processor. One cup of walnut halves will make a half cup of ground walnuts.

ZESTING CITRUS

To make grated lemon, lime, or orange peel you can use a microplane zester or the small holes of a box grater. Grate off only the yellow, green, or orange part; once you hit the white, rotate to the next part of the fruit.

MAKING VANILLA SUGAR

Vanilla sugar can be found in most supermarkets and always in kosher stores. You can also make your own by placing 2 whole vanilla beans in a jar with 2 cups of sugar and let it sit for 1 week, shaking occasionally.

PITTING CHERRIES

There are many ways to pit cherries, including purchasing a cherry pitter. As I oppose utensils that have only one use, after trying a few techniques, I decided I liked the "paper clip" method. To pit cherries using a paper clip, you will want to wear gloves. Take a clean paper clip and pull up one end to straighten it. Use the end of the clip to press into the center of the pit through the stem end, which loosens the pit. Use your fingers to split the cherry open and remove the pit.

FREEZING AND STORING DESSERTS

Because kosher bakers are not permitted to bake on the Sabbath, we recognize the importance of baking in advance and freezing desserts. Although each recipe in this book contains specific storage instruction for that dessert, you should be aware of some general storage and freezing guidelines. Generally, desserts containing cream fillings, custards, uncooked eggs, or fruit should always be stored in the refrigerator, covered with plastic wrap, for up to three days. Dry desserts such as cakes, cookies, and bar cookies can be stored at room temperature wrapped in plastic or in an airtight container or freezer bag for up to five days. Those desserts with unbaked cream fillings and fresh fruit do not freeze very well. I have also found that cakes containing baked fruits end up a little mushy when thawed, though there are some fruit desserts in this book that can be frozen with success. Layer cakes, cookies, bar cookies, baked fruit pies, tart and pie doughs all freeze very well and are best when used within three months. If a cake is frosted or glazed, first freeze on a cookie sheet for one hour and then wrap in plastic wrap and return to freezer for up to three months. Unfrosted cakes should be wrapped tightly in plastic. Freeze cookies in freezer bags to take up less space. Unless otherwise specified, frozen desserts should be thawed overnight in the refrigerator or at room temperature for 2 to 3 hours before serving. The challah chapter in part 3 has its own directions for storing and freezing challahs.

The Ten Commandments
of Kosher Baking

1 Only parve desserts, those not containing dairy, can be served following a meat meal.

2 All desserts must be able to be made in advance of Shabbat and holidays. Thou shalt keep room in your refrigerator and freezer for this purpose.

3 Always bake for more people than you invited—people show up.

4 Know your audience and bake accordingly.

5 Shave five minutes off cake baking time and two minutes off cookie baking time in every recipe and check for doneness—you can always *add* baking time, but you cannot take it away.

6 Every baking disaster can be fixed—if it doesn't look right, plate it in the kitchen.

7 Pick your five favorite dessert recipes and always have those ingredients on hand.

8 Keep some sticks of margarine in your freezer—it behaves more like cold butter for cookies and pie or tart doughs.

9 Substitute soy milk for dairy cream in any recipe unless the recipe requires that the cream be whipped.

10 All desserts shall be worth the calories and so delicious you'll be content to eat only one piece.

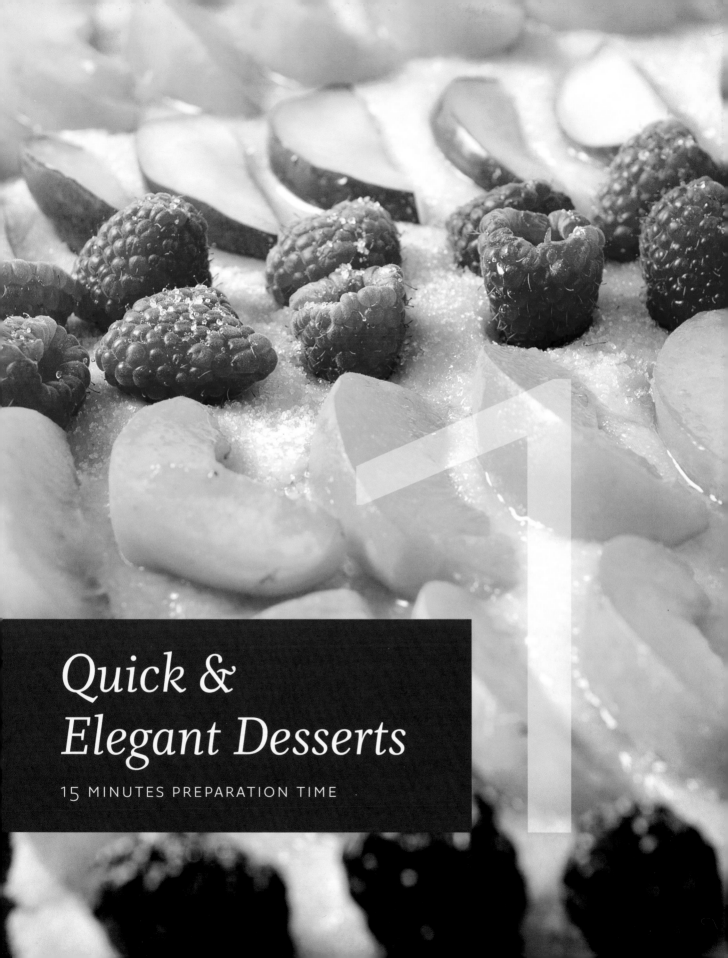

Quick & Elegant Desserts

15 MINUTES PREPARATION TIME

This part contains quick, delicious, and beautiful desserts.

You may have thought that baking takes too much time and effort. These recipes will prove otherwise. All of the desserts in this part are ready for the oven in approximately fifteen minutes or less. If you are new to baking, the recipes in this part require equipment you probably have and demand no fancy techniques. If you are an experienced baker, you will find yourself turning to part 1 when you have used up nearly all of your cooking time with other parts of the meal and you need to prepare a quick dessert, but one that is as tasty as everything else you made.

There may be occasions when you are baking for many people and need to serve multiple desserts or when you simply want to present a variety of flavors and textures to your family or guests. This part is divided into cookies, cakes, pastries, tarts, and pies, so you have many choices of fast-and-easy yet still elegant desserts.

Chocolate Chip Mandelbread

MAKES ABOUT 30 COOKIES

STORAGE

Place in an airtight container or freezer bags and store at room temperature for up to five days or freeze up to three months.

My best friend Limor Decter always has these cookies on hand (fresh or in the freezer) and she is constantly giving them out. Anyone would be lucky to be her friend since she visits and cooks for any friend who is sick, not once during an illness, but over and over again. The recipe results in cookies that are chewy on the inside. For crisper cookies, add another two to three minutes to the second baking time.

_____

3 cups all-purpose flour

1 cup sugar

2 teaspoons baking powder

Dash of salt

¼ cup orange juice

3 large eggs

½ cup canola or vegetable oil

1 teaspoon pure vanilla extract

10 ounces parve semisweet chocolate chips

_____

1 Preheat the oven to 350°F. Line a jelly roll pan or large cookie sheet with parchment.

2 In a large bowl, mix together the flour, sugar, baking powder, salt, orange juice, eggs, oil, and vanilla until it forms a dough. Add the chocolate chips and mix again to evenly distribute the chips.

3 Divide the dough in half and shape each half into a log, about 10 to 12 inches long by 3 to 5 inches wide. Flatten each loaf slightly. Place the 2 loaves on the prepared pan, about 5 inches apart.

4 Bake for 35 minutes, or until the loaves look golden on top. Slide the parchment and logs off the pan onto the counter. Slice each loaf crosswise into ¾- to 1-inch-thick slices. Don't worry if the insides of the cookies seem unbaked. Place a new piece of parchment on the pan and place the sliced cookies on the parchment cut-side down. Place the pan in the oven and bake 4 minutes more. Slide the parchment off the cookie sheet onto a cooling rack and let the cookies cool.

Chocolate Chunk Biscotti

MAKES ABOUT 40 BISCOTTI

STORAGE

Place in an airtight container or freezer bags and store at room temperature for up to five days or freeze up to three months.

My son Jake says this is his favorite dessert in the entire book.

2 cups all-purpose flour

½ cup parve unsweetened cocoa

½ cup sugar

1 teaspoon baking soda

4 large eggs

1 teaspoon pure vanilla extract

10 ounces parve bittersweet chocolate, chopped in ½-inch pieces

1 Preheat the oven to 350°F. Line a large cookie sheet with parchment.

2 In a large bowl, whisk together the flour, cocoa, sugar, and baking soda. Add the eggs and vanilla and mix well. Stir in the chopped chocolate. You will have a thick dough.

3 Divide the dough in half and with your hands shape each half into a log 3 inches wide by 12 to 14 inches long. Place the logs on the prepared cookie sheet and flatten slightly on the top. Bake for 30 minutes, until the outside of the loaves is hard to the touch. Let cool for 10 minutes.

4 Slide the parchment and logs off the cookie sheet onto the counter. Line the cookie sheet with a new piece of parchment. Using a sharp knife, cut each log crosswise into ¾-inch thick slices. Place the slices cut-side down on the cookie

sheet. Return the pan to the oven and bake for 5 minutes for chewy cookies and 10 minutes for harder cookies. Slide the parchment off the cookie sheet onto a cooling rack and let the cookies cool.

Lemon Rosemary Biscotti Sticks

MAKES ABOUT 32 BISCOTTI STICKS

STORAGE

Place in an airtight container or freezer bags and store at room temperature for up to five days or freeze up to three months.

Everyone always asks how I came up with these. I was walking through the produce section of the grocery store thinking about lemon biscotti when I noticed the fresh herbs. On a whim, I grabbed the fresh rosemary. The biscotti loaves spread while baking and you end up with longer and skinnier cookies than typical biscotti. Therefore, use your largest cookie sheet or jelly roll pan.

2 cups all-purpose flour

1¼ cups plus ¼ teaspoon sugar, divided

1 teaspoon baking powder

2 teaspoons lemon zest (grated outer peel) (from 1 lemon)

2 large eggs plus 1 yolk (reserve 1 white to glaze tops
    of biscotti)

1½ teaspoons pure vanilla extract

1 tablespoon fresh squeezed lemon juice (from zested lemon)

1 teaspoon finely chopped fresh rosemary leaves

1 Preheat the oven to 350°F. Line a cookie sheet or jelly roll pan with parchment.

2 In a large bowl, whisk together the flour, 1¼ cups sugar, baking powder, and lemon zest. Add the 2 whole eggs plus 1 egg yolk, vanilla, lemon juice, and rosemary and mix with a wooden spoon or with the paddle attachment of a stand mixer until the dough comes together.

3 Divide the dough in half. Form 2 logs, about 3 x 8 inches each. Place the logs on the prepared pan, leaving space between them. Beat the reserved egg white and brush

BAKING GREEN
Instead of disposable parchment, you can place a reusable silicone mat on top of your cookie sheet and simply wipe it clean after each use. Silpat is one brand of silicone mat. You can find them in cooking stores.

it on the tops of the two loaves. Sprinkle the remaining ¼ teaspoon sugar on top of the loaves.

4 Bake for 25 to 30 minutes, or until slightly golden on top. Slide the parchment and logs off the cookie sheet onto the counter. Let sit 5 minutes. Place a new sheet of parchment on the cookie sheet.

5 Cut each log crosswise into ½-inch thick slices. Don't worry if the center of the cookies is gooey. Place the sliced cookies cut-side down onto the parchment-lined cookie sheet and place back in the oven. Bake for 12 to 15 minutes, until browned a little on the edges. The longer you bake the cookies the harder they become, so if you want chewier cookies bake them 12 rather than 15 minutes. Slide the parchment off the cookie sheet onto a cooling rack and let the cookies cool.

Double Chocolate Chip Cookies

MAKES ABOUT 3 DOZEN

STORAGE

Place baked cookies into an airtight container or freezer bags and store at room temperature for up to five days or freeze up to three months.

I have given you two ways to bake these cookies: one allows you to bake them right away, and the other allows you to freeze the dough and bake the cookies later in smaller batches. I usually keep rolls of dough (marked "dairy" or "parve") in my freezer so that, if I have unexpected visitors, I can just slice and bake my own cookies, which are ready to share in no time. I also like to shape the dough into logs, let them set up for 2 hours in the freezer, then slice them because the cookies all come out the same size—vestiges of my days catering when I actually sold these cookies in Geneva, Switzerland, to people who wanted a taste of America.

½ cup (1 stick) parve margarine

½ cup sugar

½ cup light brown sugar

2 large eggs

1 teaspoon pure vanilla extract

1 cup raw oats (not quick-cooking kind)

1⅓ cups all-purpose flour

½ teaspoon baking powder

½ teaspoon baking soda

¼ teaspoon salt

1½ cups parve chocolate chips

3½ ounces parve semisweet or bittersweet chocolate

Don't sweat the burnt edges of cookies or crusts. Use a vegetable peeler to shave off the burnt parts.

1. Preheat the oven to 400°F. Line two cookie sheets with parchment.

2. In a large bowl, beat the margarine, sugar, and brown sugar with a stand or hand-held electric mixer, or by hand with a whisk, until creamy. Add the eggs and vanilla and beat until smooth.

3. Place the oats into the bowl of a food processor fitted with a metal blade. Process until the oats are ground to a powder. Add the powdered oats, flour, baking powder, baking soda, and salt to the egg and sugar mixture and mix until combined.

4. Add the chocolate chips to the batter and mix in. Using the small holes of a box grater or microplane zester, grate half of the bar of semisweet chocolate into a medium bowl or over a cutting board. Add the grated chocolate to the bowl with the dough. Place the other half of the chocolate bar in the food processor bowl that you used for the oatmeal and process until the chocolate is in very small pieces. Add the pieces and any powdered chocolate in the bowl to the cookie dough and mix just until all the chocolate chips and pieces are distributed throughout the dough.

5. To bake right away: Using a small spoon, scoop up some cookie dough, 1 to 2 tablespoons as desired, roll it into a ball between your palms, flatten slightly, and place on a parchment-lined cookie sheet, about 1½ inches apart. Bake for 12 to 14 minutes, until the cookies are just set. They should be firm on the outside edge, but can still be very soft in the center. They will continue to harden slightly after they come out of the oven. Slide the parchment onto a rack and let cool. Eat immediately or freeze the baked cookies, once completely cooled, in a freezer bag or container.

6. To freeze the dough and bake the cookies later: Divide the dough into 3 portions. Shape each portion into a long log about 1½ inches in diameter. Wrap each in plastic wrap and then roll each on the counter a few times to make them as round as possible. Place in the freezer for at least 2 hours and up to three months. When

you're ready to bake, take a roll out of the freezer and preheat the oven to 400°F. On a cutting board, use a sharp knife to cut the frozen dough into ¼-inch slices. Place on a parchment-lined cookie sheet and bake for 12 to 14 minutes, until they are firm on the outside edge, but still very soft in the center. Slide the parchment off the cookie sheet onto a cooling rack and let the cookies cool.

Sablé Galette Cookies

MAKES ABOUT 18 BARS
STORAGE

Place baked cookies into an airtight container or freezer bags and store at room temperature for up to five days or freeze up to three months.

This is the easiest cookie you will ever bake. It is made as one large cookie that you cut after baking. Sablé means sand-blasted, which describes the grainy texture of these cookies perfectly. I saw cookies like these during my travels around Brittany in the northwest region of France, where they use enormous amounts of butter in everything they bake. For a Sephardic twist, I like to add orange blossom water to this parve version of the famous French cookie.

2 cups all-purpose flour
1 cup (2 sticks) parve margarine, cut into
    tablespoons
Dash of salt
½ cup plus 1 teaspoon sugar, divided
2 large egg yolks, divided
½ teaspoon pure vanilla extract
2 tablespoons orange blossom water
    (optional)
1 tablespoon cold water plus ½ tablespoon
    water, divided

1 Preheat the oven to 350°F. Place the flour, margarine, salt, and ½ cup of the sugar in the bowl of a food processor fitted with a metal blade. Pulse about seven times, or until the mixture looks like sand. You can also do this by hand in a large bowl with two knives or a pastry cutter. Add 1 egg yolk, the vanilla, orange blossom water, if using, and the tablespoon of cold water. Process or mix just until the dough comes together.

2 Place a large piece of parchment on the counter and grease lightly using the paper or foil that wrapped the margarine. Dump the dough onto the greased parchment and, using a rolling pin, roll into a large circle, about 9 inches in diameter.

3 To decorate the edge of the cookie, using the flat end of the handle of a wooden spoon, or the tip of your index finger, make indentations one after the other all around the outside of the circle.

4 Whisk together the remaining egg yolk with the ½ tablespoon of water. Brush the top of the cookie with egg wash. Using the tines of a fork, make one set of lines straight across the top of the cookie. Make another set about 2 inches below the first. Repeat until you have four to five sets of lines. Now rotate the parchment a quarter turn to the right and make four to five additional sets of lines, each about 2 inches apart. The new set of lines should cross the first set of lines on an angle, creating a diamond-shaped grid.

5 Sprinkle the top of the cookie with the remaining teaspoon of sugar. Slide the parchment onto a cookie sheet and bake for 35 to 37 minutes, until the edges start to look golden. Remove from the oven and immediately cut the cookie into 8 or 12 large wedges or about eighteen 1 x 3-inch bars, if you like. If you wait until the cookie cools to cut it, you will not get nice clean edges.

Amaretto Cookies

MAKES ABOUT 3 DOZEN

STORAGE

Place baked cookies into an airtight container or freezer bags and store at room temperature for up to five days or freeze up to three months.

If you've ever been to Italy and sipped on a cappuccino or an espresso, you may have been lucky enough to enjoy these almond-flavored cookies, which are a favorite of mine. If any of these crisp cookies are still sitting around after five days, freeze them. You can crush them up in a food processor and sprinkle on ice cream or use in my Toasted Almond Layer Cake (page 166).

———

One 8-ounce bag slivered almonds (about 1¾ cups)

1 cup sugar

1 tablespoon all-purpose flour

2 large egg whites

1 tablespoon amaretto (almond-flavored liqueur)

———

1 Preheat the oven to 325°F. Line a large jelly roll pan with parchment. Spread the almonds on the sheet and toast for 20 minutes, stirring the nuts after 10 minutes. When the almonds are golden and fragrant, remove the pan from the oven and slide the parchment off the pan. Let cool for 5 minutes.

2 Place the toasted almonds into the bowl of a food processor fitted with a metal blade. Process until the nuts are ground to a powder. Place the ground nuts in a medium bowl. Add the sugar, flour, egg whites, and amaretto and mix until combined. I like to use my hands, but a wooden spoon is a neater option. Line two jelly roll pans or cookie sheets with parchment.

3 Wet your hands and take walnut-sized clumps of dough and roll them into balls about 1 inch in diameter. Place the balls on the prepared baking sheets, about 2 inches apart. Be sure not to overcrowd the cookies; they spread while baking. You can bake in batches. Bake for 25 to 30 minutes, 25 minutes for chewier cookies and 30 for crunchier cookies. Slide the parchment off the cookie sheet onto a cooling rack and let the cookies cool.

When my friend Maria Sloan was testing this recipe for me, she decided to adapt it for Passover, and was happy with the results. To make these cookies for Passover, simply substitute potato starch for the flour.

Chewy Chocolate Velvet Cookies

MAKES ABOUT 5 DOZEN 1½-INCH COOKIES

STORAGE

Place baked cookies into an airtight container and store at room temperature for up to five days. They do not stay chewy if frozen.

These cookies are crunchy on the outside and very rich and chewy on the inside.

2½ cups confectioners' sugar

1 cup parve unsweetened cocoa

3 tablespoons all-purpose flour

4 large egg whites

---

1 Preheat the oven to 350°F. Line two cookie sheets with parchment.

2 In a medium bowl, sift together the confectioners' sugar, cocoa, and flour. Set aside.

3 In a large bowl, beat the egg whites with a hand-held or stand electric mixer on medium speed until thick and foamy, not stiff. Add the sugar and cocoa and flour mixture and mix on low speed until combined. Turn the speed up to high and beat for 1 minute, until stiff.

4 Using two small spoons, scoop up about 1 tablespoon of the batter with one spoon and use the back of the second spoon to place it on the cookie sheet. Leave about 1 inch between the cookies. Bake for 14 minutes, or until puffed. Slide the parchment off the cookie sheet onto a cooling rack and let the cookies cool.

Pistachio Financiers

MAKES 2 DOZEN

STORAGE

Place into an airtight container or freezer bags and store at room temperature for up to five days or freeze up to three months.

When I lived in Europe, little almond financiers, mini rectangles shaped like gold bars, were everywhere. Here is a mini cupcake-shaped version with pistachio nuts. If you shell the nuts yourself, rub them between the palms of your hands to remove the nuts' excess brown skin.

1 cup plus 24 additional shelled, unsalted pistachio nuts (about ⅔ pound total of nuts in their shells)

⅓ cup all-purpose flour

⅔ cup sugar

3 large egg whites

½ cup (1 stick) parve margarine

1 Preheat the oven to 350°F. Place mini muffin paper cups into 24 mini muffin cups.

2 Place the 1 cup of pistachio nuts in the bowl of a food processor fitted with a metal blade. Process the nuts into tiny pieces.

3 Transfer the nut pieces to a medium bowl. Using a silicone spatula, mix in the flour, sugar, and egg whites. Heat the margarine in the microwave oven for 45 seconds, or until melted, and fold in three parts to the batter. Mix well.

4 Using the tablespoon on your measuring spoon set, spoon the batter into the mini muffin molds, filling each two-thirds full. Place a pistachio nut in the center of the top of each. Bake for 20 minutes, or until a toothpick inserted into one of the cakes comes out clean. Let cool.

Fudgy Brownies

MAKES 16 TO 20 BROWNIES

STORAGE

Store covered with plastic or in an airtight container at room temperature for up to five days or freeze for up to three months.

Brownies are the easiest chocolate dessert you can make and are always a crowd-pleaser.

———

Parve margarine, for greasing pan

6 ounces parve semisweet or bittersweet chocolate, chopped or broken into 1-inch pieces

1 cup sugar

⅓ cup canola or vegetable oil

¼ cup parve plain soy milk

2 large eggs

1 teaspoon pure vanilla extract

¼ teaspoon salt

½ teaspoon baking powder

¼ cup parve unsweetened cocoa

1 cup all-purpose flour

———

1 Preheat the oven to 350°F. Line an 8-inch square baking pan with foil, letting some hang over the sides of the pan about two inches. Grease the bottom and sides with margarine.

2 Melt the chocolate, either on the stovetop or in the microwave, following the "Melting chocolate" instructions (see Foolproof Tips and Techniques).

3 When the chocolate is melted, whisk in the sugar and oil. Next, whisk in the soy milk, eggs, and vanilla. Add the salt, baking powder, and cocoa and whisk again. Finally, add the flour and whisk well.

4 Pour into the pan and spread evenly. Bake for 30 minutes, or until the top looks dry. Let cool in the pan. Lift the foil to remove the brownie from the pan and cut into squares.

◇ Chocolate Almond Toffee Bars

MAKES TWENTY-FOUR 3 X 1-INCH BARS OR ABOUT 28 SQUARES

STORAGE

> *Store covered with plastic or in an airtight container at room temperature*
> *for up to five days or freeze for up to three months.*

I developed these gluten-free bars for my friend Andrea Neusner and her five-year-old daughter Miranda, both of whom have celiac disease, which prevents their bodies from tolerating any gluten. When I brought several gluten-free desserts to their house one night, I was so happy when Miranda asked her mom if there were any kinds she could eat—and Andrea said that for once, she could have all of them.

———

    1 cup (2 sticks) parve margarine
    1 large egg yolk
    ¾ cup light brown sugar
    2 cups store-bought or fresh-ground almond flour (see "Making almond
        flour," page xxvii)
    ½ cup potato starch
    7 ounces parve semisweet or bittersweet chocolate, chopped or broken
        into 1-inch pieces
    ⅓ cup pecan halves, roughly chopped

———

1 Preheat the oven to 350°F. Cut a piece of parchment to fit in the bottom of a 9 x 13-inch pan. Use one of the margarine wrappers to grease the pan. Press in the parchment rectangle and then use the other margarine wrapper to grease the top of the parchment and sides of the pan.

2 In a medium bowl, beat the margarine and brown sugar until creamy. Whisk in the almond flour, egg yolk, and potato starch until combined.

3 Using a silicone spatula, scoop up clumps of the sticky dough and spread it across the bottom of the pan, as evenly as you can.

4 Bake for 40 minutes, or until the dough appears set. Let cool for 15 minutes.

5 Melt the chocolate either on the stovetop or in the microwave, following the "Melting chocolate" instructions (see Foolproof Tips and Techniques).

6 When the chocolate is melted, pour over the top and use a silicone spatula to spread gently to cover the entire top to the edges. Sprinkle with the pecan pieces. Let cool and then cut into 3 x 1-inch bars or squares.

Orange Tea Cake

SERVES 12 TO 15

STORAGE

Once the glaze has dried, store covered in plastic at room temperature for up to five days or freeze for up to three months.

When I was a guest on the Chicago radio talk show *Walking on Air with Betsy and Sal*, I gave this recipe to the hosts to test and discuss on a show about baking tips. Sally complained on air that the cake wasn't very pretty. As it turned out, she forgot to add the glaze. Her family ate up the entire cake right out of the oven before she could even read that part of the recipe. Make the glaze.

CAKE

Spray oil containing flour or spray oil plus 2 tablespoons flour
    for greasing and flouring pan
1 Earl Grey tea bag
½ cup boiling water
2 cups plus 2 teaspoons sugar, divided
4 large eggs
1 cup canola or vegetable oil
2½ cups all-purpose flour
2 teaspoons baking powder
Dash of salt
1 teaspoon pure vanilla extract
1 tablespoon orange zest (grated outer peel) (from 1 orange)
¼ cup fresh orange juice (from zested orange)

GLAZE

1 Earl Grey tea bag
½ cup boiling water
1 cup confectioners' sugar

1 Preheat the oven to 350°F. Grease and flour a large Bundt pan.

2 To make the cake: Steep the tea bag in the ½ cup of boiling water. Add 2 teaspoons of the sugar and stir until dissolved. Let steep while you prepare the batter.

3 In a large bowl, mix together the remaining 2 cups of sugar, the eggs, oil, flour, baking powder, salt, vanilla, orange zest, and orange juice with a whisk or electric mixer on medium speed. Lift the tea bag and squeeze excess liquid into the cup to make the tea as strong as possible, and then discard the tea bag. Pour the tea into the batter and mix vigorously by hand or for 2 minutes with an electric mixer on medium speed until all the ingredients are combined and the batter is creamy.

4 Pour the batter into the prepared Bundt pan and bake for 1 hour or until a skewer inserted in the cake comes out clean. Remove from the oven and let cool for 10 minutes in the pan. Turn the cake onto a rack and let cool completely.

5 To make the glaze: Place the tea bag in the ½ cup of boiling water and let steep 2 minutes. Sift the confectioners' sugar into a bowl. Add 2 tablespoons of the brewed tea and whisk until the sugar has dissolved and you have a white glaze you can pour. Let the glaze sit 5 minutes to thicken and use a whisk to drizzle over the cake.

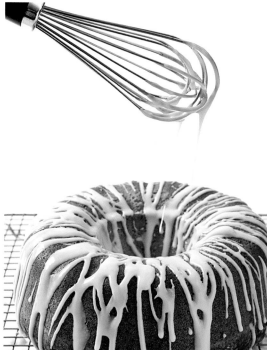

Vanilla Pound Cake

SERVES 12 TO 15

STORAGE

Store covered in plastic at room temperature for up to five days or freeze wrapped in plastic for up to three months.

As its name suggests, this is a very dense, delicious cake that is a great afternoon snack. If you are looking for a lighter cake, see the Vanilla Sheet Cake recipe on page 33. My daughter Emily gets credit for the mocha variation.

———

Spray oil containing flour or spray oil plus 2 tablespoons flour
    for greasing and flouring pan

½ cup (1 stick) margarine

½ cup solid vegetable shortening

2 cups all-purpose flour

2 cups sugar

½ teaspoon salt

1 teaspoon baking powder

4 large eggs, beaten

1 teaspoon pure vanilla extract

⅔ cup parve plain soy milk, divided

———

1 Preheat the oven to 350°F. Grease and flour a large Bundt pan.

2 In a large bowl, beat the margarine and shortening until creamy with a stand or hand-held electric mixer on medium-high speed. Use a silicone spatula to scrape down the bowl and mix again. In a medium bowl, combine the flour, sugar, salt, and baking powder. Add half of these dry ingredients to the batter and mix. The batter will be crumbly. Add the eggs, vanilla, and ⅓ cup of the soy milk to the batter and mix together. Add the rest of the dry ingredients and mix until combined. Finally, add the rest of the soy milk and mix until just combined. Pour the batter into the prepared Bundt pan and smooth the top with a silicone spatula. Bake for 1 hour, or until a skewer inserted in the cake comes out clean. Let cool for 10 minutes in the pan and then turn the cake out onto a rack to cool to room temperature.

MOCHA MARBLE POUND CAKE

1 Complete Steps 1 and 2 for the Vanilla Pound Cake.

2 In a medium bowl, combine ¼ cup parve unsweetened cocoa, 1 tablespoon finely ground coffee, and 1 teaspoon sugar. Add one-third of the vanilla batter and whisk well.

3 Using a quarter-cup measuring cup, scoop up some of the vanilla batter and place it in the Bundt pan. Scoop up another ¼ cup of the vanilla batter and place in the pan, about 2 inches away from the other scoop. Repeat until you have 4 scoops in the pan, spaced as evenly as you can. Do not spread the scoops of batter together.

4 Using another quarter-cup measuring cup, scoop up some of the mocha-flavored batter and place it between two of the vanilla batter clumps. Repeat with another 3 scoops of the mocha batter, until you have alternating batters in the bottom of the pan. For the next layer, place a scoop of the vanilla batter on top of the mocha batter and then a scoop of the mocha batter on top of the vanilla until you have used up the batters.

5 Take a knife, place it into the batter, and pull it through the center of the batter all around in a circle. You do not want to mix the two batters together, just marble gently.

6 Bake the cake, following the instructions in Step 2 for Vanilla Pound Cake.

Everyone's Favorite Chocolate Cake

SERVES 12 TO 15

STORAGE

Store covered in plastic at room temperature for up to five days or freeze wrapped in plastic for up to three months.

Here is the one dessert that you can throw together in ten minutes that will satisfy everyone. My kids like it for breakfast. The inspiration for this recipe came from Suzanne Hope Diamond, a friend of my brother-in-law Steve. Steve baked it the Shabbat after I left Camp Ramah in Palmer, Massachusetts, where I teach cooking to special-needs and other campers each summer. This cake helped me celebrate the completion of the program. For frostings, see page 293.

Spray oil containing flour or spray oil plus 2 tablespoons flour
    for greasing and flouring pan
2 cups sugar
2 cups all-purpose flour
¾ cup parve unsweetened cocoa
2 teaspoons baking powder
2 teaspoons baking soda
1 teaspoon salt
1 cup orange juice, without pulp
½ cup canola or vegetable oil
1 teaspoon pure vanilla extract
3 large eggs
1 cup boiling water

1 Preheat the oven to 350°F. Grease and flour a Bundt or tube pan.

2 In a large bowl, mix together the sugar, flour, cocoa, baking powder, baking soda, and salt. Add the orange juice, oil, vanilla, and eggs and mix for 2 minutes, until everything is thoroughly combined. Add the boiling water in 3 parts, gently mixing it in with a silicone spatula or wooden spoon (if you use an electric mixer, be careful, the water splatters).

3 Pour into the prepared pan and bake for 50 to 60 minutes, or until a skewer inserted in the cake comes out clean. Let cool for 10 minutes in the pan and then turn the cake out onto a rack to cool to room temperature.

Chocolate Mint Cake

SERVES 12 TO 15

STORAGE

Once the glaze has dried, store covered in plastic at room temperature for up to five days or freeze wrapped in plastic for up to three months.

I love the combination of chocolate and mint but my son Joey is a purist and wants nothing but chocolate flavor in his chocolate cake. You can easily omit the mint in the cake and the glaze. This is also a great vegan chocolate cake because it contains no eggs.

CAKE

Spray oil containing flour or spray oil plus 2 tablespoons flour for greasing and flouring pan

3 cups all-purpose flour

½ cup parve unsweetened cocoa

2 teaspoons baking soda

1 teaspoon salt

2 cups sugar

2 tablespoons white vinegar

½ cup canola or vegetable oil

1 teaspoon pure vanilla extract

2 teaspoons mint extract

1 cup water

1 cup parve plain soy milk

GLAZE

7 ounces parve semisweet or bittersweet chocolate, chopped or broken into 1-inch pieces

3 tablespoons parve margarine

1 tablespoon canola or vegetable oil

2 tablespoons parve plain soy milk

¾ teaspoon mint extract

1   Preheat the oven to 350°F. Grease and flour a Bundt or tube pan.

2   In a large bowl, whisk together the flour, cocoa, baking soda, salt, and sugar. Add the vinegar, oil, vanilla, mint extract, water, and soy milk. Beat until combined, about 1 minute, scraping down the sides of the bowl as necessary.

3   Pour the batter into the greased pan and bake for 1 hour or until a skewer inserted in the cake comes out clean. Let cool for 10 minutes in the pan. Turn the cake out onto a rack to cool to room temperature.

4   To make the glaze: Melt the chocolate and margarine in a small, heavy saucepan on low heat, stirring often with a wooden spoon. When the chocolate has melted, remove the pan from the heat. Add the oil, 2 tablespoons of soy milk, and ¾ teaspoon of mint extract and whisk until very smooth and shiny.

5   To glaze the cake, slide a large piece of aluminum foil underneath the wire rack with the cake. You can also place the cake on your serving plate and place a few small pieces of waxed or parchment paper all around under the cake. Pour the glaze slowly over the cake; make sure some glaze runs down the sides of the hole in the center. Use a silicone spatula to smooth the glaze and cover the entire cake. Let the glaze set 5 minutes. If you used a rack, you can now place the cake on a serving plate. (I use my hands to lift the cake from underneath.) If you used waxed paper to catch the extra glaze, remove the paper.

Pecan Coffee Cake

SERVES 12 TO 15

STORAGE

Store covered in plastic at room temperature for up to five days or freeze wrapped in plastic for up to three months.

When I told my kids I made "coffee cake," they assumed there was coffee in the cake. I explained that it is a kind of cake one eats along with coffee; they had no idea what I was talking about. I guess they have seen me eat *every* kind of cake with a cup of coffee.

Spray oil, for greasing pan

½ cup (1 stick) parve margarine

8 ounces parve cream cheese

3 tablespoons parve sour cream

1¼ cups sugar

2 large eggs

1 teaspoon pure vanilla extract

2 cups all-purpose flour

1 teaspoon baking powder

¼ teaspoon baking soda

¼ teaspoon salt

¼ cup parve plain soy milk

2 teaspoons ground cinnamon

¼ cup light brown sugar

½ cup chopped pecans

1 Preheat the oven to 350°F. Grease a 10-inch springform pan with spray oil.

2 In a large bowl, beat the margarine and cream cheese by hand with a whisk or with a stand or hand-held electric mixer on medium speed until soft and creamy, about 1 minute. Scrape down the bowl with a silicone spatula and mix in the sour cream. Next, mix in the sugar and, when fully combined, mix in the eggs and vanilla. Add the flour, baking powder, baking soda, and salt and whisk or mix on low speed until combined. Add the soy milk and mix until just combined. The batter will be thick.

3 In a small bowl, combine the cinnamon, sugar, and chopped pecans.

4 Using a silicone spatula, scoop half of the batter into the pan and spread evenly. Sprinkle half of the pecan mixture over the entire top of the batter. To get the rest of the batter to evenly cover the pecan mixture, use a large spoon or measuring cup to scoop up the batter and disperse all around the pan on top of the nut mixture. Use the spatula to gently spread the batter to cover. Sprinkle the rest of the cinnamon mixture on the top.

5 Bake for 50 minutes, or until a skewer inserted in the cake comes out clean. Let cool for 5 minutes. Run a knife around the sides of the pan and remove the sides. Enjoy warm or at room temperature. I like to serve this cake in slices, which are prettier than the whole cake.

Apple Upside-Down Cake

SERVES 15 TO 20

STORAGE

Store covered in plastic at room temperature for up to four days or freeze wrapped in plastic for up to three months.

I already had several apple desserts in this book when Judy Lerner sent me this recipe, a favorite of hers and anyone who has tried it. Judy says that she likes to share the recipe so she doesn't always have to make it and bring it to friends; they can make it themselves and bring it to her.

Spray oil, for greasing pan

1½ teaspoons ground cinnamon

2 cups plus 3 tablespoons sugar, divided

2 cups all-purpose flour

5 large eggs

1 cup canola or vegetable oil

1 teaspoon pure vanilla extract

4 apples (McIntosh, Gala, Fuji, Golden Delicious)

1 tablespoon confectioners' sugar

1 Preheat the oven to 350°F. Grease a 9 x 13-inch pan with spray oil.

2 In a small bowl, mix the cinnamon with 3 tablespoons of the sugar. Sprinkle on the bottom of the prepared pan.

3 In a large bowl, beat the flour, remaining 2 cups of sugar, eggs, oil, and vanilla with a stand or hand-held electric mixer on medium-high speed or by hand until well mixed. Peel and core the apples, halve them and then cut into ¼-inch-thick slices. Place the slices on top of the cinnamon and sugar in the pan in 3 long rows of overlapping slices. Pour the batter over the apples and spread evenly.

4 Bake for 1 hour, or until the top is browned and a skewer inserted comes out clean. Let cool for 30 minutes and then turn over onto a large serving platter or tray. Serve at room temperature. Just before serving, sift the confectioners' sugar over the top. The sugar will seep into the apples and heighten the taste.

Honey Cake with Pecan Swirls

SERVES 16

STORAGE

Store covered in plastic at room temperature for up to five days or freeze wrapped in plastic for up to three months.

I admit that I am not a huge fan of honey cake. The versions presented to me when I was a child tasted like cardboard. The first time I ate decent honey cake was when my kids baked it in preschool for Rosh Hashanah. It was actually moist. I decided that the Jewish baking world did not need yet another simple honey cake so I created this updated (*and moist!*) version.

———

Spray oil containing flour or spray oil plus 2 tablespoons flour for greasing and flouring pan

1 cup pecan halves

½ plus ⅓ cup sugar, divided

1 tablespoon ground cinnamon

⅔ cup brewed espresso or very strong coffee (or 1 teaspoon instant coffee granules dissolved in ⅔ cup boiling water)

¾ cup honey

½ cup canola or vegetable oil

⅓ cup dark brown sugar

2 large eggs

2 cups all-purpose flour

¼ teaspoon ground cloves

¼ teaspoon ground cinnamon

¼ teaspoon ground ginger

¾ teaspoon baking powder

¾ teaspoon baking soda

———

1 Preheat the oven to 350°F. Grease and flour a 12-inch loaf pan.

2 Place the pecan halves in a bag and crush them with a rolling pin until the largest pieces are between ¼ and ½-inch long. Add the ½ cup sugar and 1 tablespoon cinnamon to the bag and shake to combine.

3 In a large bowl, whisk together the coffee and honey. Add the oil, ⅓ cup of the white sugar, the brown sugar, and eggs and whisk well. Add the flour, cloves, cinnamon, ginger, baking powder, and baking soda and beat with a stand or hand-held electric mixer on medium speed for 2 minutes, or mix vigorously by hand, until you have a smooth batter.

4 Scoop up 1 cup of the batter and pour into the pan. Tilt the pan in a circle so the batter covers the entire bottom. Sprinkle on ⅓ cup of the nut mixture, covering the entire batter. Repeat with another cup of batter and ⅓ cup of the nut mixture. Repeat again. Pour the remaining batter on top and spread gently to cover the nuts.

5 Bake for 1 hour, or until a skewer inserted comes out clean. Let cool for 10 minutes in the pan and then turn out onto a rack to continue cooling. This cake is good either warm or at room temperature.

Pumpkin Cake

SERVES 12 TO 15

STORAGE

Store covered in plastic at room temperature for up to five days or freeze wrapped in plastic for up to three months.

This recipe is for those of you who think desserts cannot be healthy. Pumpkin is rich in antioxidants, vitamins, and minerals that fight disease and, my favorite benefit, slow the aging process.

———

Spray oil containing flour or spray oil plus 2 tablespoons flour
    for greasing and flouring pan
½ cup (1 stick) parve margarine
1 cup sugar
1 cup canned pumpkin purée (not pumpkin pie filling)
1 teaspoon pure vanilla extract
2 large eggs
2 cups all-purpose flour
½ teaspoon salt
1 teaspoon baking powder

1 teaspoon baking soda

1 teaspoon ground cinnamon

1 teaspoon ground ginger

½ teaspoon ground cloves

½ teaspoon ground nutmeg

2 teaspoons confectioners' sugar

---

1 Preheat the oven to 350°F. Grease and flour a Bundt or tube pan.

2 In a large bowl, beat the margarine and sugar with a stand or hand-held electric mixer on medium-high speed until creamy. Add the pumpkin purée and beat again. Use a silicone spatula to scrape down the bowl. Add the vanilla and eggs and mix well. Add the flour, salt, baking powder, baking soda, cinnamon, ginger, cloves, and nutmeg. (At this point I wrap plastic wrap around the top of the mixer and over the rim of the bowl, or cover with a clean dish towel, so that the flour does not escape and hit me in the face when I turn on the mixer.) Mix all the ingredients together. Use a silicone spatula to scoop the batter into the pan and then smooth the top.

3 Bake for 45 minutes, or until a skewer inserted comes out clean. Let cool for 10 minutes in the pan and then turn out onto a rack and let cool completely. To serve, sift the confectioners' sugar over the top.

Date Cake

SERVES 16

STORAGE

Store covered in plastic at room temperature for up to five days or freeze
wrapped in plastic for up to three months.

I received this recipe from Limor Decter, who says that her mother-in-law, Barbara Decter Schlussel, makes it every Rosh Hashanah. Limor says it is a Sephardic recipe, but Limor is the Sephardi, not Barbara. I was surprised by the lack of spices in this cake, but the dates provide all the taste you need.

———

Spray oil, for greasing pan

2 cups pitted dates

½ cup boiling water

½ cup (1 stick) parve margarine, melted

2 large eggs

1 cup all-purpose flour

¾ cup sugar

1 teaspoon baking powder

1 teaspoon baking soda

———

1 Preheat the oven to 350°F. Grease a 9-inch loaf pan with spray oil.

2 Chop the dates roughly into ½- to ¾-inch pieces. Place the chopped dates and boiling water in a large heatproof bowl. Let sit 5 minutes.

3 Mix in the melted margarine, eggs, flour, sugar, baking powder, and baking soda. Pour the batter into the prepared loaf pan and bake for 45 minutes or until a skewer inserted in the cake comes out clean. Let cool for 10 minutes in the pan and then remove to a rack to cool completely.

Lime Poppy Seed Pound Cake

SERVES 12 TO 15

STORAGE

Once the glaze has set and cake completely cooled, store covered in plastic at room temperature for up to five days or freeze wrapped in plastic for up to three months.

I created this cake for my husband Andy, who loves poppy seed anything. I decided to use lime to flavor the cake rather than lemon because limes don't get enough attention.

CAKE

Spray oil containing flour or spray oil plus 2 tablespoons flour
for greasing and flouring pan

1¼ cups sugar

2 tablespoons lime zest (grated outer peel) (from 3 limes)

4 large eggs

1 tablespoon fresh lime juice (from ½ lime)

2 teaspoons pure vanilla extract

1 cup canola or vegetable oil

½ cup (1 stick) parve margarine, melted

1⅔ cups all-purpose flour

1 teaspoon baking powder

½ teaspoon salt

1 tablespoon poppy seeds

GLAZE

⅔ cup sugar

¼ cup lime juice (from 1½ limes)

½ teaspoon pure vanilla extract

Does the whole cake not look as pretty as you hoped? Maybe there is a burnt edge or a section that did not pop out of the pan cleanly? Slice and plate the cake in the kitchen, add some berries to the plate, and then bring it to your guests. They need never see the whole cake.

1. Preheat the oven to 350°F. Grease and flour a Bundt or tube pan.

2. In a large bowl, or the bowl of a food processor fitted with a metal blade, whisk or pulse the sugar and lime zest until mixed. Add the eggs, lime juice, and vanilla and process or whisk for a few seconds to combine. Add the melted margarine and oil and process or whisk for 10 seconds. Add the flour, baking powder, and salt to the batter and process or whisk again. Add the poppy seeds and process or whisk to just mix in.

3. Use a silicone spatula to pour the batter into the prepared pan. Bake for 50 to 60 minutes, or until a wooden skewer inserted comes out clean. (Do not discard the skewer; you will use it to glaze the cake.) Cool in the pan for 10 minutes. Remove from the pan and let cool on a rack.

4. Place the ingredients for the glaze in a small, heavy-bottomed saucepan and bring to a boil. Turn the heat down to medium and cook uncovered, stirring often, for 4 to 5 minutes, until the glaze thickens.

5. Place the cake on aluminum foil or on a metal rack over a cookie sheet. Take the skewer you used to test the cake and poke holes all around the top and sides of the cake. Use a pastry brush to brush the glaze all around the cake, making sure to cover all the sides, including the sides facing the inside of the cake. Use up all of the glaze; it usually takes two times around to brush the entire cake.

Blueberry Cake

SERVES 12 TO 15

STORAGE

Store covered in plastic at room temperature for up to four days. The cake can be frozen wrapped in plastic, but is a bit mushy when thawed.

I added cumin to this dessert to see how it would taste because I like cumin, ginger, and cinnamon in my food. Several people remarked that there was something interesting about the cake that they just could not identify. You can dress up this cake with raspberry or blackberry sauce (see page 294). Just pour some sauce on half your dessert plate and place a square of the cake in the center. Sprinkle a few fresh red berries around the plate and you will have a beautiful plated dessert.

CAKE

Spray oil containing flour or spray oil plus 2 tablespoons flour
    for greasing and flouring pan
⅓ cup orange juice
4 large eggs
¾ cup canola or vegetable oil
1 tablespoon pure vanilla extract
1½ cups sugar
2½ cups all-purpose flour
1 tablespoon baking powder
¼ teaspoon salt
¼ teaspoon ground cinnamon
¼ teaspoon ground ginger
¼ teaspoon ground cumin

BLUEBERRY FILLING

3 cups fresh or one 10-ounce bag frozen blueberries
1 tablespoon sugar
1 tablespoon all-purpose flour
¼ teaspoon ground ginger

1 Preheat the oven to 375°F. Grease and flour a 9 x 13-inch baking pan.

2 To make the cake: Whisk together the orange juice, eggs, oil, and vanilla in a large bowl. Add the sugar, flour, baking powder, salt, cinnamon, ginger, and cumin and mix well with a silicone spatula or wooden spoon. You will have a very thick batter.

3 To make the filling: place the blueberries, sugar, flour, and ginger in a medium bowl and toss to combine.

4 Using a silicone spatula, spread half of the batter into the prepared baking pan. Scatter the blueberry mixture and any sugar and flour remaining at the bottom of the bowl all around the batter. Scoop up the remaining batter and, a little at a time, drop it on top of the blueberry layer. You may not have enough batter to completely cover the blueberry layer; just do your best and spread very gently.

5 Bake for 55 to 60 minutes, or until a skewer inserted in the cake comes out clean. Let cool for 10 minutes in the pan and then turn onto a rack to cool completely.

Banana Bread

SERVES 16

STORAGE

Store covered in plastic at room temperature for up to five days or freeze wrapped in plastic for up to three months.

Banana bread is probably among the first five desserts I ever baked; I simply cannot bring myself to eat bananas that have turned black or let them go to waste.

Spray oil containing flour or spray oil plus 2 tablespoons flour
   for greasing and flouring pans

3 medium-sized ripe bananas

¾ cup (1½ sticks) parve margarine

½ cup sugar

2 large eggs

1½ teaspoons pure vanilla extract

2 cups all-purpose flour

1 teaspoon baking soda

¾ teaspoon salt

½ cup parve plain soy milk

1 Preheat the oven to 325°F. Grease and flour a 12-inch loaf pan.

2 Purée the bananas in a food processor or in a medium bowl with a hand blender or potato masher. Set aside.

3 In a large bowl, beat the margarine and sugar with a stand or hand-held electric mixer on medium-high speed or whisk by hand until creamy. Add the banana purée, eggs, and vanilla and mix well. Add the flour, baking soda, and salt and mix again. Add the soy milk and mix until combined.

4 Pour the batter into the loaf pan and bake for 70 minutes, or until a skewer inserted in the center comes out clean. Cool for 15 minutes in the pan and then remove to a rack to cool completely.

Corn Bread

MAKES FORTY 2-INCH SQUARES

STORAGE

Store covered in plastic at room temperature for up to five days or freeze wrapped in plastic for up to three months.

I had always thought of corn bread as a bread and not a dessert. Then one year on the Shabbat after Thanksgiving my kids kept asking for corn bread when my husband and I were eating pumpkin and cranberry desserts. This recipe was adapted from one I got years ago from Rickie Bobeck. It's designed for a crowd; it makes two 9 x 13-inch pans. You can also halve the recipe, but why bother? It freezes very well.

Spray oil containing flour or spray oil plus 2 tablespoons flour
   for greasing and flouring pans

4 cups all-purpose flour

2 cups yellow corn meal

1½ cups sugar

1 teaspoon salt

2 tablespoons baking powder

4 large eggs

1 cup parve whipping cream

2½ tablespoons canola or vegetable oil

2 cups parve plain soy milk

½ cup (1 stick) parve margarine, melted

————

1 Preheat the oven to 350°F. Grease and flour two 9 x 13-inch baking pans.

2 In a large bowl, sift together the flour, corn meal, sugar, salt, and baking powder. In a medium bowl, whisk together the eggs, whipping cream, oil, and soy milk. Pour the wet ingredients into the dry ingredients. Add the melted margarine and stir until just combined.

3 Bake for 1 hour, or until a skewer comes out clean. The corn bread should be a little brown on top. Serve warm or at room temperature.

Vanilla Sheet Cake

MAKES ONE 9 X 13-INCH SHEET CAKE (SERVING 20) OR 18 CUPCAKES

STORAGE
Store covered with plastic or in an airtight container at room temperature
for up to five days or freeze for up to three months.

I use this cake for birthday parties where each kid gets about a 4 by 4-inch stack of cake layers to build his or her own layer cake and then decorate it with many colors of icing. I trim the cake sides straight, cut the cake into nine or twelve squares and then turn the individual squares on their sides and slice each into three or four layers. One year I spent every Sunday for three months straight doing baking parties for seven-year-old girls. My kids were thrilled because they got to eat all the sides and trimmings. You can also use this recipe to make cupcakes. For icing options, see pages 296–99.

————

Spray oil containing flour or spray oil plus 2 tablespoons flour
   for greasing and flouring pan

4 large eggs

2 cups sugar

1 cup canola or vegetable oil

2½ cups all-purpose flour

¾ cup parve plain soy milk

2 teaspoons baking powder

Dash of salt

1 teaspoon pure vanilla extract

————

1 Preheat the oven to 350°F. Grease and flour a 9 x 13-inch rectangular pan.
2 In a large bowl, whisk together the eggs, sugar, oil, flour, soy milk, baking powder, salt, and vanilla.
3 Pour into the prepared pan and bake for 55 to 60 minutes, or until a skewer inserted in the cake comes out clean. Let cool for 10 minutes in the pan and then turn onto a rack to cool completely.

VANILLA CUPCAKES

1 Preheat the oven to 350°F. Place paper liners in 18 muffin cups.
2 Follow Step 2 for Vanilla Cake, above.
3 Pour the batter evenly into the muffin cups, two-thirds to three-quarters full. Bake for 30 to 35 minutes, or until a toothpick inserted in a cupcake comes out clean. Let cool for 10 minutes in the pan and then place the cupcakes on a rack to cool completely.

Chocolate Cupcakes

MAKES 18 CUPCAKES

STORAGE

Store covered with plastic or in an airtight container at room temperature for up to five days or freeze for up to three months.

These are not your typical cupcakes. My nephew had just turned six and was coming to visit. I was told that Beni loved chocolate so I set out to make chocolate cupcakes with icing. I decided that I wanted something more dense than my basic chocolate sponge cake recipe but not as gooey as my brownie recipe. After staring at the two recipes for 10 minutes, trying to understand the science behind gooey versus spongy cakes, I came up with a plan. The first try was great. Sadly, one of the cupcakes broke in half when I removed it from the muffin pan so I just *had* to eat it. It tasted like one of those restaurant-style warm chocolate cakes. I instantly baked a second batch. To serve to grownups for an elegant dessert, serve warm with a chocolate or berry sauce or a frosting such as

the Quick Buttercream Icing, Traditional Buttercream Icing, or Vanilla Cream Cheese Frosting (pages 296–99).

---

8 ounces parve semisweet or bittersweet chocolate,
    chopped or broken into 1-inch pieces

½ cup canola or vegetable oil

1½ cups sugar

½ cup parve plain soy milk

3 large eggs

1 teaspoon pure vanilla extract

½ teaspoon salt

½ teaspoon baking powder

½ cup parve unsweetened cocoa

1½ cups all-purpose flour

---

1 Preheat the oven to 350°F. Place 18 paper muffin cups in a muffin pan or pans.

2 Melt the chocolate on the stovetop or in the microwave, following the "Melting chocolate" instructions (see Foolproof Tips and Techniques).

3 When the chocolate is melted, whisk in the oil and sugar. Add the soy milk, eggs, and vanilla and whisk again. Add the salt, baking powder, and cocoa and whisk again. Finally, add the flour and mix well with a wooden spoon or silicone spatula. The batter will be thick.

4 Using a ¼- or ⅓-cup measuring cup to scoop up batter, fill the muffin cups about two-thirds to three-quarters full, dividing the batter evenly among the 18 muffin cups.

5 Bake for 30 to 33 minutes, or until a toothpick comes out with only a little chocolate on it. Let cool for 10 minutes in the pan and then remove the cupcakes to a rack. Serve warm or at room temperature. They may be reheated in a 200°F oven for 20 minutes or in the microwave for 30 seconds.

Black & Blue Muffins

MAKES 18 MUFFINS

STORAGE

Store covered with plastic or in an airtight container at room temperature for up to five days or freeze for up to three months.

My son Sam likes to eat these for breakfast so I make a batch and freeze them. He often refuses to share them with his brothers. I sometimes substitute ½ cup whole-wheat flour for ½ cup of the white flour to add some fiber. Sam doesn't notice the change.

———

1 cup (2 sticks) parve margarine

1 cup sugar

¼ cup light brown sugar

2 large eggs

1 tablespoon honey

1 teaspoon pure vanilla extract

¼ teaspoon ground cinnamon

2 cups all-purpose flour (or 1½ cup white flour and
    ½ cup whole-wheat flour)

¼ teaspoon salt

2 teaspoons baking powder

½ cup parve plain soy milk, divided

6 ounces (½ pint) blueberries

6 ounces (½ pint) blackberries, cut in half if large

———

1 Preheat the oven to 350°F. Place paper liners in 18 muffin cups.

2 In a large bowl, beat the margarine, sugar, and brown sugar with a stand or hand-held electric mixer on medium-high speed or by hand with a whisk until creamy, scraping down the sides of the bowl with a spatula as necessary. Add the eggs, honey, vanilla, and cinnamon and beat again briefly.

3 In a separate bowl, whisk by hand the flour, salt, and baking powder. Add half the dry mixture to the bowl with the other ingredients and whisk until just combined. Add half the soy milk and whisk again. Repeat with the rest of the dry ingredients and the soy milk. Add the fruit and mix in gently with a wooden spoon.

4 Spoon the batter into the muffin cups, filling each about two-thirds full. Tap the pan on the counter to even out the batter in the cups. Bake for 35 minutes, or until a toothpick inserted comes out clean. Let cool for 10 minutes in pan and then remove to a rack to cool completely.

Summer Fruit Triangles

MAKES 10 TRIANGLES

STORAGE

> *Store covered with plastic or in an airtight container at room*
> *temperature for three days. These pastries can be reheated in a 200°F*
> *oven for 30 minutes.*

This is one of the easiest desserts to make and it contains no added sugar. I have even made these in kids' cooking classes. It uses ultra-convenient parve frozen puff pastry squares, which I always keep on hand in the freezer. You can vary this recipe with different fruits; just measure about two cups chopped fruit.

———

Ten 4 x 4-inch parve frozen puff pastry squares

3 plums, cut into ½-inch pieces

1 peach, cut into ½-inch pieces

3 large strawberries, cut into ¼-inch dice

2 teaspoons cornstarch

½ teaspoon ground cinnamon, divided

1 large egg

Frozen parve puff pastry is a great product to keep in your freezer. You can make many different quick desserts with it.

1 Preheat the oven to 400°F. Line a baking sheet with parchment.

2 Thaw the puff pastry at room temperature for 30 to 45 minutes or use the "Quick thaw method for puff pastry" (see Foolproof Tips and Techniques). The squares are ready to use when you can bend the stack of squares slightly. As you peel off each square, the other layers will thaw as you work.

3 Place the cut fruit in a bowl. Add the cornstarch and ¼ teaspoon of the cinnamon and toss to coat.

4 Place some water in a small bowl. Peel off a puff pastry square, dip your fingers in the water, and wet all the edges of the square. Place about 2 tablespoons of the fruit mixture in the center of the square.

Fold the square into a triangle and pinch tightly along the edges to seal them. Place the triangle on the prepared cookie sheet. Repeat with the remaining pastry squares and fruit.

5 In a small bowl, beat the egg with remaining ¼ teaspoon cinnamon. Use a pastry brush to brush the tops of the pastries. Bake for 30 minutes or until golden brown.

Chocolate Chip Pastry Sticks

MAKES 18 TO 20 STICKS

STORAGE

Store covered with plastic or in an airtight container at room temperature for four days or freeze for up to three months.

These sticks taste fine at room temperature, but you can reheat them in a toaster oven or, on Shabbat, you can place them on foil in a low, 200°F oven.

Flour for sprinkling

One 17.3-ounce box parve frozen puff pastry sheets (2 sheets total)

2 large egg yolks

3 tablespoons parve plain soy milk, divided

½ teaspoon pure vanilla extract

¾ cup mini parve chocolate chips or 1 cup regular-size parve chocolate chips

---

1 Preheat the oven to 400°F. Line 2 cookie sheets with parchment.

2 Thaw the puff pastry at room temperature for 45 minutes or use the "Quick thaw method for puff pastry" (see Foolproof Tips and Techniques). The dough is ready to use when you can unroll it easily without breaking it.

3 In a small bowl, whisk together the egg yolks, 2 tablespoons of the soy milk, and the vanilla. Set aside. Place a piece of parchment (about 9 inches long) on the counter and sprinkle it with some flour. Unroll 1 sheet of pastry dough onto the parchment and, using a rolling pin, roll it out until it is about 9 inches long by 7 inches wide. If your rolling pin starts to stick to the pastry, rub a little flour directly on the rolling pin. Use a pastry brush to brush the egg mixture all over the pastry. (Do not use all of the egg mixture; you will use it twice more.) Sprinkle the chips

all over so that the dough is well covered. Use your hands to press the chips gently into the dough.

4 Place another piece of parchment on the counter, sprinkle it with flour and unroll the second piece of pastry onto it. Roll it out to 9 x 7 inches and brush with the egg mixture. Place your hand under the parchment of the second pastry, lift it up and turn it over on top of the chip-covered dough. Press the top dough into the chips. Remove the top parchment. If you like, you can trim the sides of the dough so that each side is straight.

5 Using a non-serrated knife, slice the dough in half across the longer side to create two 9 x 3½-inch pieces. Slice each half into 1-inch strips; you will have about 18 to 20 strips when you are done. Place the strips on the prepared cookie sheets, 1 inch apart. Add the remaining 1 tablespoon of soy milk to the remaining egg mixture and stir. Brush the top of each chocolate chip strip with the egg mixture.

6 Bake for 15 to 20 minutes, or until golden on top. So that the sticks brown evenly, turn the cookie sheets after 10 minutes and switch racks after 15 minutes. These are best served immediately or reheated later in a low 200°F oven.

Apricot Pastries

MAKES 40 PASTRIES

STORAGE

*Store covered with plastic or in an airtight container at room temperature
for four days or freeze for up to three months.*

These are very cute mini pastries that I like to keep in the freezer and thaw as needed. You can use either the 4 x 4- or 3 x 3-inch frozen pastry squares. I prefer the 3-inch squares because the resulting pastries are smaller.

———

10 parve frozen 3 x 3- or 4 x 4-inch puff pastry squares
   (about ¾ of a package)
½ to ⅔ cup apricot butter or apricot preserves
2 teaspoons vanilla sugar (to make your own, see page xxviii)

———

1 Preheat the oven to 400°F. Thaw the puff pastry squares at room temperature for 30 to 45 minutes or use the "Quick thaw method for puff pastry" (see Foolproof

Tips and Techniques). The squares are ready to use when you can bend the stack of squares slightly. As you peel off each square, the other layers will thaw as you work.

2 Line 2 large cookie sheets with parchment. Place some water in a small bowl. Take one of the pastry squares and cut it into 4 equal squares. Place ¼ teaspoon of apricot butter or jam in the center of each small square. Wet your finger and moisten one corner of an apricot-filled square. Fold the opposite corner over the apricot filling and then take the wet corner and fold it over the dry pastry corner and press to close, leaving some of the apricot filling to stick out over and under where the dough is pressed together.

3 Place on cookie sheet and repeat with the remaining apricot filling and squares, placing the pastries 1 inch apart on the cookie sheets. Sprinkle with the vanilla sugar. Place in the freezer for 10 to 15 minutes (this will help them hold together better).

4 Bake for 15 to 20 minutes, or until lightly browned. If any of the pastries open during baking, wait 3 to 4 minutes for them to cool, then use your fingers to reseal them, holding in place a few seconds.

Almond Puff Pastry Twists

MAKES ABOUT 50 STICKS

STORAGE

Store covered with plastic or in an airtight container at room temperature for four days or freeze for up to three months.

These are sweet, crunchy, and nutty puff pastry sticks. I sometimes make a savory version to serve with soup using black and white sesame seeds, caraway seeds, and salt, omitting the sugar and nuts.

———

1 sheet parve frozen puff pastry (from a 17.3-ounce box)
½ cup sliced almonds (with skin on)
⅓ cup vanilla sugar (to make your own, see page xxviii)
Flour, for sprinkling
1 large egg, beaten

1 Preheat the oven to 425°F. Line 2 baking sheets with parchment.

2 Thaw the puff pastry at room temperature for 45 minutes or use the "Quick thaw method for puff pastry" (see Foolproof Tips and Techniques). The dough is ready to use when you can unroll it easily without breaking it.

3 Place the sliced almonds in the bowl of a food processor fitted with a metal blade and process the nuts until they are ground into small pieces, not into a powder. Transfer to a small bowl and add the vanilla sugar and toss together.

4 Place a piece of parchment on the counter and sprinkle with 1 tablespoon of flour. Place the puff pastry sheet on the parchment and roll it out until the pastry is a rectangle, about 12 x 14 inches. If your rolling pin starts to stick to the pastry, rub a little flour directly on the rolling pin. Use a pastry brush to brush the pastry completely with the beaten egg (reserving some egg for the other side). Sprinkle half the almond mixture on the pastry and press gently with your fingers so the mixture sticks to the pastry. Set another piece of parchment over the dough and flip the dough and parchment over. Carefully remove the top parchment. Brush the second side with the egg and sprinkle on the rest of the almond-sugar mixture. Once again, press gently.

5 Cut the dough lengthwise into 3 long strips approximately 4 x 14 inches. Then cut them crosswise into ½ to ¾ x 4-inch strips. Peel off each strip, stretch slightly, and then twist them with your fingers 2 to 3 times. Place on prepared baking sheets 1 inch apart.

6 Bake for 12 to 14 minutes, or until the tops start to look brown. Slide the parchment off the baking sheet onto a rack and let the pastries cool to room temperature completely.

Apple Pastry

SERVES 15

STORAGE

Store covered with plastic or in an airtight container at room temperature for three days.

This is one of my "fallback" recipes if I am looking to bake something easy that I know I will have the ingredients for. I always keep puff pastry in my freezer and I always have some kind of apples around. I like to serve this for breakfast or brunch.

1 sheet frozen parve puff pastry (from a 17.3-ounce box)

¼ cup sugar

2 teaspoons ground cinnamon

Flour, for sprinkling

2 tablespoons parve margarine, melted

½ cup applesauce

4 apples, peeled and cored (McIntosh, Gala, Fuji, or Granny Smith)

1 Preheat the oven to 425°F.

2 Thaw the puff pastry at room temperature for 45 minutes or use the "Quick thaw method for puff pastry" (see Foolproof Tips and Techniques).

3 In a small bowl, combine the sugar and cinnamon.

4 Place a piece of parchment about 16 inches long on the counter. Sprinkle with flour. Place the pastry sheet on the floured parchment and, with a rolling pin, smooth out the creases, keeping the rectangle shape. Roll the dough out to about 14 x 16 inches. If your rolling pin starts to stick to the pastry, rub a little flour directly on the rolling pin. Cut the dough lengthwise into 3 long strips, about 4½ x 16 inches each. (Leave them in place, as you will use the same parchment for baking the pastries.) Cut ½ inch off each long side of each strip and set aside. You will have 3 large 16 x 3-inch-wide strips and six 16 x ½-inch-wide strips.

5 Brush about an inch of the borders of the large pieces of pastry with some of the melted margarine. Place a ½-inch strip on one long side of the pastry and another ½-inch strip on the other long side to form a raised border. Repeat with the remaining two large strips and four narrower strips. Spread one-third of the applesauce on each pastry in between the borders.

6 Cut the apples into very thin slices. Place the apple slices overlapping in between the borders, with the apple slices facing the long way, trimming the apple slices to fit if necessary. Sprinkle a tablespoon of cinnamon sugar over the top of the apples in each pastry. Slide the parchment onto a cookie sheet.

7 Bake for 20 minutes, or until the edges are golden. Let cool for 10 minutes and then cut each long strip across into 5 pieces. Serve warm or at room temperature.

Cinnamon Palmiers

MAKES 32 TO 36 PASTRIES

STORAGE

*Store covered with plastic or in an airtight container at room temperature
for four days or freeze for up to three months.*

I have always loved these pastries no matter what they are called: I knew them as
"elephant ears" growing up but the French call them "palmiers."

———

One 17.3-ounce box parve frozen puff pastry sheets
⅔ cup sugar
4 teaspoons ground cinnamon
Flour, for sprinkling

———

1 Preheat the oven to 400°F. Thaw the puff pastry at
   room temperature for 45 minutes or use the "Quick
   thaw method for puff pastry" (see Foolproof Tips and
   Techniques). The dough is ready to use when you can
   unroll it easily without breaking it.

2 In a small bowl, combine the sugar and cinnamon.

3 Place parchment on the counter and sprinkle with flour.
   Unroll one pastry sheet and place on the parchment
   with the creases at right angles to a rolling pin. Use the
   rolling pin to smooth out the creases and to roll out the
   rectangle about 2 inches larger on each side.

4 Sprinkle one-fourth of the cinnamon sugar on the
   dough, covering it. Place a second piece of parchment
   on top and use a rolling pin to roll over the dough twice
   in each direction, pressing the cinnamon sugar into the
   dough. Place your hand under the parchment and flip it
   over. Peel off the top piece of parchment and then cover
   the exposed side of the dough with another one-fourth
   of the cinnamon sugar. Return the parchment to the
   dough and then roll over it with your rolling pin to press
   the cinnamon sugar into the dough. Remove the top
   piece of parchment from the dough.

5 Use a dull knife to score (mark, but do not cut completely through) a line horizontally across the middle of the dough. One side at a time, roll tightly from the outside toward the scored line in the middle, using either your fingers or the parchment to help you roll. Stop rolling at the middle line. Repeat with the other side. Fold the sides of parchment up over the rolled dough, roll up the parchment around the dough, and place in the freezer. Repeat with the second sheet of dough, following Steps 3 through 5.

6 Take the spare piece of parchment you removed from the dough and place it on a cookie sheet.

7 Remove the first roll from the freezer, slice crosswise into ¾-inch slices, and place cut-side down on the cookie sheet 2 inches apart. The pastries will appear dry; do not worry about that.

8 Bake for 14 minutes. Turn the palmiers over and bake another 5 minutes, watching so they do not burn. Both sides should be equally golden. Slide the parchment off the cookie sheet onto a cooling rack and let the cookies cool to room temperature.

9 Remove the second roll from the freezer, and slice as you did the first roll. Bake as you did the first batch.

Vanilla Bean Crispy Treats

MAKES SIXTEEN 2-INCH-SQUARE BARS

STORAGE

Store in an airtight container at room temperature for five days.

Okay, so Rice Krispie Treats are truly desserts for dummies, but everyone—kids and adults—loves them. When I lived in Switzerland, a group of American ex-patriate friends would get together to make them to remind them of home. I wanted to update the classic recipe so I tried vanilla bean. My kids were fighting over them. They are very addictive. Feel free to double the recipe and place into a 9 x 13-inch pan. If needed, you can use vanilla extract in this recipe, but the fresh vanilla bean taste is very strong and is what makes these special.

———

2 tablespoons parve margarine, plus extra to grease pan

1 vanilla bean, split lengthwise and scraped (reserve seeds),
   or 2 teaspoons pure vanilla extract

One 7-ounce package large marshmallows

4 cups crisp rice cereal

1 Grease an 8-inch square baking pan.

2 Place the margarine in a large microwave-safe bowl and heat in the microwave for 30 seconds or until melted. Add the vanilla seeds to the margarine and whisk to mix in.

3 Add the marshmallows to the bowl and return to the microwave and cook until the marshmallows melt and puff up, about 1 to 1½ minutes. Use a silicone spatula to mix the marshmallows into the margarine. Add the cereal and mix it into the marshmallow mixture.

4 Place the batter in the prepared pan and use a spatula to spread as evenly as you can. Let cool to room temperature and then cut into pieces.

Mocha Brownie Fudge

MAKES ABOUT 4 DOZEN SMALL SQUARES

STORAGE

Store covered or in an airtight container in the refrigerator for up to five days or freeze for up to three months.

These are basically a baked fudge candy, too thick to be brownies, but great as a candy.

———

4 ounces parve unsweetened chocolate

½ cup canola or vegetable oil

1 tablespoon instant coffee granules or ground coffee

1¼ cups sugar

¼ teaspoon salt

1 teaspoon pure vanilla extract

2 large eggs

⅔ cup all-purpose flour

———

1 Preheat the oven to 400°F. Line an 8-inch square baking pan with foil, allowing some to extend up and over the sides. (You can also use 2 sheets of foil about 16 inches long each, place on the counter in a "T," and place into the pan.) Press into the corners.

2   In a medium saucepan, heat the chocolate, oil, and coffee granules over medium heat, stirring frequently until the chocolate is melted and the coffee granules have dissolved. Remove from the heat. With a wooden spoon, mix in the sugar and salt. Add vanilla and eggs and mix again. Add the flour and stir until the batter is smooth and starting to come away from the sides of the saucepan. Spread the batter evenly in the baking pan.

3   Bake for 25 minutes or until the top is set. Immediately place the pan in the refrigerator on top of a dish towel to protect the refrigerator shelf. When completely cooled, use the ends of the foil to lift the fudge up and out of the pan. Remove the foil and place on a cutting board. Cut into small 1- to 1½-inch squares.

◇ *Fruit Soup with Triple Sorbet Garnish*

SERVES 6 TO 8 (WILL DEPEND ON MELON SIZE)

STORAGE

Store covered in the refrigerator for up to three days.

In 1994, I ate a similar dessert in the Burgundy region of France and remembered it for ten years until I developed my own version. You may add other fruit to the bowls. To make this a no-sugar-added dessert, simply omit the honey.

---

1 large ripe honeydew melon, peeled, seeded, and cut in chunks

1 teaspoon honey

3 ripe unpeeled peaches, pitted

6 ounces fresh raspberries

½ pint each of coconut, mango, and raspberry or mixed berry or other fruit sorbet

---

1   Place the honeydew into the bowl of a blender or food processor fitted with a metal blade. Process until completely puréed. Pour into a large container or bowl. Add the honey and stir.

2   Place the peaches into the bowl of the blender or food processor and process until completely puréed. Use a fine mesh strainer to strain the peach purée into the container with the puréed melon. Mix well and refrigerate until well-chilled before serving.

3 To serve, ladle the soup into shallow soup bowls. Carefully scatter the raspberries among the bowls so that you can still see them and they do not sink. Take a melon baller and scoop one ball each of the three sorbet flavors and carefully place into the bowls. Depending on the size of your bowls, you can add more than three sorbet balls to the bowl.

◇ Strawberry Gazpacho

SERVES 5 TO 6

STORAGE

Store in the refrigerator for up to three days.

Although in today's global world we get strawberries all year-round, I would highly recommend making this soup when strawberries are in season and they are more flavorful. You can also serve it as a first course or in shot glasses for a cocktail party. You can omit the sugar if desired.

---

2 pounds strawberries, washed and hulled (about 1 quart plus ½ pint)

14 mint leaves, divided

1 teaspoon fresh lemon juice

3 tablespoons confectioners' sugar (or more depending on tartness
   of fruit)

2 teaspoons orange blossom water (optional)

1½ cups whole raspberries or ¼-inch diced fruit, such as kiwi, mango,
   and/or apricot

---

1 Place the strawberries in a blender or the bowl of a food processor fitted with a metal blade and purée until smooth, scraping down the bowl to get all the pieces puréed. Add 8 of the mint leaves, the lemon juice, confectioners' sugar, and orange blossom water and process again until well mixed. Taste to see if it needs any more sugar and add to taste.

2 Cut the remaining 6 mint leaves into very thin slices.

3 To serve, ladle the purée into small bowls and scoop up ¼ cup of fruit and add to each bowl. Sprinkle some of the sliced mint leaves on top.

Tarts, Pies, & Cobbler

Quick Apricot Tart

MAKES ONE 8- OR 10-INCH TART, 10 OR 12 SERVINGS,
   OR SIX 3-INCH INDIVIDUAL TARTS

STORAGE
   Store covered with plastic at room temperature for up to three days.

You can do so many creative things with this recipe. You can bake it in an 8- or 10-inch round baking pan or a tart pan of equal size with a removable bottom. You can double the recipe and bake it on a cookie sheet or jelly roll pan, making rows of different fruit, and slice it into squares to serve. I have also used 3-inch tart rings (that have no bottom) and served it plated with raspberry or blackberry sauce (see page 294). You can also use plums, raspberries, blackberries or blueberries, or any combination thereof, to make this recipe your own creation or reflect the fruit in season.

Spray oil, for greasing pan

4 to 5 fresh apricots, halved and pitted

1¼ cups all-purpose flour

½ cup plus 2 tablespoons sugar, divided

½ teaspoon ground ginger

½ teaspoon baking powder

6 tablespoons parve margarine, cut into 12 small pieces

1 large egg, beaten

1 teaspoon pure vanilla extract

1 Preheat the oven to 375°F. Grease an 8- to 10-inch round baking or tart pan with spray oil.

2 Cut each apricot half into 4 slices.

3 Place the flour, ½ cup of the sugar, the ginger, and baking powder in the bowl of a food processor fitted with a metal blade. You can also mix the ingredients by hand in a large bowl with a whisk. Add margarine pieces and process or whisk for 10 seconds until the mixture looks like sand. Add egg and vanilla and process just

until the dough comes together. If making by hand, use your hands to knead the dough together. Take a handful of the dough, flatten it in your hand and then press it into the pan. Continue with the rest of the dough, covering the bottom evenly.

4 Starting at the outside of the pan, press the side of your finger into the dough to make indentations for the fruit. Starting at the outside edge of the pan, place the fruit wedges into the indentations tightly next to each other and press gently. Repeat with another ring inside the first ring of fruit and repeat until you reach the center. Sprinkle the remaining 2 tablespoons of sugar on top of the fruit.

5 Bake for 45 minutes, or until the pastry is lightly browned on the edges. Let cool to room temperature in the pan. Run a knife around the edges of the pan, then place a plate on top of the pan. Flip the tart over onto the plate, then turn over right-side up onto a serving plate. If you used a tart pan with a removable bottom, place your hand under the pan and lift the tart out of the outer ring. Slice into 10 or 12 wedges.

FANCY INDIVIDUAL TARTS

1 Preheat the oven to 375°F. Grease the insides of six 3-inch tart rings with a little soft margarine and place the rings on a parchment-lined cookie sheet.

2 Follow Step 3 for Quick Apricot Tart, above, and press the dough into the rings until it fits tightly in the rings.

3 Cut apricot half into 3 slices. Press the side of your finger into the dough to make indentations for the fruit in any design you like. Place the fruit into the indentations. Sprinkle the remaining 2 tablespoons of sugar on top of the fruit.

4 Bake for 30 to 40 minutes, or until the edges are brown. To serve, lift the rings off the tarts.

Cranberry Pumpkin Frangipane Tart

SERVES 8

STORAGE

Store covered in plastic at room temperature for up to three days.

This dessert is a big hit on Thanksgiving as it has the typical tastes of the holiday. It is prepared like a cake but looks like a French-style tart.

———

Spray oil, for greasing pan

5 tablespoons parve margarine

¼ cup plus 2 tablespoons light brown sugar

1½ cups almond flour (see "Making almond flour," page xxvii)

¼ cup all-purpose flour

½ cup sugar

4 large egg whites

⅓ cup canned pumpkin purée (not pumpkin pie filling)

2 cups fresh cranberries

¼ cup dried cranberries

———

1 Preheat the oven to 375°F. Grease a 9-inch springform pan with spray oil.

2 In a small saucepan, heat the margarine and ¼ cup of the brown sugar over medium heat until the margarine melts. You can also heat the margarine with the brown sugar in the microwave for 1 minute or until melted. Stir and set aside.

3 Place the almond flour into a medium bowl. Add the flour and white sugar and whisk together. Add the egg whites and pumpkin and whisk again. Add the margarine/brown sugar mixture in two parts and mix well after each addition. Pour the batter into the pan.

4 In a small bowl, combine the fresh and dried cranberries and remaining 2 tablespoons of brown sugar. Sprinkle on the top of the batter.

5 Bake for 40 to 45 minutes, or until the edges are browned. Serve warm or at room temperature. To serve, run a knife along the edge of the tart, remove the sides of the springform pan, and cut into wedges.

Plum-Cherry Mini Tarte Tatins

MAKES 12 MINI TARTS

STORAGE

This can be made 1 day in advance and stored in the refrigerator.

A tarte tatin is typically a French upside-down apple tart with caramelized apples (see Apple Tarte Tatin, page 121). These tarte tatins are definitely tart but everyone seemed to like them that way.

Spray oil, for greasing muffin pan

1 sheet frozen parve puff pastry
(from a 17.3-ounce box)

10 medium-size fresh plums,
halved and pitted

⅓ cup sugar

2 tablespoons parve margarine

Dash of ground nutmeg

Dash of ground cinnamon

12 pitted cherries, fresh or frozen
(see "Pitting cherries,"
page xxviii)

Flour, for sprinkling

1 Preheat the oven to 400°F. Grease a 12-cup muffin pan with spray oil.

2 Remove one sheet of puff pastry sheet from the box and thaw it at room temperature for 30 to 45 minutes or use the "Quick thaw method for puff pastry" (see Foolproof Tips and Techniques). The dough is ready to use when you can unroll it easily without breaking it.

3 Cut each of the plum halves into five ¼-inch wedges (10 wedges per whole plum). Place the sugar and margarine in a large heavy frying pan over medium heat and stir until the margarine and sugar have melted. Add the nutmeg, cinnamon, and plum wedges and cook for 2 minutes on high heat. Turn off the heat. Slice each of the cherries into 6 pieces and add to the plum mixture and stir to combine. Set aside to cool.

4 Place a piece of parchment the size of the pastry sheet on the counter and sprinkle some flour on it. Working on the parchment, roll the pastry sheet out to about 1 inch larger than its original size.

5 Using a glass or round cookie cutter that is a little larger than the muffin holes, cut 12 circles out of the dough.

6 Divide the plum-cherry mixture evenly into the 12 cups of the muffin pan. Place a pastry circle into each muffin compartment on top of the fruit. Bake for 25 minutes, or until the pastry is golden. Let cool in the pan to room temperature.

7 To serve, you will need 2 soup spoons. Use one spoon to scoop under the fruit and use the second to help you carefully place the tart onto a plate with the pastry on the bottom. Spoon any extra juice around the plate.

Four Quick Fruit Pies

ONE PIE SERVES 8

STORAGE

Store covered in plastic in the refrigerator for up to four days or freeze for up to three months.

My neighbor saw me at the store buying ready-made frozen pie crusts and was shocked— she thought she'd caught me doing something illicit. Although it's great to make your own crust when you can (see recipe on page 125 if you want to try), there's no shame in using store-bought. For those of you who don't have the time or expertise to make their own crusts, here you will find four possible pie fillings to choose from and three possible toppings. One method is to use a second pie crust and crumble it in your hands to scatter on top of the fruit. The second way is to cut out dough shapes from the second crust and place on top of the fruit. The third method is to make a streusel crumb topping. Mix and match pie fillings and toppings as you like.

---

1 frozen parve 9-inch deep-dish pie shell (2 if using Crust Crumble
  Topping or Crust Shapes)
Pie filling of your choice (see "4 Easy Pie Fillings," pages 59–60)
Pie topping of your choice (see "3 Easy Pie Toppings," page 60)

---

1 Preheat the oven to 350°F. Place an oven rack on the bottom shelf. Remove the pie shells from the freezer and separate (they come two to a package). If you're not using the second crust for the pie topping, return it to the freezer, wrapped in plastic.

2 Follow the directions opposite for the filling of your choice. Scoop up the pie filling into one of the pie shells. Top the pie with one of the 3 Easy Pie Toppings on page 60. For apple pie, I like to use dough circles, which look like apples; for blueberry pie, I like the homemade Crumb Topping; for peach, the Crumb Topping or Crust Crumble Topping; but for strawberry-rhubarb, I do not use any topping at all because the red color is so pretty.

3 Place the pie on a jelly roll pan and place in the oven. Bake for 1 hour, or until the crust is golden and the filling bubbly. Serve warm or at room temperature.

4 Easy Pie Fillings

APPLE PIE FILLING

    6 apples, peeled and cored
    Juice of ½ lemon
    ½ cup light brown sugar
    ¼ teaspoon ground cinnamon
    Dash of salt
    3 tablespoons all-purpose flour

Cut the apples into ¼-inch slices and place in a medium bowl. Add the lemon juice and stir. Add the brown sugar, cinnamon, salt, and flour, and toss to combine.

BLUEBERRY PIE FILLING

    16 ounces (1 pint) blueberries (measure 3½–4 cups), rinsed, dried,
        and stems removed
    Juice of ½ lemon
    ½ cup sugar
    Dash of salt
    ¼ teaspoon ground nutmeg
    3 tablespoons cornstarch

Place the blueberries and lemon juice in a medium bowl and stir. Add the rest of the ingredients and toss to combine.

PEACH PIE FILLING

    8 ripe peaches (about 2 pounds), peeled, stoned, and cut into
        ¼-inch slices
    Juice of ½ lemon
    ½ cup light brown sugar
    3 tablespoons cornstarch
    ½ teaspoon ground cinnamon
    Dash of salt

Place the peaches and lemon juice in a medium bowl and stir. Add the rest of the ingredients and toss to combine.

STRAWBERRY-RHUBARB PIE FILLING

10 stalks rhubarb, leaves removed, cut into 1-inch pieces

18 large strawberries

20 raspberries

⅓ cup sugar

3 tablespoons all-purpose flour

Dash of salt

Place the ingredients for the filling in a medium bowl and toss to combine.

3 Easy Pie Toppings

CRUMB TOPPING

6 tablespoons parve margarine

¼ cup light brown sugar

1 cup all-purpose flour

¼ teaspoon salt

Mix all the ingredients together in a bowl by hand or in a food processor and then sprinkle on top of the pie filling.

CRUST CRUMBLE TOPPING

1 frozen parve 9-inch deep-dish pie shell

Remove the pie crust from its pan, lift up pieces of the dough, and crumble them in your hands over the pie filling. Use about three-quarters of the pie crust.

CRUST SHAPES

1 frozen parve 9-inch deep-dish pie shell

1 large egg white, beaten

1 teaspoon sugar

Using a 2-inch round cookie cutter, cut out circles and place on top of the pie filling. You can use other shapes and even mini cookie cutters as well. You can overlap them if you like. Brush the crust edge and the circles or shapes with the egg white and sprinkle on the sugar.

Pumpkin Pie

SERVES 8

STORAGE

Store covered in the refrigerator for up to four days.

———

1 frozen parve 9-inch deep-dish pie shell

2 cups canned pumpkin purée (not pumpkin pie filling)

½ cup parve whipping cream

⅓ cup parve plain soy milk

2 large eggs

⅓ cup sugar

⅓ cup dark brown sugar

1 tablespoon all-purpose flour

1½ teaspoons ground cinnamon

¾ teaspoon ground ginger

½ teaspoon ground nutmeg

¼ teaspoon salt

———

1 Preheat the oven to 350°F. Remove the pie shell from the freezer and let thaw for 10 minutes. Place the pie shell on a jelly roll pan. Prick with a fork. Bake for 12 to 16 minutes, or until lightly browned. Remove from oven and set aside.

2 In a large bowl, whisk together the pumpkin, whipping cream, soy milk, and eggs. Add the white and brown sugars and whisk again. Add the flour, cinnamon, ginger, nutmeg, and salt, and whisk well. Pour into the baked pie shell. Bake for 50 minutes or until set. Let cool to room temperature and then chill until serving.

Far Breton

SERVES 8 TO 12

STORAGE

Store covered in plastic in the refrigerator. This dessert lasts a maximum of two days if you use the raspberries (they get too soft) or four days if you use the raisins.

A *far* is a creamy custard dessert from the Brittany region of France. It is typically made with prunes, but I prefer fresh raspberries or raisins.

———

1½ cups fresh raspberries or raisins

2 tablespoons rum

1 tablespoon pure vanilla extract, divided

2 cups parve plain soy milk

⅔ cup all-purpose flour

⅔ cup sugar

5 large eggs

———

1 Preheat the oven to 450°F. Grease an 8- or 9-inch round baking pan.

2 Place the raspberries or raisins in a small bowl. Add the rum and ½ tablespoon of the vanilla and stir. Set aside. In a microwave-safe bowl, heat the soy milk until hot but not boiling (about 45 seconds in the microwave at high power).

3 In a large bowl, beat the flour, sugar, eggs, and the remaining ½ tablespoon of vanilla with a stand or hand-held electric mixer on medium speed or with a whisk until smooth, about 1 minute, scraping down the bowl as necessary. Add the soy milk and beat or whisk until combined. Pour the batter into the prepared pan. With a slotted spoon, remove the raspberries or raisins from the soaking liquid and scatter all around the batter. Discard the liquid.

4 Bake for 10 minutes. Reduce the heat to 350°F and bake another 40 to 45 minutes, or until the center is set and the edges are browned. Let cool in the pan and serve at room temperature or chilled.

Orange Mocha Pecan Pie

SERVES 8

STORAGE

Store covered in plastic at room temperature for up to four days or freeze up to three months.

This pie was inspired by one I found in the 1994 *Bon Appétit* Thanksgiving issue. (If you're looking for a great dairy pie, check that one out.) I had to play with the ingredients to make it parve and I wanted the orange flavor found in that crust, but with the convenience of using a ready-made pie shell.

----

1 frozen parve 9-inch deep-dish pie shell

2 tablespoons parve margarine

3 tablespoons parve unsweetened cocoa

1½ tablespoons finely ground coffee or instant coffee granules

3 tablespoons parve plain soy milk

1 teaspoon orange zest (grated outer peel) (from 1 orange)

1 teaspoon fresh orange juice (from zested orange)

1 cup light corn syrup

1 cup sugar

3 large eggs

1 teaspoon pure vanilla extract

¼ teaspoon salt

1¼ cups pecan halves, chopped or crushed into ½-inch pieces

----

1 Preheat the oven to 350°F. Remove the pie shell from freezer and let thaw 10 minutes. Place on a jelly roll pan. Prick with a fork. Bake for 12 to 16 minutes, or until lightly browned. Remove from the oven and set aside.

2 In a large microwave-safe bowl, heat the margarine in the microwave for 45 seconds or until melted. Whisk in the cocoa, ground coffee, and soy milk. Add the orange zest and juice, corn syrup, sugar, eggs, vanilla, and salt. Whisk until well blended. Stir in the pecans.

3 Pour the filling into the pie shell. Bake until puffed and set, about 1 hour. Transfer to a rack and cool completely.

Chocolate Chip Pie

SERVES 8

STORAGE

Store covered in plastic at room temperature for up to four days or freeze up to three months.

The inspiration for this very easy recipe came from my friend Trudy Jacobson. Though she made this pie with a homemade crust, this version calls for pre-made crust for an especially quick and easy dessert.

———————

1 parve frozen 8- or 9-inch pie shell

½ cup (1 stick) parve margarine, at room temperature

1 cup dark brown sugar

2 teaspoons pure vanilla extract

2 large eggs

½ cup all-purpose flour

1½ cups parve chocolate chips, divided

———————

1 Preheat the oven to 350°F. Take the pie shell out of the freezer. In a large bowl, beat the margarine and the brown sugar with a stand or hand-held electric mixer on medium-high speed until creamy. Add the vanilla, eggs, flour and 1 cup of the chocolate chips and beat again to mix well.

2 Pour the filling into the unbaked pie shell and smooth the top. Bake for 45 minutes or until the center is set. Remove from the oven and let cool.

3 Melt the remaining ½ cup of chips in a double boiler, or heat in the microwave for about 45 seconds or until melted. Use a spoon or whisk to drizzle chocolate lines over the top of the pie.

Pear & Berry Cobbler

SERVES 20

STORAGE

Store covered with plastic in the refrigerator for up to four days. This reheats well in a 200 to 250°F oven for 30 minutes.

I like to make this cobbler for Sukkot, the Fall holiday when we eat outside in temporary huts, when the air is cool at night and I can bring a warm dessert outside to my chilly guests. I also make this when I want to feed a crowd. To re-warm the cobbler, I put it in a low oven that I leave on during Shabbat or on holidays, after I take out my main course, and it is warm enough by dessert time. You can be as creative as you want with the combinations of fruit. This recipe is a good way to use up fruit that has been sitting around a while. It works with any combination that totals about 6 to 7 cups of chopped fruit.

FILLING

> 5 pears, cored (peel on)
> 2 cups fresh berries or one 10-ounce bag frozen berries
>   (blueberries, blackberries, and/or raspberries)
> ¾ cup sugar
> 2 teaspoons pure vanilla extract
> ¼ cup all-purpose flour

TOPPING

> ¾ cup raw oats (not quick-cooking kind)
> 12 tablespoons parve margarine
> 1½ cups sugar
> 2 large eggs
> 1 teaspoon pure vanilla extract
> ¾ cup all-purpose flour
> ¾ teaspoon baking powder
> Dash of salt

1 Preheat the oven to 375°F. Cut the pears into ¾- to 1-inch pieces. Place the pears and berries in an 11 x 14-inch oven-proof glass dish or other pretty oven-to-table baking dish. Add the sugar, vanilla, and flour, and toss to combine.

2 To make the topping: Place the oatmeal in the bowl of a food processor fitted with a metal blade and process until finely ground. In a large bowl, beat the margarine and sugar with a stand or hand-held electric mixer on medium-high speed until creamy. Add the eggs and vanilla and beat again. Add the flour, ground oatmeal, baking powder, and salt, and beat briefly to just combine.

3 Using 2 large spoons, spoon clumps of the dough on top of the fruit mixture. The dough will not cover the entire pan; the dough clumps melt and spread while baking.

4 Bake for 45 minutes, or until the top is browned and looks crisp. Serve warm or at room temperature.

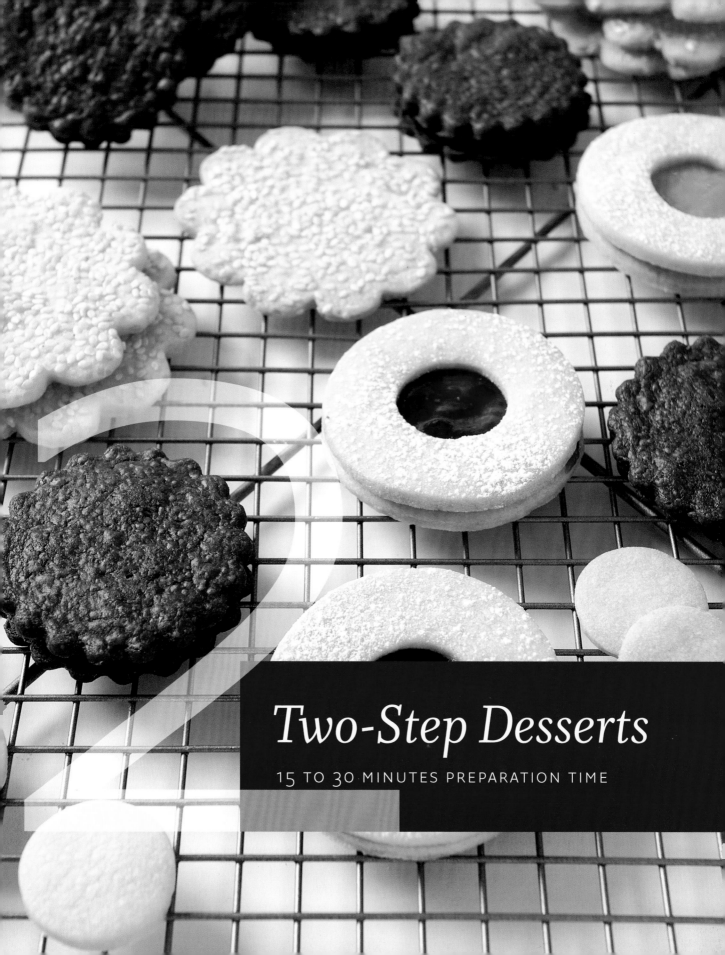

Two-Step Desserts

15 TO 30 MINUTES PREPARATION TIME

The desserts in this part are for when you a have a little more time to devote to baking, or you may have mastered the desserts in the first section and are ready to try something a little more ambitious. Most of the desserts in this part are not much harder than those in the first part, but they require more planning because they have two steps and take around 15 to 30 minutes preparation time. Generally each step is no longer than 15 minutes and there are ways to break down the steps to make things easier for yourself on the day you make a dessert. Those desserts that involve chilling dough do not have to be made in one day. You can make the dough one day and then complete the dessert within a few days. Even the layer cakes can either be made at one time or over several days. You can freeze the cake layers or in some cases complete the cake and freeze that.

Cookies, Biscotti, & Bar Cookies

Shortbread

MAKES ABOUT 4 DOZEN

STORAGE

Store covered with plastic or in an airtight container at room temperature for five days or freeze for up to three months.

These are basic, crisp "butter"-type cookies that you roll and cut into shapes. You can decorate them by dipping in or drizzling with melted chocolate, dipping into Poured Fondant Icing (see page 299), or decorating with Quick Buttercream Icing (page 296).

———

1 cup confectioners' sugar

2 cups plus 2 tablespoons all-purpose flour

1 cup (2 sticks) parve margarine, cut into tablespoons

Flour, for dusting parchment and dough

———

1   Place the confectioners' sugar and flour in the bowl of a food processor fitted with a metal blade. Pulse for 10 seconds. Add the margarine and process until the dough comes together into a ball. You can also mix by hand by cutting the margarine into the dry ingredients with a pastry cutter or two knives, then using your hands to squeeze the dough until it comes together. Divide the dough into 2 balls, wrap each in plastic, and press to flatten into discs. Place the dough in the freezer for 20 minutes or overnight.

2   Preheat the oven to 400°F. If kept in the freezer overnight, let the dough thaw just until you can press it gently.

3   Take two pieces of parchment and sprinkle a little flour on one, place one disc of dough on top, and then sprinkle a little more flour on top of the dough. Place the second piece of parchment on top of the dough and roll on top of the parchment until the dough is about ¼-inch thick. Every few rolls, peel back the top parchment

Don't worry if the cookie dough is a little dry when you roll it out, just keep working with the rolling pin and bring the crumbly pieces into the dough.

and sprinkle a little more flour on the dough. Remove the top parchment and use it to line a cookie sheet. Line another cookie sheet with fresh parchment.

4 Use cookie cutters to cut out cookies, then a metal flat-blade spatula to lift the cookies and place on the prepared cookie sheets. Re-roll any scraps and cut more cookies. If the dough becomes too soft and gets stuck to the bottom parchment, place in freezer until it gets harder. Repeat with the second disc of dough.

5 Bake for 10 to 12 minutes, or until the cookies begin to brown on the bottom. Check halfway through baking to see if the cookies in the back are browning faster than those in the front; if so, just turn the cookie sheet around. Slide the parchment off the cookie sheet onto a cooling rack and let the cookies cool.

Lemon Tea Cookies

MAKES ABOUT 4 DOZEN

STORAGE

Store covered with plastic or in an airtight container at room temperature for five days or freeze for up to three months.

One year I sold several cooking-class gift certificates for people to give to family and friends over the holidays. A woman bought a class to take with her grown children so they could spend time together. She asked me to teach them to make lemon cookies so I invented these.

1 cup confectioners' sugar

2 cups plus 2 tablespoons all-purpose flour

Zest (grated outer peel) of 1 large lemon

1 cup (2 sticks) parve margarine, cut into tablespoons

Flour, for dusting parchment and dough

1 Place the confectioners' sugar, flour, and zest in the bowl of a food processor fitted with a metal blade or stand mixer with a whisk. Pulse or mix for 10 seconds. Add the margarine and process or mix until the dough comes together into a ball. You can also mix by hand by cutting the margarine into the dry ingredients with a pastry cutter or two knives, then using your hands to squeeze the dough until it comes together.

2 Divide the dough into 2 balls, wrap each in plastic wrap, and press to flatten into discs. Place the dough in the freezer for 20 minutes or overnight.

3 Preheat the oven to 400°F. If kept in the freezer overnight, let the dough thaw just until you can press it gently.

4 Take two pieces of parchment and sprinkle a little flour on one, place one of the discs of dough on top, and then sprinkle a little more flour on top of the dough. Place the second piece of parchment on top of the dough and roll on top of the parchment until the dough is about ¼-inch thick. Every few rolls, peel back the top parchment and sprinkle a little more flour on the dough. Remove the top parchment and use to line a cookie sheet. Line another cookie sheet with fresh parchment.

5 Use cookie cutters to cut out cookies, then a metal flat-blade spatula to lift the cookies and place on the prepared cookie sheets. Re-roll any scraps and cut out more cookies. If the dough becomes too soft and gets stuck to the bottom parchment, place in freezer until it gets harder. Repeat with the second disc of dough.

6 Bake for 10 to 12 minutes, or just until the cookies begin to brown on the bottom. Check halfway through baking to see if the cookies in the back are browning faster than those in the front; if so, just turn the cookie sheet around. Slide the parchment off the cookie sheet onto a cooling rack and let the cookies cool.

Linzer Tarts

MAKES ABOUT 2 DOZEN
STORAGE

*Store covered with plastic or in an airtight container at room temperature
for five days or freeze for up to three months.*

These are sandwich cookies with jam inside that you can see through a cutout in the top.
I make these using round cookie cutters in two different sizes, but you can also use a
cookie cutter with a cutout in the middle (called a "linzer cookie cutter" and sold on-line
and in baking stores) or, for the top cookie, you can use mini cookie cutters in different
shapes and make one to three decorative cutouts. Don't forget to bake the mini cookies
you cut out and eat them yourself as soon as they cool.

1 cup (2 sticks) parve margarine, cut into
    tablespoons
1 cup confectioners' sugar
2 cups plus 2 tablespoons all-purpose flour
1 teaspoon pure vanilla extract
Flour, for dusting parchment and dough
½ cup red raspberry jam
½ cup apricot jam
2 tablespoons confectioners' sugar, to dust
    cookies (optional)

1 Place the margarine, sugar, flour, and vanilla in the
  bowl of a food processor fitted with a metal blade or
  stand mixer with a whisk. Process or mix until all the
  ingredients come together into a ball. You can also
  mix by hand by cutting the margarine into the dry
  ingredients, then using your hands to squeeze the dough
  until it comes together. Divide the dough into 2 balls,
  wrap each in plastic wrap, and press to flatten into discs.
  Place in the freezer for 20 minutes or overnight.

2 Preheat the oven to 400°F. Remove the dough from the
  freezer and let thaw just until you can press it gently.

3   Take two pieces of parchment and sprinkle a little flour on one, place one of the dough discs on top, and then sprinkle a little more flour on top of the dough. Place the second piece of parchment on top of the dough and roll on top of the parchment until the dough is about ¼-inch thick. Every few rolls, peel back the top parchment and sprinkle a little more flour on the dough. Remove the top parchment and use it to line a cookie sheet. Line a second cookie sheet with parchment.

4   Use a large round cookie cutter to cut out large circles. Re-roll any scraps and cut out more large circles. Use a smaller round cutter to cut out the centers of half of the large circles. Use a metal flat-blade spatula to place the cut cookies onto the prepared cookie sheets. Use a knife to lift the center circles out of half of the large cookies and place on the cookie sheet to bake. You should have large cookies, rings, and mini circles. Do the same for the other disc of dough.

5   Bake for 10 to 12 minutes, or just until the cookies begin to brown on the bottom. Check halfway through baking to see if the cookies in the back are browning faster than those in the front; if so, just turn the cookie sheet around. Slide the parchment off the cookie sheet onto a cooling rack and let the cookies cool.

6   Spread some jam, about ¾ to 1 teaspoon, just to cover the large cookie circles, and then place a cookie ring on top (bottom side on the jam) to create a sandwich. Press lightly. I usually make half the cookies with red raspberry jam and half with apricot because they look better on a platter with two colors. The mini circles are for you to enjoy as reward for your hard work. To serve, sift some confectioners' sugar on the top of the cookies, if desired.

Sesame Cookies

MAKES 5 TO 6 DOZEN

STORAGE

Store covered with plastic or in an airtight container at room temperature for five days or freeze for up to three months.

I was sitting at a hotel pool in Jerusalem when the waiter brought me my afternoon cappuccino topped with whipped cream (decadent) along with some very cute cookies. My favorite had sesame seeds on top so I invented these cookies. I use a scalloped flower-shaped cookie cutter but you can use any shape. My friend Jen Klein, whose sons have allergies to nuts but not sesame, was very excited about these cookies. She said they tasted too elegant to be cut into whimsical shapes like stars. I will eat them no matter their shape.

---

1 cup (2 sticks) parve margarine, cut into tablespoons

2 cups plus 2 tablespoons flour

1 cup confectioners' sugar

1 teaspoon toasted sesame oil

Flour, to dust parchment and dough

½ cup sesame seeds

---

1 Place the margarine, flour, confectioners' sugar, and sesame oil in the bowl of a food processor fitted with a metal blade or stand mixer with a whisk. Process or mix until all the ingredients come together into a ball. You can also mix by hand by cutting the margarine into the dry ingredients with a pastry cutter or two knives, then using your hands to squeeze the dough until it comes together. Divide the dough into 2 balls, wrap each in plastic wrap, and press to flatten into discs. Place the dough in the freezer for 20 minutes or overnight.

2 Preheat the oven to 400°F. If kept in the freezer overnight, let the dough thaw just until you can press it gently.

3 Take two pieces of parchment and sprinkle flour on one, place one of the dough discs on top, and then sprinkle a little more flour on top of the dough. Place the second piece of parchment on top of the dough and roll on top of the parchment until the dough is about ¼-inch thick. Every few rolls, peel back the top parchment and sprinkle a little more flour on the dough. Remove the top parchment and use to line a cookie sheet. Line a second cookie sheet with fresh parchment.

4　Place the sesame seeds on a small plate.

5　Use any shape cookie cutter about 2 inches wide to cut out the cookies. Re-roll any scraps and cut out more cookies. Pick up each cookie using a metal flat-blade spatula and place the top of the cut cookie on the sesame seeds. Press gently until it is completely covered with seeds. Place the cookies seed-side up on the prepared cookie sheets. Repeat with the second disc of dough.

6　Bake for 10 to 12 minutes, or until the edges and bottoms look a little brown. Check halfway through baking to see if the cookies in the back are browning faster than those in the front; if so, just turn the sheet around. When the cookies are done, slide the parchment off the cookie sheet onto a cooling rack and you can then use the cookie sheets for your next batch.

Coffee Cardamom Shortbread

MAKES 3 TO 4 DOZEN

STORAGE

Store covered with plastic or in an airtight container at room temperature for five days or freeze for up to three months.

Cardamom is a Middle Eastern spice that is used to flavor thick Turkish coffee. These cookies, eaten alongside a strong cup of coffee, can help you replicate the Middle Eastern coffee experience.

———

2 cups all-purpose flour

1 cup confectioners' sugar

1 cup (2 sticks) parve margarine, cut into tablespoons

4 teaspoons instant coffee granules (not espresso powder or finely ground coffee)

1 teaspoon ground cardamom

———

1　Place the flour, confectioners' sugar, margarine, coffee granules, and cardamom into the bowl of a stand mixer or food processor and mix until the dough comes together. You can also mix by hand by cutting the margarine into the dry ingredients with a pastry cutter or two knives, then using your hands to squeeze the dough until it comes together.

2 Gather the dough into a ball and divide into four pieces. Shape each quarter into a round or square log, depending on whether you want round or square cookies, about 6 to 7 inches long by 1 to 1½ inches wide. To make a round log, cover with plastic wrap and roll on the counter. To make the roll square, wrap in plastic and then press each side on the counter, while rubbing from side to side until each side is squared. Place the logs in the freezer for 20 minutes or overnight.

3 Preheat the oven to 400°F. Line 2 cookie sheets with parchment. When the dough is chilled, remove from the freezer and unwrap. Using a sharp knife on a cutting board, slice the dough into ⅓- to ½-inch slices. Place the cookies on the prepared cookie sheets, about 1½ inches apart.

4 Bake for 12 to 14 minutes, until the bottoms of the cookies begin to brown. Check halfway through baking to see if the cookies in the back are browning faster than those in the front; if so, just turn the cookie sheet around. Slide the parchment off the cookie sheet onto a cooling rack and let the cookies cool.

Chocolate Sandwich Cookies

MAKES 2 TO 3 DOZEN 2-INCH COOKIES

STORAGE

Store covered with plastic or in an airtight container at room temperature for five days or freeze for up to three months.

For these cookies, I like to use cookie cutters that are fluted or heart-shaped. I once tried stars but it was too difficult to get the filling into the points.

COOKIES

1½ cups all-purpose flour, plus extra to dust parchment and dough

½ cup parve unsweetened cocoa

1¼ cups confectioners' sugar

1 cup (2 sticks) parve margarine, cut into tablespoons

FILLING

10 ounces parve semisweet or bittersweet chocolate, chopped or broken into 1-inch pieces

3 tablespoons parve margarine

4 tablespoons parve plain soy milk

1 teaspoon pure vanilla extract

4 tablespoons confectioners' sugar

1 Place the flour, cocoa, and confectioners' sugar in the bowl of a food processor fitted with a metal blade. Process a few seconds to mix. Add the margarine pieces and process until the dough comes together. You can also mix by hand by cutting the margarine into the dry ingredients with a pastry cutter or two knives, then using your hands to squeeze the dough until it comes together.

2 Divide the dough into 2 balls, wrap in plastic, and flatten into discs. Place in the freezer for 20 minutes or overnight.

3 Preheat the oven to 400°F. If kept in the freezer overnight, let the dough thaw just until you can press it gently. Take two pieces of parchment and sprinkle flour on one, place the dough on top, and then sprinkle a little more flour on top of the dough. Place the second piece of parchment on top of the dough and roll on top of the parchment until the dough is about ¼-inch thick. Every few rolls, peel back the top parchment and sprinkle a little more flour on the dough. Remove the top parchment and use to line a cookie sheet. Line a second cookie sheet with fresh parchment.

4 Use small, no larger than 2-inch, cookie cutters to cut cookies. Use a flat metal-blade spatula to transfer the cut cookies onto the prepared cookie sheets. Re-roll any dough scraps between two sheets of parchment and cut. Repeat with the second disc of dough.

5 Bake for 10 minutes or until just set. Let cool on the cookie sheets for 2 minutes and then slide the parchment off the sheets to cool. Meanwhile, prepare the chocolate filling.

6 Melt the chocolate and margarine in a heatproof bowl set over a saucepan of simmering water (or use a double boiler) until melted and smooth. Heat the soy milk in the microwave for 15 seconds. Remove the bowl with the chocolate from the heat and add the heated soy milk, vanilla, and confectioners' sugar to the chocolate. Mix well and then place in the refrigerator for 15 minutes before using. If you can pour the filling, it is not yet thick enough to use.

7 To assemble the cookies, spread about ½ to 1 teaspoon of the chocolate filling on the bottom of one cookie and cover with the bottom of another. You can also use a pastry bag to squeeze the filling onto the cookies. Squeeze the cookies gently to spread the filling to the edges. Let sit at room temperature for 30 minutes to set.

Oatmeal Raisin Cookies

MAKES 4 TO 5 DOZEN
STORAGE
Store covered with plastic or in an airtight container at room temperature for five days or freeze for up to three months.

My kids are strongly adverse to raisins baked or cooked in anything so I give you a range of raisin amounts, depending on how much you like them. These cookies are best when chewy; I only bake one batch at a time so I can monitor them closely to make sure they do not overbake.

———

3 cups raw oats (not quick-cooking kind), divided
1 cup (2 sticks) parve margarine
1 cup light brown sugar
½ cup sugar
2 large eggs
2 teaspoons pure vanilla extract
1 cup all-purpose flour
1 teaspoon baking powder
1 teaspoon baking soda
½ teaspoon ground cinnamon
¼ teaspoon salt
½ to 1 cup raisins, to taste

———

1 Preheat the oven to 350°F. Line a cookie sheet with parchment. You will bake these cookies one sheet at a time.

2 Place ½ cup of the raw oats in a food processor fitted with a metal blade and grind to a powder. In a large bowl, beat the margarine with a stand or hand-held electric mixer on medium-high speed or by hand with a whisk until creamy. Add

the brown and white sugars and beat again until well mixed. Add the eggs and vanilla and beat. Add the ground oats, the remaining 2½ cups whole oats, flour, baking powder, baking soda, cinnamon, and salt and mix well. Add the raisins and mix in well.

3   Place in the refrigerator for a minimum of 20 minutes or overnight.

4   Using 2 small spoons, scoop up about a tablespoon of cookie dough and place on the prepared cookie sheet, 2 to 3 inches apart. I keep the dough in the refrigerator as the first batch bakes.

5   Bake for 15 minutes, or until the cookies are brown on the edges but are still soft if you poke your finger into one. Remove from the oven and slide the parchment onto a cooling rack. Do not worry if they appear soft when you remove them from the oven; they will firm up as they cool but stay chewy. Let cookie sheet cool for five minutes and then bake the next batch of cookies.

Bubba (Jam Button) Cookies

MAKES ABOUT 5 DOZEN 1½-INCH COOKIES
STORAGE
Store covered with plastic or in an airtight container at room temperature for five days or freeze for up to three months.

My mother-in-law gave me this recipe many years ago when I got married and I never made them because they seemed too boring. I was out for dinner at a fancy restaurant for my birthday one year and on the tray of petit fours was a little cookie with a little jam on it. Andy got excited because they looked liked his bubba's (grandmother's) cookies. So I finally tried them out and when I asked my husband whether they tasted like his grandmother's cookies he said they're even better. You can make them with just jam or add nuts and cinnamon. It takes some patience to shape all the cookies, so find some helpers.

———

1 cup (2 sticks) parve margarine

½ cup sugar

2 large egg yolks

1 tablespoon pure vanilla extract

2 cups all-purpose flour

⅓ cup jam, any flavor (I like apricot)

OPTIONAL

> 3 tablespoons ground walnuts (see "Making ground walnuts," page xxviii)
>
> ½ teaspoon ground cinnamon

————

1 Preheat the oven to 350°F. Line 2 large cookie sheets with parchment.

2 In a large bowl, beat the margarine with a stand or hand-held electric mixer on medium-high speed, or by hand with a whisk, until soft, scraping down the bowl several times. Add the sugar and beat until it is mixed in. Add the egg yolks and vanilla and beat again, scraping down the bowl as necessary. Add the flour and mix until the dough comes together.

3 Take a small piece of dough and form a ball about 1 to 1¼ inches in size. Flatten the ball between the palms of your hands and then use the tip of your finger to make a ½-inch depression in the center. Place on the prepared cookie sheets 1 inch apart.

4 When all the cookies are formed and placed on the cookie sheets, use a small spoon (a demitasse spoon works great, or a ¼-teaspoon measuring spoon) to scoop up some jam, a little less than ¼ teaspoon, and use your finger to push the jam from the spoon into the depression on the top of each cookie. You want to just fill the hole. If desired, combine the walnuts and cinnamon and sprinkle on top of the jam.

5 Bake for 20 to 22 minutes, or until the cookies are golden on the bottoms; the tops will remain light. Slide the parchment and cookies onto racks to cool.

Peanut Butter Cookies

MAKES 5 TO 6 DOZEN 1½-INCH COOKIES

STORAGE

> *Store covered with plastic or in an airtight container at room temperature for five days or freeze for up to three months.*

These chewy, nutty cookies are for people who really love peanut butter.

————

> ½ cup raw oats (not quick-cooking kind)
>
> 1 cup creamy peanut butter

½ cup sugar

½ cup light brown sugar

¼ cup all-purpose flour

½ cup (1 stick) parve margarine, cut into 12 pieces

1 large egg

1 teaspoon pure vanilla extract

————

1 Place the oatmeal in the bowl of a food processor fitted with a metal blade and process to a powder. Add the peanut butter, white and brown sugars, flour, margarine, egg, and vanilla and process until the ingredients are mixed together. The dough will be gooey.

2 Scoop the dough into a bowl, cover with plastic wrap and place in the refrigerator for a minimum of 20 minutes. (It can be left longer, if more convenient; I have kept the dough in the refrigerator up to 2 days.)

3 Preheat the oven to 400°F. Line 2 cookie sheets with parchment. You will bake the cookies in several batches. Take the dough out of the refrigerator. Using a teaspoon, scoop up heaping teaspoons of dough and roll them into balls. Place them on the cookie sheets, 1½ inches apart, and flatten. Keep the dough in the refrigerator as the first batches bake.

4 Bake for 12 minutes, or until the edges are a little brown; the centers will still be soft. Slide the parchment and cookies onto a rack to cool. Let the cookie sheets cool for 5 minutes. Form the rest of the dough into balls, place on the cookie sheets, flatten, and bake.

Almond Anise Biscotti

MAKES ABOUT 8 DOZEN

STORAGE

Store covered with plastic or in an airtight container at room temperature for five days or freeze for up to three months.

These are the classic type of biscotti made in Italy. You can bake them hard for dipping into espresso or tea, or chewier, as you like. In my house, I have to bake them both ways to keep both the crispy-cookie camp and the chewy-cookie camp happy.

1 cup slivered almonds

4 tablespoons parve margarine, at room temperature

1 cup sugar

¼ cup light brown sugar

2 large eggs

1 teaspoon anise seeds

1 teaspoon pure vanilla extract

1 teaspoon almond extract

2½ cups all-purpose flour

1½ teaspoons baking powder

———————

1 Preheat the oven to 350°F. On a large, parchment-lined jelly roll pan, toast the almonds in the oven for 15 minutes or until golden and fragrant, shaking the pan midway through. Let cool for 5 minutes and then chop roughly.

2 In a mixing bowl, beat together the margarine and the sugars with a stand or hand-held electric mixer on medium-high speed or by hand with a whisk until creamy. Add the eggs and mix. Add the anise seeds, vanilla and almond extracts and mix again. Add the flour and baking powder and mix. Finally, add the toasted and chopped almonds and mix or knead with your hands until the almonds are distributed throughout the dough.

3 Re-line the same cookie sheet you used to toast the almonds with parchment.

4 Divide the dough into 4 equal pieces and then shape each into a narrow log, about 2 inches wide and 8 to 9 inches long. Place on the cookie sheet, 3 inches apart. Use a silicone spatula to smooth the tops and sides of the logs. Bake for 30 minutes. Slide the parchment and logs onto a cutting board to cool for 10 minutes. Reduce the oven temperature to 300°F. Using a sharp serrated knife, slice the logs into ¼- to ⅓-inch-thick slices. Place the slices cut-side down on top of a new piece of parchment on the cookie sheet. Bake for 7 to 10 minutes; 7 for soft, 10 for crunchier cookies. Slide the parchment and cookies onto a rack to cool.

Hamentaschen

MAKES ABOUT 4 DOZEN

STORAGE

Store covered with plastic or in an airtight container at room temperature
for five days or freeze for up to three months.

I am not a huge fan of hamentaschen, the triangle-shaped filled cookie eaten on the holiday of Purim. The cookies are made to remind us of the three-pointed hat worn by Haman, the villain of the Purim story who sought to destroy all the Jews. Often the cookie dough is too dry, the fillings typical and boring. I knew I had to have some hamentaschen recipes in this book so I was determined to find a good one. After trying several recipes over the past few years, I went back to the basics with my husband Andy's family recipe that his brother Steve always uses with great success.

---

3 large eggs

1 cup sugar

½ cup canola or vegetable oil

1 teaspoon orange juice

3½ teaspoons baking powder

3 cups all-purpose flour, plus extra for sprinkling

1 cup fruit jam or preserves, canned apricot or poppy seed pie filling, or homemade Lemon Curd (see page 86)

---

1 Preheat the oven to 350°F. Line 2 large cookie sheets with parchment.

2 In a large bowl, mix together the eggs, sugar, oil, and orange juice, and mix well. Add the baking powder and flour and mix until the dough comes together. I like to use my hands for this because it kneads the dough well. Divide the dough in half.

I prefer the lighter-colored stainless steel or aluminum cookie sheets. Cookies baked on the darker, often non-stick, cookie sheets will bake faster because the darker sheets retain heat better. If you are using a dark sheet, check the cookies one or two minutes earlier.

3 Take another two pieces of parchment and sprinkle flour on one, place one dough half on top, and then sprinkle a little more flour on top of the dough. Place the second piece of parchment on top of the dough and roll on top of the parchment until the dough is about ¼-inch thick. Every few rolls, peel back the top parchment and sprinkle a little more flour on the dough.

4 Use a glass or round cookie cutter about 2 to 3 inches in diameter to cut the dough into circles. Place a teaspoon of the filling in the center and then fold in 3 sides to form a triangle, leaving a small opening in the center. Pinch the 3 corners very tightly. Place on the prepared cookie sheets. Repeat with the rest of the dough and re-roll and cut any dough scraps you have.

5 Bake for 12 to 16 minutes, or until the bottoms are lightly browned. The baking time often depends on the type of cookie sheet used: cookies on darker sheets bake faster. Just watch the cookies until they look done—you do not want them to be brown on top because then they will be too hard. Slide the parchment onto racks to cool the cookies.

Lemon Curd

2 large eggs plus 1 egg yolk

½ cup sugar

Zest (grated outer peel) of ½ lemon

3 tablespoons fresh lemon juice (from 2 large lemons)

3 tablespoons parve margarine

———

In a double boiler, combine the whole eggs, egg yolk, and sugar. Add the lemon zest and juice and stir. Cook the curd uncovered over simmering water, stirring occasionally, until a thick mixture is formed, about 25 minutes. Be patient and do not stir too much. If the water in the double boiler boils too fast, turn down the heat. Remove the bowl from the heat and whisk in the margarine in small pieces. Cool for 5 minutes and then cover with plastic and refrigerate overnight. To use immediately, place the bowl of lemon curd in a larger bowl containing about 2 inches of ice and 1 cup of cold water. Let the smaller bowl sit in the ice for 15 minutes and the curd will be ready to use.

Orange Poppy Seed Hamentaschen

MAKES ABOUT 4 DOZEN

STORAGE

Store covered with plastic or in an airtight container at room temperature for five days or freeze for up to three months.

When I told my husband Andy about my new ideas for hamentaschen, he said that what he truly loves is the old-fashioned poppy seed version. I told him that the Jewish world already has enough recipes for poppy seed hamentaschen and he just repeated that he would still like to see it in the book. So I added orange flavor to the dough and filling and some seeds to the dough so they would look a little different.

DOUGH

3 large eggs

1 cup sugar

½ cup canola or vegetable oil

1 teaspoon orange zest (grated outer peel) (from 1 orange)

1 teaspoon fresh orange juice (from zested orange)

1 teaspoon poppy seeds

3½ teaspoons baking powder

3 cups all-purpose flour, plus extra for sprinkling

FILLING

½ cup poppy seeds

2 tablespoons sugar

1 teaspoon orange zest (grated outer peel) (from 1 orange)

¾ teaspoon ground cinnamon

1 large egg white

2 tablespoons honey

2 teaspoons all-purpose flour

———————

1 Preheat the oven to 350°F. Line 2 large cookie sheets with parchment.

2 To make the dough: In a large bowl, mix together the eggs, sugar, oil, orange zest, orange juice, and poppy seeds. Add the baking powder and flour and mix until the dough comes together. I like to use my hands for this because it kneads the dough well. Divide the dough in half.

3 To make the filling: In a bowl, mix together the poppy seeds, sugar, zest, cinnamon, egg white, honey, and flour.

4 Take another two pieces of parchment and sprinkle flour on one, place one dough half on top, and then sprinkle a little more flour on top of the dough. Place the second piece of parchment on top of the dough and roll on top of the parchment until the dough is about ¼-inch thick. Every few rolls, peel back the top parchment and sprinkle a little more flour on the dough.

5 Use a glass or round cookie cutter about 2 to 3 inches in diameter to cut the dough into circles. Place a teaspoon of filling in the center and then fold in 3 sides to form a triangle, leaving a small opening in the center. Pinch the 3 corners very tightly. Place on the prepared cookie sheets. Repeat with the rest of the dough and re-roll and cut any dough scraps you have.

6 Bake for 12 to 16 minutes, or until the bottoms are lightly browned. After 12 minutes, watch the cookies closely to avoid over-baking them; you do not want them to be brown on top because then they will be too hard. Slide the parchment onto racks to cool the cookies.

Chocolate Candy Hamentaschen

MAKES ABOUT 4 DOZEN

STORAGE

Store covered with plastic or in an airtight container at room temperature for five days or freeze for up to three months.

When I edited *Kids in the Kitchen* for the *Kosher by Design* book series, I made a delicious cookie that used chocolate-covered raisins instead of chocolate chips and I loved the change. So when I was ruminating about chocolate hamentaschen and wanted something different, I tried the chocolate-covered raisins and loved the sweet, chewy filling. It reminds me of a candy bar I loved as a child.

3 large eggs

1 cup sugar

½ cup canola or vegetable oil

1 teaspoon orange juice

1 teaspoon pure vanilla extract

1 tablespoon baking powder

2¼ cups all-purpose flour, plus extra for sprinkling

¾ cup parve unsweetened cocoa

1 cup parve chocolate-covered raisins

1 Preheat the oven to 350°F. Line 2 large cookie sheets with parchment.

2 In a large bowl, mix together the eggs, sugar, oil, orange juice, and vanilla. Add the baking powder, flour, and cocoa and mix until the dough comes together. I like to use my hands for this because it kneads the dough well. Divide the dough in half.

3 Take another two pieces of parchment and sprinkle flour on one, place one dough half on top and then sprinkle a little more flour on top of the dough. Place the second piece of parchment on top of the dough and roll on top of the parchment until the dough is about ¼-inch thick. Every few rolls, peel back the top parchment and sprinkle a little more flour on the dough.

4 Use a glass or round cookie cutter about 2 to 3 inches in diameter to cut the dough into circles. Place 4 chocolate-covered raisins in the center and then fold in 3 sides to form a triangle, leaving a small opening in the center. Pinch the 3 corners very tightly. Place on a prepared cookie sheet. Repeat for the rest of the dough and re-roll and cut any dough scraps you have.

5 Bake for 12 to 16 minutes, until the bottoms are lightly browned. Slide the parchment onto racks to cool the cookies.

Lemon Bars

MAKES 35 SQUARE BARS

STORAGE

Store covered with plastic or in an airtight container at room temperature for five days or freeze for up to three months.

I did not discover lemon bars until my early twenties when I was practicing law in a law firm and the wife of one of the partners would send them in every once in a while. I love to eat the hard and gooey edges that are trimmed off to cut perfect squares.

CRUST

2 cups all-purpose flour

½ cup confectioners' sugar

1 cup (2 sticks) parve margarine, frozen for 15 minutes and cut into tablespoons, plus extra for greasing pan and parchment

½ teaspoon salt

FILLING

6 large eggs

2 cups sugar

⅓ cup all-purpose flour

½ teaspoon baking powder

⅓ cup fresh lemon juice (from 3 lemons)

1 tablespoon lemon zest (grated outer peel) (from 1 to 3 lemons, depending on size)

———

2 teaspoons confectioners' sugar, for dusting baked bars

———

1 Preheat the oven to 350°F. Grease a 9 x 13-inch pan with some margarine. Place a piece of parchment in the pan that is large enough to go up the sides and hang over a few inches. Grease the top and sides of the parchment with some margarine.

2 To make the crust: In the bowl of a stand mixer fitted with a wire whisk or a food processor fitted with a metal blade, place the flour, confectioners' sugar, margarine, and salt. You can also mix the ingredients together by hand with a wooden spoon. Mix until the dough comes together. Take handfuls of dough, flatten between your palms and then press into the bottom of the pan. When all of the dough is in the pan, place the pan in the freezer for 10 minutes.

3 Remove from the freezer and bake in the oven for 25 minutes or until the edges look golden.

4 While the crust is baking, make the filling. Place the eggs, sugar, flour, baking powder, lemon juice and zest in a medium bowl and whisk well. When the crust is baked, remove from the oven and reduce the temperature to 325°F. Whisk the filling again and pour over the crust. Return to the oven and bake for 30 minutes.

5 Remove from the oven and let cool completely. Use the overhanging parchment to lift the lemon bar out of the pan and slide onto a cutting board. Place the 2 teaspoons confectioners' sugar in a sifter or sieve and dust the top of the lemon bar. Trim off about ¼ inch of the sides (and eat them immediately) and then cut into squares or long bars.

Pecan Bars

MAKES 35 SQUARE BARS

STORAGE

Store covered with plastic or in an airtight container at room temperature for five days or freeze for up to three months.

This recipe represents my nod to the American South.

CRUST

2 cups all-purpose flour

¼ cup confectioners' sugar

½ teaspoon salt

½ cup (1 stick) parve margarine, frozen for 15 minutes, plus extra for greasing pan and parchment

½ cup solid vegetable shortening, frozen for 15 minutes

FILLING

3 cups pecan halves

½ cup pure maple syrup

1 cup light brown sugar

½ cup sugar

¼ cup parve plain soy milk

1 Preheat the oven to 350°F. Grease a 9 x 13-inch pan with some margarine. Place a piece of parchment in the pan that is large enough to go up the sides and hang over a few inches. Grease the top and sides of the parchment.

2 To make the crust: In the bowl of a food processor fitted with a metal blade or a mixer, place the flour, confectioners' sugar, and salt. Pulse or mix for 10 seconds to combine. Cut the margarine and shortening into 1-inch pieces and add to the bowl. Process or mix just until the mixture comes together. (You can also make the dough by hand by cutting the margarine and shortening into the dry ingredients with a pastry cutter or two knives and then mixing it with a wooden spoon or by hand until the dough comes together.)

3 Take pieces of the dough, flatten them between your palms, and then press into the prepared pan. Try to evenly cover the bottom of the pan. Place the pan in the freezer for 10 minutes.

4 Remove from the freezer and bake for 22 minutes or until the edges look golden.

5 Meanwhile, prepare the filling. Place the pecan halves in a freezer bag, close tightly and then hit them with a rolling pin or bottom of a saucepan to break them into small pieces. Do not completely crush them. Place the maple syrup and both sugars in a heavy saucepan and place over medium heat. After the sugars melt, add the pecan pieces and soy milk. Bring to a boil, reduce to low heat, and cook for 3 minutes. Turn off the heat and leave the filling in the saucepan until the dough is baked.

6 When the crust is baked, remove it from the oven and reduce the temperature to 325°F. Pour the filling over the dough and spread evenly. Return to the oven and bake for 20 minutes. Remove from the oven and cool completely. Use the overhanging parchment to lift the pecan bar out of the pan and place on a cutting board. Trim off about ¼ inch of the sides and then cut into squares.

Raspberry Bars

MAKES 35 SQUARE BARS
STORAGE

*Store covered with plastic or in an airtight container at room temperature
for five days or freeze for up to three months.*

My friend, and great baker, Lisa Silverman and I have baked huge trays of these bars several times for synagogue events. Lisa always insists on sprinkling chocolate chips (about 1 cup) over the jam, but I like them simpler. Then again, Lisa complains that both my banana bread and pumpkin cake need chocolate chips too.

2 cups plus 2 tablespoons all-purpose flour

1 cup confectioners' sugar

1 cup (2 sticks) parve margarine, frozen for 15 minutes, plus extra for
    greasing pan and parchment

1 teaspoon pure vanilla extract

FILLING

12 ounces (1½ cups) seedless red raspberry jam

———

1 Preheat the oven to 350°F. Grease a 9 x 13-inch pan with some margarine. Place a piece of parchment in the pan that is large enough to go up the sides and hang over a few inches. Grease the top and sides of the parchment.

2 To make the crust: Place the flour and sugar into the bowl of a food processor fitted with a metal blade. Process for 10 seconds. Cut the margarine into pieces and add to the bowl along with the vanilla. (You can also make the crust by hand by cutting the margarine into the dry ingredients with a pastry cutter or two knives.) Process or hand mix with a wooden spoon until the dough comes together.

3 Divide the dough into 2 parts, ⅓ and ⅔ of the dough. Wrap the smaller piece in plastic, flatten, and place in the freezer. Take the larger piece and break it into pieces and scatter over the parchment. Press the pieces into the pan as evenly as you can. Place in the oven and bake for 15 minutes.

4 Remove from the oven and let cool for 15 minutes. Use a silicone spatula to spread the jam all over the crust in the pan. Remove the other dough piece from the freezer and, using the large holes of a box grater, grate the remaining dough over the filling. Use your hands to spread the grated dough all over to cover the filling.

5 Bake for 30 minutes, or until the edges start to brown. Let cool. Trim off about ¼ inch of the sides and then cut into squares or long bars.

Cakes, Cupcakes, & Scones

Iced Lemon Pound Cake

MAKES ONE 9-INCH CAKE, 12 SERVINGS

STORAGE

Once the icing has dried, store covered in plastic at room temperature for up to five days or freeze wrapped in plastic for up to three months.

This cake was inspired by my favorite lemon pound cake recipe from *Cook's Illustrated*. I had to play around with ingredients to come up with a butter-free version that had enough lemon flavor and the right moistness. I also added the white glaze.

CAKE

Spray oil containing flour or spray oil plus 2 tablespoons flour
   for greasing and flouring pan
½ cup (1 stick) parve margarine
1½ cups sugar
2 tablespoons lemon zest (grated outer peel) (from 2 to 3 lemons)
1 tablespoon fresh lemon juice (from 1 lemon)
4 large eggs
½ cup parve plain soy milk
1 cup canola or vegetable oil
1½ cups all-purpose flour
1½ teaspoons baking powder
¼ teaspoon salt

LEMON ICING

½ cup sugar
¼ cup lemon juice (from 2 large lemons)
½ cup confectioners' sugar

1 Preheat the oven to 350°F. Grease and flour a 9-inch loaf pan.
2 Melt the margarine in a microwave-safe bowl in the microwave, about 1 minute. Set aside.

3   Place the sugar and lemon zest in the bowl of a food processor fitted with a metal blade and process for a few seconds to mix (or use a stand mixer with the whisk attachment or whisk by hand). Add the lemon juice, eggs, soy milk, oil, and melted margarine and process or whisk until combined. Add the flour, baking powder, and salt to the batter and mix until combined.

4   Pour the batter into the prepared pan and bake for 1 hour, or until a skewer inserted in the center comes out clean. Cool the cake in the pan for 10 minutes and then remove to a rack to cool.

5   To make the lemon icing: Bring the sugar and lemon juice to boil, lower the heat to medium and cook uncovered for 2 minutes, stirring to make sure the sugar is dissolved. Pour into a heatproof bowl and let cool for 5 minutes. Sift the confectioners' sugar into the sugar syrup and whisk to combine. Pour on top of the cake and let cool completely.

Upside-Down Raspberry Cake

MAKES ONE 9-INCH CAKE, 8 TO 12 SERVINGS
STORAGE

Store covered with plastic in the refrigerator for up to three days.

You will like the combination of fresh and baked raspberries in this dessert. Plan to make this when you can find good quality raspberries. When I was in cooking school in Paris, we used gorgeous raspberries that were the size of quarters in our desserts.

———

½ cup (1 stick) parve margarine, very soft

3 cups fresh or frozen raspberries, plus 1 cup fresh raspberries to decorate

1½ cups plus 3 tablespoons plus 1 teaspoon sugar, divided

5 large eggs, separated

¼ ounce (1 envelope) active dry yeast

3 tablespoons warm water

1¼ cups all-purpose flour

1 Preheat the oven to 375°F. Take a 9-inch springform pan and detach the bottom. Cover the top of the pan bottom with aluminum foil and then wrap the excess foil under the bottom. Attach the pan sides to the bottom, lock in place, and then unwrap the foil and wrap up around the sides of the pan. Use 1 tablespoon of the margarine to grease the bottom and sides of the pan.

2 In a small bowl, toss the 3 cups of raspberries with the 3 tablespoons of sugar. Place in the bottom of the pan and spread to evenly cover the bottom.

3 With a stand or hand-held electric mixer or by hand with a whisk, beat the egg yolks with the 1½ cups sugar in a large bowl for 5 minutes on high speed, or until the mixture is thick. Scrape the bowl down halfway through.

4 In a separate small bowl, mix the yeast with 1 teaspoon sugar and warm water. Let sit 5 minutes. Add to the egg and sugar mixture and mix. Add the remaining 7 tablespoons of soft margarine and whisk well.

5 In a separate bowl, use an electric mixer on high speed to beat the egg whites until stiff and then fold into the batter.

6 Pour the batter on top of the raspberries. Bake for 45 minutes or until a skewer inserted in the cake comes out clean. Let cool.

7 To serve, run a sharp knife along the sides and then remove the outer ring of the springform pan. Place a serving plate on top of the cake and then turn the cake over onto the plate. Remove the bottom of the pan. Just before serving, scatter 1 cup of fresh raspberries on top.

Carrot Cake with Cinnamon Honey Cream Cheese Frosting

MAKES ONE 8- OR 9-INCH FOUR-LAYER CAKE, 12 SERVINGS

STORAGE

Store in the refrigerator for up to five days and then wrapped tightly in the freezer for up to three months.

When I created this cake, I could not believe how great it was on the first try. I had never made a carrot cake before. I never loved carrot cake because people put so much *chazerei* (Yiddish for "stuff") into it—nuts, pineapple, and coconut. This cake is a four-layer cake; you will cut each cake into two layers. In cooking school, we learned to place cardboard circles under all layer cakes. It makes it easier to lift the cake to ice the sides and takes up less space to store—you don't have to store a large serving platter in your refrigerator. You can buy them in cooking supply, cake decorating, or craft stores. If you do not have one, just place the cake directly on your serving plate.

CAKE

Spray oil containing flour or spray oil plus 2 tablespoons flour for
    greasing and flouring pan

4 large eggs

1 cup sugar

1 cup dark brown sugar

1 cup canola or vegetable oil

½ cup orange juice

2 teaspoons pure vanilla extract

1½ cups all-purpose flour

½ cup whole-wheat flour

1½ teaspoons baking powder

1 teaspoon salt

2 teaspoons ground cinnamon

3 cups peeled and thinly grated carrot (from about 5 large carrots)

CINNAMON HONEY CREAM CHEESE FROSTING

12 ounces parve cream cheese

1½ teaspoons pure vanilla extract

2¼ teaspoons cinnamon

3 tablespoons honey

7 cups confectioners' sugar

1½ tablespoons parve plain soy milk

———

1 Preheat the oven to 350°F. Grease and flour two 8- or 9-inch round pans.

2 In a medium bowl, beat the eggs and sugars with a stand or hand-held electric mixer on medium speed for 3 minutes, or by hand with a whisk, until thick. Add the oil, orange juice, and vanilla and mix on low speed or gently by hand to combine.

3 In a separate medium bowl, whisk the flour, whole-wheat flour, baking powder, salt, and cinnamon. Add half of the dry ingredients to the bowl with the eggs/sugar and mix on low speed or gently by hand to combine. Add the rest of the flour mixture and mix until just combined.

4 Using the side of a box grater, grate the carrot into small threads, about ¾ inch long. Add to the batter and mix in well.

5 Divide the batter between the 2 prepared round pans. Bake for 40 minutes, or until a skewer inserted in the cakes comes out clean. Cool in the pans for 10 minutes and then turn out onto a rack to cool completely. While the cakes are cooling, take the cream cheese out of the refrigerator so it will soften.

6 When the cakes are cool, use a sharp knife to trim the top and sides of the cakes so that they are even (eat the trimmings). Following the instructions in "Slicing cake layers" (see Foolproof Tips and Techniques), slice each cake in half to create four layers.

7 To make the frosting: Place the cream cheese, vanilla, cinnamon, and honey in a large bowl and beat with a hand-held or stand electric mixer at high speed or by hand with a whisk to combine. Add the confectioners' sugar in three parts, mixing in each addition completely on medium speed or vigorously with a whisk before adding the next one. When using a stand mixer, I wrap plastic wrap all around the top of the mixer and around the bowl after the second and third additions of sugar so that my hair and all kitchen surfaces are not covered in white. Add the soy milk and beat for 30 seconds until the frosting looks creamy.

8 Cut out a cardboard circle that's about an inch or so larger than the diameter of your cake. Place the top of the first cake top-side down onto the cardboard circle on a serving plate. Scoop up about ¾ to 1 cup of the frosting and place in the center of the cake. Working from the center of the cake toward the outside edge of the cake, use a silicone spatula to spread the frosting back and forth across the top of

the cake (you will do the sides later). Use more icing if necessary; if you spread too little, you will pick up crumbs and then have to clean them off. (Use a separate bowl for the icing that has crumbs in it—you can snack on that later.)

9 Place the bottom of the first cake, bottom-side up, on top of the icing. Add another ¾ to 1 cup of icing and spread. Place the top of the second cake, top-side down on top of the icing. Add icing to cover. Finally, place the bottom of the second cake, bottom-side up, on top of the icing. Look at the cake to see if it is even. If not, press a little on any side that seems too high.

10 Take some icing and cover the top of the cake. Next, cover the sides, using up about 3 tablespoons of icing each time. After the cake is evenly covered, pour boiling hot water over a long, flat

The frosting for this cake can be made in advance and stored covered in the refrigerator for up to five days.

metal spatula (sometimes called a "metal icing spatula") to heat it. Dry it slightly and use to smooth the cake's top and the sides. If you have a pastry bag and a star tip, you can place any leftover icing in the bag and make a design of your choice on the cake. I like to make a border around the edge and then lines across the cake. If you want to avoid the final step of smoothing the icing altogether, sprinkle finely chopped walnuts or pistachios on the top and sides.

11 Place in the refrigerator until serving.

White Cake with Seven-Minute Frosting

MAKES ONE 9-INCH FOUR-LAYER CAKE, 16 TO 20 SERVINGS
STORAGE

> *Store in the refrigerator for up to five days and then wrapped tightly in the freezer for up to three months.*

This cake is great for birthdays or anniversaries or simply when you want to impress your friends and family. You can embellish it with chocolate shavings (a vegetable peeler works great for this), sprinkles of your choice, chopped nuts, edible flowers, shredded coconut or decorate with store-bought parve icing, or just leave it as a grand white cake. I would avoid strawberries as they bleed too much onto the icing.

Spray oil containing flour or spray oil plus 2 tablespoons flour
  for greasing and flouring pan

2 large eggs plus 6 whites

2 cups canola or vegetable oil

1 cup parve plain soy milk

2 cups sugar

2½ cups all-purpose flour

2 teaspoons baking powder

2 teaspoons pure vanilla extract

¼ teaspoon cream of tartar

SEVEN-MINUTE FROSTING

1½ cups sugar

⅓ cup warm water

3 large egg whites, at room temperature

1 tablespoon light corn syrup

Dash of salt

1 teaspoon pure vanilla extract

1 Preheat the oven to 350°F. Grease and flour two 9-inch round baking pans.

2 Separate the 2 whole eggs and place the yolks in one large bowl and all of the whites in another (you will have 8 egg whites altogether). Into the bowl with the egg yolks, add the oil, soy milk, sugar, flour, baking powder, and vanilla. Beat by hand with a whisk or with an electric mixer for 1 minute.

3 Beat the egg whites with the cream of tartar until stiff peaks form. Fold half of the whites into the batter and, when almost mixed in, fold in the rest of the whites and mix until combined. Divide the batter between the 2 prepared pans and bake for 40 minutes, or until a skewer inserted into the cakes comes out clean. Let cool for 10 minutes, remove from the pans onto a wire rack and then let cool completely.

4 While the cakes are baking, make the seven-minute frosting. Pour a few inches of water into the bottom of a double boiler or a medium saucepan and bring to a boil, then reduce the heat to medium. Off heat, place the sugar and ⅓ cup warm water in the top of the double boiler or in a metal or other heatproof bowl that can sit on top of the saucepan without falling in. Whisk to dissolve the sugar. Add the egg whites, corn syrup, and salt and beat for 1 minute with an electric mixer on

medium-high speed. Place over the gently boiling water and beat with an electric mixer on high speed for a full 7 minutes. If the water starts to bubble too much, turn the heat down. Remove from heat, add vanilla and beat until the frosting is thick and has soft peaks, another 30 seconds.

5 When the cakes are cool, use a sharp knife to trim the tops and sides of the cakes so that they are even (eat the trimmings). Slice each cake into two layers, following the method described in "Slicing cake layers" (see Foolproof Tips and Techniques).

6 Place one cake bottom, bottom side down, on a serving plate, reserving the second cake bottom to use for the top of the cake. Spread about ¾ cup of frosting on the top of the cake. Working from the center of the cake toward the outside edge of the cake, use a silicone spatula to spread the frosting back and forth across the top of the cake (you will do the sides later). Add the second cake half and more frosting. Do the same for the next half. Place the second cake bottom, bottom-side up, on top. Spread the frosting all around the sides of the cake and then cover the top of the cake with frosting.

7 Heat a long, flat metal spatula under boiling water, dry slightly, and use to smooth the top and sides. Store in the refrigerator.

◇ *Chocolate Almond Cake with Chocolate Glaze*

MAKES ONE 10-INCH CAKE, 12 TO 16 SERVINGS

STORAGE

Store in the refrigerator for up to five days and then wrapped tightly in the freezer for up to three months.

This is a dense, nutty, chocolate cake covered in chocolate. I often bake this on Passover.

CAKE

1 cup whole blanched almonds

Parve margarine for greasing pans

10 ounces parve semisweet or bittersweet chocolate

½ cup ground walnuts (see "Making ground walnuts," page xxviii)

3 large eggs plus 2 whites

¾ cup sugar

7 ounces parve semisweet or bittersweet chocolate, chopped or broken
   into 1-inch pieces

1 cup parve whipping cream

½ teaspoon pure vanilla extract

1 Preheat the oven to 350°F. Place the almonds on a parchment-lined jelly roll pan and toast for 15 minutes, or until the almonds are browned and fragrant.

2 Take a 10-inch springform pan and detach the bottom. Trace the bottom onto a piece of parchment and cut out. Cover the top of the pan bottom with aluminum foil and then wrap the excess foil under the bottom. Attach the pan sides to the bottom, lock in place, and then unwrap the foil and wrap up around the exterior sides of the pan. Grease the bottom and sides of the pan. Press the parchment circle into the bottom of the pan. Grease the top of the parchment circle.

3 Break the chocolate into small pieces and place in the bowl of a food processor fitted with a metal blade. Add the toasted almonds, ground walnuts, whole eggs, egg whites, and sugar and process until the mixture becomes a smooth batter. Make sure there are no large chocolate chunks in the batter.

4 Spread the batter in the prepared pan and bake for 40 minutes or until set. Let cool for 20 minutes.

5 To make the glaze: Melt the chocolate either on the stovetop or in the microwave, following the "Melting chocolate" instructions in Foolproof Tips and Techniques.

6 In a small saucepan over low heat, bring the cream and vanilla just to a boil. Pour the cream into the melted chocolate. Beat with an electric mixer on medium speed or vigorously by hand with a whisk for 2 minutes to thicken the glaze.

7 Release the sides of the pan. Use a wide knife or long metal spatula to separate the parchment circle from the foil and slide the cake and parchment onto a serving platter. Place small pieces of waxed paper under and around the bottom of the cake to catch any extra glaze. Pour the glaze over the cake and use a silicone spatula to smooth the top and cover all the sides. Store in the refrigerator until serving. Remove the waxed paper pieces and serve.

Six-Layer Chocolate Ganache Cake

MAKES ONE 9-INCH SIX-LAYER CAKE, 12 TO 20 SERVINGS

STORAGE

Store in the refrigerator for up to five days and then wrapped tightly in the freezer for up to three months.

In this elegant dessert, ganache—a thick chocolate filling—is spread between six chocolate cake layers. Because this cake is rich, it can be sliced thinly to serve a crowd. You can make the cake a day before you assemble it—simply wrap it in plastic to keep fresh. You can even make the sugar syrup four days in advance (store it covered at room temperature). If you are pressed for time when assembling the cake, you can cut each cake in half rather than thirds and make a four-layer cake.

CAKE

    Spray oil containing flour or spray oil plus 2 tablespoons flour
        for greasing and flouring pan

    3 cups all-purpose flour

    ¾ cup parve unsweetened cocoa

    2¼ cups sugar

    1 teaspoon baking soda

    1 teaspoon baking powder

    1 teaspoon salt

    3 large eggs

    ¾ cup canola or vegetable oil

    1 teaspoon pure vanilla extract

    1 cup water

    1 cup parve plain soy milk

SUGAR SYRUP

    ½ cup water

    ⅔ cup sugar

GANACHE

    20 ounces parve semisweet or bittersweet chocolate, plus extra
        for decorating cake, if desired

    2 teaspoons pure vanilla extract

1¼ cups parve plain soy milk

4 tablespoons parve margarine

1. Preheat the oven to 350°F. Grease and flour two 9-inch round pans.

2. In a large bowl, mix together the flour, cocoa, sugar, baking soda, baking powder, and salt. Add the eggs, oil, vanilla, water, and soy milk. Beat by hand with a whisk or with a hand-held or stand electric mixer on medium speed until combined, about 1 minute, scraping down the sides of the bowl as necessary.

3. Divide the batter evenly between the two prepared pans. Bake for 45 minutes, or until a skewer inserted in the cakes comes out clean.

4. Meanwhile, prepare the sugar syrup. Place the water and sugar in a small heavy pot over medium heat. Stir to dissolve the sugar and bring to a rolling boil. Remove from heat. Let sit at room temperature until you are ready to use.

5. When the cakes are baked, remove from oven and let cool for 10 minutes. Remove the cakes from the pans and let cool completely on a rack while you prepare the ganache.

6. To make the ganache: Break the chocolate into small pieces and melt on the stovetop or in the microwave, following the "Melting chocolate" directions in Foolproof Tips and Techniques.

7. When the chocolate is melted, whisk in the vanilla. Heat the soy milk until hot, not boiling. Add to the chocolate mixture a little at a time and whisk well after each addition. Add the margarine and whisk until very smooth. Cover with plastic and place in the refrigerator for 15 minutes.

8. When the cakes have cooled, take each cake and trim the top and sides to make them even (eat the scraps). Following the instructions in "Slicing cake layers" (see Foolproof Tips and Techniques), slice each cake into three pieces so that you will have six layers.

9. Set aside one of the cake bottoms to use as the top of the cake. Place the other cake bottom, bottom-side down, on your serving plate and put some pieces of waxed paper under the cake to catch the drippings. Take a pastry brush, dip into the sugar syrup and brush the top of the cake layer all around to moisten it. Scoop up about ¾ cup of the ganache and, using a silicone spatula, spread evenly on that layer of cake; use just enough ganache to cover the layer. Add the next piece of cake, moisten with syrup, and spread another ¾ cup of ganache. Repeat with all layers until you get to the cake bottom that you reserved for the top. Place on top,

bottom-side up, but do not moisten it with the sugar syrup. As you assemble the cake, try to make it even by looking at the cake from the side and gently pressing down to even out the cake if the cake is too tall on one side.

10 Use a long metal spatula to spread ganache on the top and sides of the cake so that the layers are no longer visible. Try to reserve 1 to 2 tablespoons of ganache to use for decorating the cake. Heat the blade of the metal spatula in very hot or boiling water and wipe lightly with a towel and then immediately slide around the sides and top of the cake to make the ganache completely smooth; you may need to reheat the blade and repeat this step a few times.

11 Place any leftover ganache in a pastry bag to make flowers, dots, or swirls on top of the cake. You can also scrape extra chocolate with a vegetable peeler on top of the cake.

12 Store in the refrigerator until serving.

Madeleines

MAKES 30 LITTLE CAKES

STORAGE

Store covered with plastic or in an airtight container at room temperature for five days or freeze for up to three months.

The classic French madeleine is a mini lemon sponge cake baked in a pan with shell-shaped molds. Honestly, the little cakes come out better in that pan, but I've also baked them in mini muffin pans and they came out nice too. This recipe makes about 30 and the madeleine pans typically contain molds for 12, so you'll need to bake a few batches unless you own multiple Madeleine pans.

———————

Spray oil containing flour or spray oil plus 2 tablespoons flour for greasing and flouring pan

4 large eggs, at room temperature

½ cup (1 stick) parve margarine

1 cup all-purpose flour

⅔ cup sugar

2 teaspoons pure vanilla extract

1½ teaspoons lemon zest (grated outer
   peel) (from 1 lemon)
1 tablespoon confectioners' sugar, sifted

1 Preheat the oven to 375°F.
2 Grease and flour the madeleine molds in
   the pan.
3 Crack the eggs into a large bowl and beat
   with an electric mixer on low speed for
   1 minute. Add the sugar in four parts,
   beating continuously on low speed and
   adding more sugar after each addition
   is mixed in. (This is easiest with a stand
   mixer, though you can use a hand-held
   too.) Add the vanilla and lemon zest, turn
   the mixer to high speed, and beat for
   5 minutes. The mixture will become thick
   and creamy.
4 Place the melted margarine in a medium
   bowl. Mix the flour into the melted
   margarine with a wooden spoon until
   thoroughly combined. It will become a
   dry-looking paste.
5 Add half of the beaten eggs to the flour
   and margarine mixture and whisk. Put
   half of this mixture back into the eggs and
   mix with a silicone spatula. Add the other half of the mixture to the eggs and mix.
   Spoon a tablespoon of the batter into each mold. Place the leftover batter in the
   refrigerator.
6 Bake for 12 minutes, or until a toothpick inserted comes out clean. Immediately
   remove the madeleines from the pan to cool on a wire rack. Re-grease and re-flour
   the pan. Repeat with the remaining batter, re-greasing and re-flouring the pan
   before each use.
7 Serve warm or at room temperature sprinkled with the sifted confectioners' sugar.

Fondant-Covered Mini Cakes

MAKES TWENTY 1½-INCH SQUARES

STORAGE

Store covered with plastic or in an airtight container at room temperature for one day.

These are those cute little icing-covered mini cakes that you see at parties and weddings. We make these in my petit-four classes. They are really sweet. You can decorate the tops with little icing flowers, if desired.

CAKE

Spray oil containing flour or spray oil plus 2 tablespoons flour
for greasing and flouring pan

4 large eggs

2 cups sugar

1 cup canola or vegetable oil

2½ cups all-purpose flour

¾ cup parve plain soy milk

2 teaspoons baking powder

Dash of salt

1 teaspoon pure vanilla extract

SUGAR SYRUP

½ cup water

⅔ cup sugar

———

½ cup raspberry or apricot jam

POURED FONDANT ICING

6 cups confectioners' sugar

½ cup water

2 tablespoons light corn syrup

1 teaspoon almond extract

———

½ recipe Quick Buttercream Icing (page 296), plain or colored, to decorate the tops (optional)

1 Preheat the oven to 350°F. Grease and flour a 9 x 13-inch rectangular pan.

2 To make the cake: Place the eggs, sugar, oil, flour, soy milk, baking powder, salt, and vanilla in a large bowl and whisk well. Pour into the prepared pan.

3 Bake for 55 to 60 minutes, or until a skewer inserted in the cake comes out clean. Let cool in the pan for 10 minutes and then turn the cake out onto a rack to cool completely.

4 While the cake is baking, make the sugar syrup. Place the water and sugar in a small saucepan over medium-high heat. Bring to a rolling boil, stirring to dissolve the sugar, and then remove from the heat.

5 Take the cooled cake and trim off the sides so that all sides are completely straight. Cut the cake into 8 equal squares. Take one piece, turn it on its side, and then cut into ¼-inch slices. Repeat with the other cake squares. Make stacks 4 cake slices high by spreading jam on top of the first, second, and third slices, finishing with a slice of cake on top. Cut into little square cakes, about 1½ x 1½ inches each.

6 When you are ready to cover the cakes, make the poured fondant icing. Place the confectioners' sugar, water, and corn syrup in a saucepan. Cook over low heat, whisking constantly, until the sugar has melted and the mixture is smooth, about 4 minutes. Remove from heat and whisk in the almond extract.

7 Place a wire rack on a foil or waxed paper–lined cookie sheet to catch fondant drippings.

8 Whisk the fondant. Place a little cake on a fork and hold it steadily over the saucepan with the fondant. Use a ladle to pour the fondant over the cake a few times until all the sides are covered, letting the fondant drip back into the pan. Place on the rack to dry and harden. When the fondant gets too thick to ladle, add some of the sugar syrup to thin it and whisk well.

9 You can decorate the tops by placing a contrasting color of Quick Buttercream Icing in a pastry bag with a star tip and making little flowers on top. These mini cakes last one day after preparing and then the fondant gets too dry.

Twinkie Cupcakes

MAKES 18 CUPCAKES

STORAGE

Store covered with plastic in the refrigerator for four days.

When I set out to create this recipe, I was thinking about a filled cupcake with some kind of cream and Twinkies came to mind. As it turns out, as of the writing of this book, Twinkies no longer have kosher certification, so this recipe is even more important. If you want the authentic Twinkies shape, there are tons of websites dedicated to how to create your own homemade Twinkies in the classic rectangular shape.

CUPCAKE

4 large eggs

1 cup canola or vegetable oil

½ cup parve plain soy milk

1 cup sugar

1¼ cups all-purpose flour

1 teaspoon baking powder

1 teaspoon pure vanilla extract

⅛ teaspoon cream of tartar

CREAM FILLING

2 tablespoons parve margarine, at room temperature

¼ cup parve cream cheese, at room temperature

1¼ cups confectioners' sugar

¼ teaspoon pure vanilla extract

¼ cup parve whipping cream

1   Preheat the oven to 350°F. Place paper liners in 18 muffin cups.

2   Separate the eggs, placing 1 yolk in a medium bowl (refrigerate the 3 remaining yolks for another use) and the 4 whites into another bowl. Into the bowl with the egg yolk, add the oil, soy milk, sugar, flour, baking powder, and vanilla. Beat with an electric mixer on medium-high speed or whisk by hand for 1 minute.

3   With an electric mixer on high speed, beat the egg whites with the cream of tartar until stiff peaks form. Using a silicone spatula, fold half of the whites into

the batter and, when almost mixed in, add the rest of the whites and mix until combined. Use a ⅓-cup measuring cup to scoop the batter into the lined muffin cups. Bake for 30 minutes, or until a toothpick inserted in the center of a cupcake comes out clean. Let cool completely in the pan.

4 To make the cream filling: Place the margarine and cream cheese in a bowl. Beat with an electric mixer on medium-high speed or by hand with a whisk until creamy, scraping down the bowl a few times. Add ½ cup of the confectioners' sugar and mix. Scrape down the bowl. Add another ½ cup confectioners' sugar and mix again. Add the final ¼ cup sugar and beat until creamy. Add the vanilla and mix.

5 In a separate bowl, use an electric mixer to beat the cream until stiff. Add the whipped cream to the filling in two parts, mixing it with a whisk and scraping down the bowl so that all of the cream is mixed in.

6 Use a round ½-teaspoon measuring spoon or a small melon baller to scoop out a ball of cupcake from the top center of the cupcake. You can scoop twice to get a deeper hole, but do not scoop down to the bottom. Remove the ball and eat if you like.

7 Fill a pastry bag with a ¼-inch round tip with the cream filling. Squeeze the cream to fill the scooped-out hole and then add some cream to the top of the cupcake. I usually squeeze a circle about 1½ inches wide on top of the cupcake, but you can add more cream if you like. Repeat with the other cupcakes. Store in the refrigerator, but let soften at room temperature for a half hour before eating.

Red Velvet Cupcakes with Vanilla Icing

MAKES 20 CUPCAKES

STORAGE

Store in the refrigerator for up to three days.

Okay, so they are more pink than red. But really, how much red food coloring are you prepared to put inside your body? This recipe represents the max I was willing to use. Add more if you like.

CUPCAKES

2½ cups all-purpose flour

2 cups sugar

2 teaspoons baking powder

½ teaspoon salt

2 teaspoons parve unsweetened cocoa

3 large eggs

1 teaspoon pure vanilla extract

1 cup canola or vegetable oil

¾ cup parve plain soy milk

1 teaspoon vinegar

1½ teaspoons red gel food coloring

VANILLA ICING

8 ounces parve cream cheese

4 tablespoons parve margarine

1 teaspoon pure vanilla extract

4 cups confectioners' sugar

1 tablespoon parve plain soy milk

1 Preheat the oven to 350°F. Place 20 cupcake papers in your muffin pans.

2 To make the cupcakes: Place the flour, sugar, baking powder, salt, and cocoa in a bowl and mix well. Add the eggs, vanilla, oil, soy milk, and vinegar and mix again. Add the food coloring and mix for 1 minute. Use a ¼- or ⅓-cup measuring cup to scoop batter into each muffin cup, about two-thirds full. Bake for 30 minutes, or until a toothpick inserted in the center comes out clean. Let cool in the pans.

3 While the cupcakes are baking, make the icing: Place the cream cheese and margarine in a bowl and beat with an electric mixer on medium-high speed until creamy. Add the vanilla and mix again. Add the confectioners' sugar, 1 cup at a time, and mix in. When the sugar is all mixed in, add the soy milk and beat for 1 minute.

4 When the cupcakes are cool, use a pastry bag and star tip to squeeze a swirl of icing in the center of each cupcake. Do not cover the entire cupcake.

Lavender & Orange Cupcakes with Purple Frosting

MAKES 24 CUPCAKES

STORAGE

Store in the refrigerator for up to three days.

I know what you are thinking: lavender is a scent for bath soap. When I was in cooking school in Paris, we used it to add color to cake decorations. Now McCormick Spices has included it in its spice line.

───────

2½ teaspoons dried lavender leaves, divided

4 large eggs

2 cups sugar

1 cup canola or vegetable oil

2½ cups all-purpose flour

¾ cup parve plain soy milk

2 teaspoons baking powder

Dash of salt

1 teaspoon pure vanilla extract

1 teaspoon orange blossom water or orange juice

1 teaspoon orange zest (grated outer peel) (from 1 orange)

PURPLE FROSTING

4 tablespoons solid vegetable shortening

4 tablespoons parve margarine

½ teaspoon pure vanilla extract

2 cups confectioners' sugar, sifted

1 tablespoon parve plain soy milk

Few drops purple food coloring

───────

1 Preheat the oven to 350°F. Place 24 paper liners into a muffin pan or pans.

2 Place 2 teaspoons of the lavender in a small plastic bag. Use the lavender bottle or a rolling pin to crush the lavender leaves. Place the crushed leaves in a large bowl. Add the eggs, sugar, oil, flour, soy milk, baking powder, salt, vanilla, orange blossom water or juice, and zest and whisk well.

3 Use a ¼- or ⅓-cup measuring cup to scoop the batter into the muffin cups, about two-thirds full. Bake for 25 to 30 minutes, or until a toothpick inserted in a cupcake comes out clean. Let cool in the pan.

4 To make the frosting: Use an electric mixer on medium-high speed to beat the shortening and margarine until creamy. Add the vanilla and mix again. Add the confectioners' sugar into the bowl in three parts, mixing well after each addition. Scrape the bowl down after each addition of sugar. (I usually cover the top of the bowl with plastic wrap so the sugar does not fly out of the bowl.)

5 Add the soy milk and beat on medium speed for 2 minutes. Add food coloring, one drop at a time, until you achieve a light purple color. Use a pastry bag with a large star tip and make a swirl in the center of each cupcake; do not cover the entire cupcake. Sprinkle the remaining lavender leaves on top of the frosting.

Basic Scones

MAKES 12 SCONES

STORAGE

Store covered with plastic or in an airtight container at room temperature for five days or freeze for up to three months. Thaw 1 hour before serving.

These are great for breakfast or to serve for an afternoon tea on a Shabbat or holiday afternoon. Serve with several flavors of jam. My husband Andy and son Joey brought them to the hospital when they visited Joey's classmate, who was recovering from surgery; the boy's mom and grandparents appreciated a home-baked snack. Don't forget the jars of jam and plastic knives.

In this recipe you can substitute ½ cup whole-wheat flour for ½ cup white flour.

Spray oil, for greasing round pan, if using

2 cups plus 2 tablespoons all-purpose flour, divided

¼ cup sugar

1 tablespoon baking powder

½ teaspoon salt

6 tablespoons parve margarine, frozen for 15 minutes

2 large eggs, divided

½ cup parve plain soy milk

1 Preheat the oven to 425°F. You can bake the dough in a 9-inch round baking pan, which is the least time-consuming method, or form individual scones and bake them on a parchment-lined cookie sheet. If you're using the round pan, grease it with spray oil and set aside. (*Note*: These do not bake as well in disposable aluminum pans.)

2 Place 2 cups of the flour, the sugar, baking powder, and salt in the bowl of a food processor fitted with a metal blade. Pulse for 10 seconds. Cut the chilled margarine into small pieces and scatter over the dry ingredients. Pulse for about 10 seconds, or until the mixture resembles sand. Or, you can cut the margarine into the dry ingredients by hand with two knives or a pastry cutter.

3 Beat 1 egg and add it and the soy milk to the flour and margarine mixture. Process or mix just until the dough starts to come together, about 5 seconds. Sprinkle 1 tablespoon of flour on the counter. Place the dough on the floured surface and gently knead in the flour until the dough is smooth. Add a little more flour if the dough seems sticky and knead it in.

4 To bake the scones in the round pan, shape the dough into a ball and flatten it into a pancake the size of your baking pan. Place the dough in the greased pan. With a sharp knife dipped in flour, score (cut halfway) the top of the dough into 8 to 12 wedges.

5 To form individual scones, divide the dough in half. Take each half and roll into a log that is about 2 inches thick. Cut the log into triangular shapes by slicing diagonally, alternating directions with each slice. Try to cut the triangles about the same size. Place on a parchment-lined cookie sheet, about 1½ inches apart.

6 Beat the remaining egg and then brush the top of the dough/scones.

7 Bake for 15 to 20 minutes, or until the top is golden. Let cool for 10 minutes and then remove from the pan or cookie sheet. If you baked them in the pan, cut on the scored lines into wedges. Serve warm or at room temperature.

FLAVORED SCONES

You can mix in ½ cup, or more to taste, of dried fruits, such as cranberries, raisins, or currants, chocolate chips, or chopped nuts. I particularly like to add these additional ingredients when I've substituted some whole-wheat flour for white, creating a flavor-packed scone.

Scones au Chocolat

MAKES 8 SCONES

STORAGE

Store covered with plastic or in an airtight container at room temperature for five days or freeze for up to three months. Thaw 1 hour before serving.

One afternoon, I was driving the kids home from school when they asked me to bake some scones. I asked them what they thought about baking scones with jam inside them. They were not too excited about that idea until Joey suggested, "Why don't you put chocolate inside them?" "Like pain au chocolat?" I asked. And then at the same time, we all yelled out "scones au chocolat!" Here they are.

————

Spray oil, for greasing pan

2 cups plus 2 tablespoons all-purpose flour, divided

¼ cup sugar

1 tablespoon baking powder

½ teaspoon salt

6 tablespoons parve margarine, frozen for 15 minutes

2 large eggs, divided

½ cup parve plain soy milk

7 ounces parve semisweet chocolate, cut into 3 x ¾-inch bars

————

1 Preheat the oven to 425°F. Grease a 9-inch round baking pan with spray oil and set aside. (*Note*: These do not bake as well in disposable aluminum pans.)

2 Place 2 cups of the flour, the sugar, baking powder, and salt into the bowl of a food processor fitted with a metal blade. Pulse for 10 seconds. Cut the chilled margarine into small pieces and scatter over the dry ingredients. Mix for about 10 seconds, or until mixture resembles sand. You can cut the margarine into the dry ingredients by hand.

3 Beat 1 egg and add it and the soy milk to the flour and margarine mixture. Process or mix just until the dough starts to come together, about 5 seconds. Sprinkle 1 tablespoon of flour on the counter. Place the dough on the floured counter and gently knead in the flour until the dough is smooth. Add a little more flour if the dough seems sticky and knead it in. Divide the dough in half.

4 Shape one-half of the dough into a ball and place on parchment sprinkled with

flour. Use a rolling pin to roll into a pancake the size of your baking pan. Place the dough into the pan. With a sharp knife dipped in flour, score (mark, but do not cut completely through) the top of the dough into 8 wedges.

5   Place a 3 x ¾-inch bar of chocolate into each triangle and press it into the dough. You can also use any smaller or broken pieces; just place them in the shape of a bar in each triangle. Take the other half of the dough and roll out into a second large pancake, as you did with the first half, and place on top of the chocolate bars. Use your fingers to press the dough between the bars and around the edges to completely cover the chocolate bars with the dough. Take your knife and score again into 8 triangles around the chocolate pieces.

6   Beat the remaining egg and brush the top of the dough. Bake for 15 to 20 minutes, or until the top is golden. Let cool for 10 minutes and then remove from the pan. Cut on the scored lines into wedges. Serve warm or at room temperature.

Apple Tarte Tatin

SERVES 8 TO 12

STORAGE

Store covered with plastic in the refrigerator for up to 3 days.

This is an upside-down apple tart and is one of my favorite French desserts. It is perfect to serve for Rosh Hashanah or Thanksgiving. I like to use the largest Granny Smith apples I can find. If you can only find the smaller ones, reduce the apple cooking time in Step 4 by 5 minutes and the baking time in Step 5 (without the pastry on top) by 5 minutes as well.

---

1 sheet parve frozen puff pastry (from a 17.3-ounce box)

10 tablespoons parve margarine

¾ cup sugar

8 Granny Smith apples

Flour for sprinkling

---

1 Preheat the oven to 400°F.

2 Thaw the puff pastry at room temperature for 45 minutes or use the "Quick thaw method for puff pastry" (see Foolproof Tips and Techniques).

3 You will need a deep, ovenproof skillet about 11 to 13 inches wide. Make sure the handle is ovenproof as well. Take a piece of parchment about 16 inches long and sprinkle some flour on it. Roll out the puff pastry sheet until it is 1 inch larger than your pan. Place the pan on top of the rolled pastry and use a sharp knife to cut a circle in the pastry the size of the pan. Remove excess dough and set the dough circle aside.

4 Place the margarine and sugar in the skillet and set over medium-low heat. Cook for 5 minutes, stirring often. Meanwhile, peel and core the apples and cut into quarters. Add the apples on their sides to the skillet in concentric circles, starting at the outside and working your way toward the center. Pack the apples tightly. Cook for 20 minutes uncovered without stirring.

5 Place the skillet in the oven for 15 minutes. Remove the skillet from the oven. Place your hand under the parchment, beneath the pastry circle, and flip the pastry over on top of the apples. Be careful, the skillet is hot! Peel off the parchment and use a sharp knife to cut a few holes in the pastry. Return the skillet to the oven and bake for 20 minutes, or until the pastry is golden.

6 Remove from oven and let rest for 10 minutes. Place a large serving plate over the pan and then flip the tart onto the plate. If any of the apples get stuck in the pan, use a spatula to scoop them out and place where they belong on the tart. Serve warm or at room temperature.

Poppy Seed Tart

SERVES 12

STORAGE

Store covered with plastic at room temperature for five days or freeze for up to three months.

The preparation of this dessert is similar to making bar cookies, but baked in a springform pan the result is more elegant.

Spray oil or parve margarine for greasing
2 cups all-purpose flour
1 cup confectioners' sugar
1 tablespoon orange zest (grated outer peel) (from 1 orange)
1 cup (2 sticks) parve margarine, frozen for 20 minutes
1 large egg yolk
1 tablespoon cold water
12 ounces ready-made poppy seed filling

1 Preheat the oven to 350°F. Grease a 9-inch springform pan.

2 Place the flour, sugar, and orange zest in the bowl of a food processor fitted with a metal blade. Process for 10 seconds. Cut the frozen margarine into pieces and add to the bowl. Process for another 10 seconds. Add the egg yolk and water and then process until the dough comes together. You can also mix by hand by cutting the margarine into the dry ingredients with a pastry cutter or two knives and then mixing in the egg and water.

3 Divide the dough in half. Take one portion of dough and wrap it in plastic, then flatten it and place it in the freezer. Take the other half and break it into pieces. Scatter the pieces over the bottom of the pan and press them in as evenly as you can. Place in the oven and bake for 15 minutes. Let cool for 15 minutes.

4 Use a silicone spatula to spread the poppy seed filling over the crust in the pan. Remove the other dough half and, using the large holes of a box grater, grate the dough over the filling. Use your hands to distribute the grated dough to cover the filling.

5 Bake for 40 to 45 minutes, or until the top starts to brown. Remove from oven and let cool.

Plum Tart

SERVES 8 TO 12

STORAGE

Store covered with plastic for three days in the refrigerator.

This tart is made with easy-to-use puff pastry crust, a custardy filling, and fresh plums. It looks like a French country tart.

1 sheet frozen puff pastry (from a 17.3 ounce box)

6 plums, a little soft, but not too ripe

4 tablespoons parve margarine, plus extra for greasing

1 large egg plus 1 yolk

⅓ cup plus 1 tablespoon sugar, divided

½ teaspoon pure vanilla extract

⅓ cup all-purpose flour, plus extra for sprinkling

¼ teaspoon baking powder

1 tablespoon parve whipping cream

1 Preheat the oven to 400°F. Move an oven rack to the lowest shelf.

2 Place a 9- or 10-inch tart ring or tart pan with a removable bottom on top of a parchment-lined cookie sheet. Take some soft margarine and with your finger, rub the margarine around the inside of the ring or pan.

3 Take the sheet of puff pastry out of the freezer. Thaw the puff pastry at room temperature for 30 to 45 minutes or use the "Quick thaw method for puff pastry" (see Foolproof Tips and Techniques).

4 Unroll the pastry on top of a piece of parchment sprinkled with a little flour. Roll the pastry about 1 inch larger than your tart ring or pan. You will need to sprinkle some flour on your rolling pin so the pastry does not stick to it. Place your hand under the parchment and flip the pastry over into the tart ring or pan, using your fingers to gently press the pastry into the corners. Peel the parchment off the pastry. Again, use your fingers to make sure the pastry is in the corners and then drape any extra dough over the top of the ring or pan. Roll your rolling pin along the top of the ring or pan to cut off the excess dough. Place the cookie sheet in the freezer for 10 minutes while you prepare the plums and filling.

5 Take each plum, cut in half around the pit, and then cut each half into ¼-inch slices.

6 In a microwave-safe bowl, heat the margarine in the microwave for 30 seconds to soften, but not completely melt it. In another bowl, place the whole egg and yolk, ⅓ cup of sugar, and vanilla and whisk. Add the flour and baking powder and mix with a wooden spoon or silicone spatula. Add the softened margarine and whipping cream and mix well. Remove the cookie sheet from the freezer and spread this mixture evenly inside the tart ring or pan.

7 Take the plum slices and, starting on the outside of the pastry, place the slices on their sides, in concentric circles. Pack the plums in tightly. Bake on the bottom oven rack for 25 minutes. Sprinkle the remaining tablespoon of sugar on top. Place back in the oven on the middle rack and bake another 10 minutes. Remove to rack to cool. If you used a tart ring without a bottom, slide the tart onto a serving plate and then pull off the ring. For a tart pan with a removable bottom, place your hand under the bottom and lift the tart up and out of the ring.

Cherry Pie

MAKES ONE 8- OR 9-INCH PIE, 8 TO 12 SERVINGS

STORAGE

*Store covered with plastic in the refrigerator for four days or freeze
for up to three months.*

People seem to love or hate cherry pie. I have found that if the filling is from real cherries, then I like it. I just can't bear that canned red goo that masquerades as cherries in many pies. My friend Betsy Brint loves cherry pie. She says that not only is it beautiful to look at, but her taste buds water thinking about the tangy tart cherries mixed with sugar to create a sweet syrupy filling.

CRUST

2 cups all-purpose flour, plus extra for sprinkling

½ teaspoon salt

2 tablespoons sugar

6 tablespoons solid vegetable shortening, frozen 30 minutes and
cut into 6 pieces

½ cup (1 stick) parve margarine, frozen for 30 minutes and cut
into tablespoons

3 tablespoons cold water

FILLING

4 cups pitted cherries (from about ¾ pound whole cherries)
(see "Pitting cherries," page xxviii)

½ cup sugar

½ teaspoon ground cinnamon

Dash of salt

3 tablespoons cornstarch

———

1 large egg white, beaten, for brushing over top crust

1 teaspoon sugar, for sprinkling over top crust

———

1 Preheat the oven to 350°F. Place an oven rack on the lowest shelf. You will need a
8- or 9-inch pie pan for this dessert.

2 To make the crust: Place the flour, salt, and sugar into the bowl of a food processor

fitted with a metal blade. Pulse for 10 seconds. If you're making the crust by hand, whisk together the dry ingredients. Add the shortening and margarine and process until the mixture looks like sand, or cut in the shortening and margarine by hand with two knives or a pastry cutter. Add the cold water and process or mix until the dough just comes together.

3 Gather into a ball and break off a little more than one-third of the dough. Wrap both pieces of dough separately in plastic and flatten. Freeze for 20 minutes.

4 To make the filling: Roughly chop the pitted cherries so that each cherry has been cut into quarters. In a medium bowl, toss the chopped cherries with the sugar, cinnamon, salt, and cornstarch to coat the cherries. Keep tossing until you do not see any cornstarch.

5 Take the smaller piece of dough out of the freezer and place it on a piece of parchment sprinkled with flour. Cover with a second piece of parchment and roll out to about 8 inches wide by 12 inches long and ¼-inch thick. Use a knife to cut the dough into long strips, about ¾-inch wide. Leave the strips on the parchment. Slide the parchment onto a cookie sheet and place in the freezer.

6 Meanwhile, remove the larger piece of dough from the freezer and place on a piece of parchment or plastic wrap sprinkled with flour. Sprinkle the top of the dough with some flour and cover with a piece of parchment. Roll on top of the parchment to roll the dough into a circle about 1 inch larger than your pie pan. Peel back the top parchment and sprinkle some more flour on the dough as you roll. Remove the top parchment. Place your hand under the parchment or plastic, lift the dough and turn it over into the pie pan. Remove the parchment or plastic. Use a knife to trim the dough. You can use the dough scraps to decorate the pie crust by rerolling the scraps and cutting them into small (under 2-inch) shapes with a cookie cutter. Place them on parchment and into the freezer for a few minutes before transferring them to the pie crust.

7 Dump the filling into the crust and spread evenly.

8 To assemble the lattice: Place half the dough strips (about 5) across the pie, about 1½ inches apart. Fold the first, third, and fifth strips back over themselves. Place another strip at right angles across the unfolded strips. Unfold the folded strips over the new strip. Now fold back the strips that were not folded before (the second, fourth and, if needed, sixth strips). Add another strip at right angles, over the unfolded strips, 1½ inches from the other, and then unfold the folded ones. Keep alternating until you have covered the pie. Trim off the edges and press to seal the edges of the lattice strips to the rim of bottom crust.

9 Use a pastry brush to brush the egg white over the crust and lattice. Sprinkle the 1 teaspoon sugar all over the top. Place on a jelly roll pan and put on the bottom rack in the oven. Bake for 1 hour, or until the top of the crust starts to brown and the cherries look bubbly.

Peach Pie for a Crowd

ONE 9 X 13-INCH PIE, 15 TO 18 SERVINGS
STORAGE

Store covered in plastic in the refrigerator for up to four days or freeze up to three months.

As my family grew larger and we invited more and more guests, I realized that I rarely baked pies. The reason was that an 8-inch pie barely fed the six of us. I created this recipe to bake a pie in a 9 x 13-inch pan.

CRUST

3 cups all-purpose flour, plus extra for sprinkling

¾ cup whole-wheat flour

1 teaspoon salt

3 tablespoons sugar

10 tablespoons solid vegetable shortening

1 cup (2 sticks) parve margarine

5 to 6 tablespoons cold water

FILLING

12 peaches (still firm), peeled and cut into ⅓-inch slices

1 cup light brown sugar

½ teaspoon ground cinnamon

⅓ cup cornstarch

———

1 large egg white, beaten, to brush on pie

2 teaspoons sugar, to sprinkle on pie

1 Grease a 9 x 13-inch pan. Place an oven rack on the lowest shelf.

2 Preheat the oven to 350°F. Place the white and whole-wheat flours, salt, and sugar into the bowl of a food processor fitted with a metal blade. Pulse for 10 seconds. If you're making the crust by hand, whisk together the dry ingredients. Add the shortening and margarine and process until the mixture looks like sand, or cut in the shortening and margarine with a pastry cutter or two knives. Add the cold water a tablespoon at a time and mix just until the dough just comes together.

3 Gather into a ball and break off a little more than one-third of the dough. Wrap both pieces of dough separately in plastic and flatten. Freeze for 20 minutes.

4 To make the filling: Place the peach slices in a medium bowl. Add the brown sugar, cinnamon, salt, and cornstarch and toss to coat the peaches until you do not see any more cornstarch.

5 Take the smaller piece of dough out of the freezer and place on a piece of parchment sprinkled with flour. Cover with a second piece of parchment and roll out about 8 inches wide by 12 inches long and ¼-inch thick. Use a knife to cut the dough into long strips, about ¾-inch thick. Leave the strips on the parchment. Slide the parchment onto a cookie sheet and place in the freezer.

6 Meanwhile, remove the larger piece of dough from freezer and place on a piece of parchment or plastic wrap sprinkled with flour. Sprinkle the top of the dough with some flour and cover with a piece of parchment. Roll on top of the parchment to roll out the dough into a rectangle about 1 inch larger than your pan. Peel back the top parchment and sprinkle some more flour on the dough as you roll. Remove the top parchment. Place your hand under the parchment or plastic, lift the dough, and turn over into the pan. Press the dough into the corners; you want the dough to come up the sides of the pan. Remove the parchment or plastic. Use a knife to trim the dough so it does not hang over the pan.

7 Dump the filling into the crust and spread evenly.

8 To make the lattice: Place half the dough strips (5 to 6) diagonally across the pie, about 1½ inches apart. Fold the first, third, and fifth strips back over themselves. Place another strip in the opposite diagonal direction (perpendicular to the first set) across the unfolded strips. Unfold the folded strips over the new strip. Now fold back the strips that were not folded before (the second, fourth, and sixth strips). Add another perpendicular strip, 1½ inches from the other, over the unfolded strips and then unfold the folded ones. Keep alternating until you have covered the pie. Trim off the edges and press to seal the edges of the lattice strips to the rim of the bottom crust.

9 Use a pastry brush to brush the egg white over the crust and lattice. Sprinkle the 2 teaspoons sugar all over the top. Bake on the bottom rack of the oven for 1 hour and 15 minutes, or until the top of the crust starts to brown and the peaches look bubbly.

Summer Fruit Galette

SERVES 8

STORAGE

Store covered in plastic in the refrigerator for up to four days.

A galette is a free-form, rustic-looking French tart. You roll out the dough into a large circle, place the fruit in the middle and then fold up the sides of the dough to partially cover the fruit. You can combine any types of fruit you like (3 cups total) to create your own signature dessert. This is a good way to use up some soft fruit you have around. I made three different flavors when I spent Shabbat at my friend Elena Neuman Lefkowitz's beautiful, brand-new house in Westhampton Beach, New York. She had not yet fully outfitted her kitchen with equipment so I rolled out the dough using a wine bottle. It worked surprisingly well.

DOUGH

1¼ cups all-purpose flour, plus extra for sprinkling

¼ teaspoon salt

6 tablespoons parve margarine, frozen for 30 minutes and
    cut into 6 pieces

1 large egg, separated

3 tablespoons ice water, divided

FILLING

3 cups fresh fruit: berries, or plums, peaches, or apricots cut into
    ½-inch pieces, or peeled and thinly sliced apples or pears

3 tablespoons sugar

2 teaspoons cornstarch

---

1 teaspoon sugar, to sprinkle on top of galette

1. To make the dough: Place the flour, salt, and margarine into the bowl of a food processor fitted with a metal blade. Pulse 10 times or cut the margarine into the flour and salt by hand using two knives or a pastry cutter.

2. Add the egg yolk (reserve the white) and 1 tablespoon of the ice water. Pulse 5 times or mix gently by hand. Add another tablespoon of the ice water and pulse another 5 times or mix again. Add the last tablespoon of water, a little at a time, pulsing or lightly mixing the dough for 10 to 15 seconds until it looks like clumps of couscous; the dough does not have to come completely together. Gather the dough into a ball.

3. Take a large piece of plastic wrap and sprinkle some flour on top. Place the dough on the floured plastic, wrap the plastic around it, and then flatten. Place the dough in the freezer for 20 minutes.

4. Preheat the oven to 425°F and place a rack on the lowest shelf of your oven.

5. Take a large piece of parchment and sprinkle it with some flour. Remove the dough from the plastic wrap and place it on top of the parchment. Sprinkle some flour on the dough and then place a second piece of parchment on top. Roll out the dough until it is about 12 to 13 inches in diameter, trying your best to keep the shape round. Peel back the top parchment and sprinkle some more flour once or twice while you are rolling.

6. To make the filling: Place the fruit in a medium bowl. In a separate small bowl, mix together the sugar and cornstarch. Sprinkle on top of the fruit and mix gently. Place the fruit in the center of the dough circle and spread it outward, leaving a 2- to 3-inch border on the outside. Take one small section of the dough border, about 2 inches, and fold it over the fruit, leaving the fruit-filled center open. Pick up another 2-inch section of the border and repeat, pressing one section into the next to seal it, so you end up with dough pleats.

7. Beat the reserved egg white and brush over the top of the dough. Sprinkle with the teaspoon of sugar. Bake for 30 minutes. Move the galette to a middle rack in the oven and bake another 10 minutes. Let cool for 20 minutes.

Challah Beer Bread Pudding
with Caramel Sauce

SERVES 12

STORAGE

Store covered in plastic in the refrigerator for up to five days.

I know it sounds strange, but I once had a dessert in a restaurant that combined sweet brioche bread with beer, vanilla ice cream, and caramel sauce and I just loved the combination. For an extra kick, serve with vanilla tofutti ice cream. I made six caramel sauces before settling on this one, which was the simplest of them all. Do not be concerned about the "globs" of caramel in the pot when you add the water—just keep cooking and stirring until they melt. The caramel sauce can be made three days in advance.

BREAD PUDDING

⅔ of a large loaf of stale challah, cut into 1-inch cubes (enough to
    mostly cover the bottom of the pan)

1½ cups full-flavored beer (from one 12-ounce bottle)

6 large eggs

1 cup sugar

2 teaspoons pure vanilla extract

2 cups parve plain soy milk

CARAMEL SAUCE

½ cup sugar

1 cup boiling water

————

1 Preheat the oven to 350°F.

2 Place the challah cubes in a 9 x 13-inch baking pan. Pour the beer over the cubes and toss to coat. Let sit 15 minutes. Place the eggs, sugar, vanilla and soy milk in a medium bowl and whisk until combined. Pour or ladle over the beer-soaked challah and bake for 50 minutes, or until the pudding is set and the edges browned.

3 Meanwhile, make the caramel sauce. Place the sugar in a heavy-bottomed saucepan over medium heat and cook, stirring often, until all of the sugar has melted and you have a deep amber-colored syrup. Remove from the heat and carefully add the boiling water. The mixture will boil up and you will see some

balls of caramel in the pot. Return the pan to medium heat and cook at a rolling boil for 10 minutes. Stir often until all of the caramel pieces have melted and you have a smooth syrup. Let cool, cover with plastic, and store at room temperature.

4 To serve, cut the pudding into squares, place on your serving plate and drizzle on the caramel sauce. Serve warm or at room temperature. The pudding can be reheated in a warm oven (200°F) for 20 minutes.

Layered Baklava with Orange Blossom Syrup

SERVES 20

STORAGE

Store covered in plastic at room temperature for up to five days.

I have always liked baklava but did not like that there was so much filo in it and not that much filling. The method I developed of layering the filo and filling takes care of that problem.

———

1⅔ cups shelled, unsalted pistachio nuts (about 1 pound pistachios
   in their shells)

1 cup slivered almonds

2¼ cups sugar, divided

½ cup ground walnuts (see "Making ground walnuts," page xxviii)
   or 1 cup walnut pieces

Spray oil

1 package frozen filo dough, thawed in the refrigerator according to
   package directions

Juice of 1 lemon

1 cup water

2 teaspoons orange blossom water

———

1 Preheat the oven to 350°F. Place an oven rack in the middle of the oven. Place the pistachios, almonds, ¼ cup of the sugar, and ground walnuts or walnut pieces into the bowl of a food processor fitted with a metal blade. Process until the mixture is ground into tiny pieces, but not completely pulverized. Place in a bowl and set aside.

2 Lightly grease a 9 x 13-inch pan with spray oil. If your sheets of filo are larger than your pan, cut the pile in half. Take 1 sheet of filo, place it in the pan and then spray with some oil. Lay another 4 sheets in the pan, spraying each sheet before placing another on top. Scoop up ¾ cup of the nut mixture and sprinkle it on top of the fifth sheet of filo. Spread as evenly as you can.

3 Place another sheet of filo on top of the nuts and spray all over with oil. One at a time, place another 4 sheets on top of each other, spraying each one. Once again,

measure ¾ cup nuts and sprinkle on top of the filo and spread. Continue this procedure until you have 5 filo layers and 4 nut layers, finishing with the filo on top. Spray the top sheet of filo with oil.

4   Take a sharp knife and make diagonal slices through the filo layers across the pan, about 1½ inches apart. Make diagonal cuts in the other direction. Place on the middle rack in the oven and bake for 30 to 40 minutes, or until lightly browned on top.

5   While the baklava is baking, make the orange blossom syrup: Bring the remaining 2 cups of sugar, the lemon juice, and water to a boil in a small saucepan. Reduce the heat to medium and cook uncovered for 5 minutes. Turn the heat to low and simmer for 7 minutes. Remove from the heat and add the orange blossom water and stir. Set aside.

6   When the baklava is baked, remove from the oven and immediately pour the syrup over it. Let cool in the pan.

Almond Pastry Squares

MAKES TWENTY-FIVE 2-INCH SQUARES
STORAGE
Store covered in plastic at room temperature for up to four days.

One of my favorite desserts that I made at cooking school in France was called a *pithivier*. It is a flower-shaped puff pastry filled with almond cream. After several tries, I decided that the flower shape was just too complicated to describe and the almond cream kept leaking out. So one day I was pressed for time and just made it into a square. The method is easy and the results as tasty as the flower-shaped version.

———

1 package parve frozen puff pastry (2 sheets from a 17.3-ounce box)

10 tablespoons parve margarine

⅔ cup plus 2 teaspoons sugar, divided

1 cup almond flour (see "Making almond flour," page xxvii)

2 tablespoons all-purpose flour, plus extra for sprinkling

3 large eggs, divided

2 teaspoons pure vanilla extract

¼ cup blanched, sliced almonds (no brown edges)

1. Thaw the puff pastry at room temperature for 45 minutes or use the "Quick thaw method for puff pastry" (see Foolproof Tips and Techniques).

2. While the puff pastry is defrosting, make the almond cream. With an electric stand or hand-held mixer on high speed or a whisk, beat the margarine in a medium bowl. Add the ⅔ cup sugar, almond flour, and flour and beat or whisk again. Add 2 of the eggs and the vanilla. Turn up the speed of the mixer to high or beat vigorously by hand until the mixture is light and airy. Cover and set aside. The cream may be made 3 days in advance and stored in the refrigerator.

3. Place a piece of parchment on the counter. Sprinkle some flour on the parchment. Unroll one sheet of puff pastry and roll it out to smooth out the lines, keeping the square shape of the pastry. Take a knife and score (mark, but do not cut completely through) a 1-inch border around the edge.

4. Place the remaining egg in a small bowl, beat it, and then brush some all around the border. Using a silicone spatula, spread the almond cream on the pastry, inside of the egg-brushed border. Try to spread it as evenly as possible.

5. Roll out the second piece of pastry on a piece of parchment sprinkled with flour. Try to roll the pastry to the same size as the first sheet of pastry. Place your hand under it and flip it over on top of the almond cream. Peel off the parchment and stretch the dough so that you can pinch the edges of the two pastry sheets together to seal the top dough to the bottom dough. Use the tines of a fork to seal the pastry tightly all around the square.

6. Brush all over with the beaten egg. (Reserve some egg to brush the top again before baking.) Carefully slide the parchment onto a cookie sheet and place in the freezer for 20 minutes.

7. Preheat the oven to 450°F. Remove the cookie sheet from the freezer and brush the dough again with the beaten egg. Sprinkle the top with the remaining 2 teaspoons of sugar and the sliced almonds. Bake for 20 minutes. Reduce the temperature to 400°F, and bake another 5 minutes until golden. Do not let the almonds burn. Serve warm or at room temperature.

Mini Carrot Soufflés with Cinnamon Crème Anglaise

SERVES 8

STORAGE

Store covered in plastic in the refrigerator for up to four days.

My friend Julie Hoffman brought a large carrot soufflé to a mutual friend's house to serve as a side dish. I found it a little too sweet for a side dish, but that did not stop me from eating three servings of it and begging for the recipe. I adapted it into a plated dessert. The sauce is a rich custardy vanilla and cinnamon-flavored crème anglaise that looks pretty when spooned around the soufflé.

SOUFFLÉS

Spray oil or extra parve margarine for greasing

1 pound carrots, peeled and cut into 1-inch chunks

½ cup parve cornflake crumbs

½ cup light brown sugar

¼ cup ground walnuts (see "Making ground walnuts," page xviii)

¼ cup chopped pecans (¼-inch pieces)

¾ cup (1½ sticks) parve margarine, melted, divided

1 tablespoon pure maple syrup

3 large eggs

½ cup sugar

¼ cup all-purpose flour

1 teaspoon baking powder

¼ teaspoon ground cinnamon

¼ teaspoon ground nutmeg

CINNAMON CRÈME ANGLAISE SAUCE

1½ cups parve plain soy milk

¼ cup parve whipping cream

1 vanilla bean, split lengthwise and scraped (reserve seeds)

4 large egg yolks

½ cup sugar

½ teaspoon ground cinnamon

1 Preheat the oven to 350°F. Grease eight 4-inch ramekins and place in a jelly roll pan.

2 Bring 8 cups of water to boil in a medium pot. Place the carrots in the boiling water and cook for 15 to 20 minutes, until soft. Drain well.

3 While the carrots are cooking, place the cornflake crumbs, light brown sugar, ground walnuts, and chopped pecans in a medium bowl and mix well. Pour 4 tablespoons of the melted margarine and the maple syrup into the bowl with the nut mixture and mix well. Spoon the mixture evenly into the 8 ramekins.

4 In a large bowl, place the eggs, ½ cup sugar, flour, baking powder, cinnamon, and nutmeg and mix well. Pour the remaining margarine into the bowl and mix again.

5 Place the drained carrots into the bowl of a food processor fitted with a metal blade and process until the carrots are completely puréed. It should look like baby food. Add the carrot purée to the egg mixture and mix well. Divide the carrot mixture among the 8 ramekins, about ⅓ to ½ cup mixture in each.

6 Place the jelly roll pan and ramekins in the oven and bake for 45 minutes, or until set.

7 While the soufflés are baking, make the cinnamon crème anglaise sauce. In a small saucepan, bring the soy milk, whipping cream, vanilla bean and scraped seeds to a boil. Meanwhile, in a large bowl, whisk together the egg yolks, sugar, and cinnamon. When the soy milk and cream boil, strain some of the liquid into the bowl with the egg mixture and whisk well. Strain the rest of the soy milk and cream into the egg mixture and whisk well. Pour back into the pan and cook on low heat, stirring constantly, for 2 minutes, or until the sauce starts to thicken slightly. Store in the refrigerator for up to four days. Serve warm or cold.

8 When the soufflés are baked, let cool for 5 minutes. To serve within an hour or two, run a knife around the edge of each ramekin and turn the soufflés out of the ramekins onto dessert plates. To serve several hours later or the next day, turn soufflés onto a cookie sheet, cover with plastic and refrigerate. When ready to serve, use a spatula to place the soufflés on dessert plates. When ready to bring to the table, spoon the sauce around each soufflé.

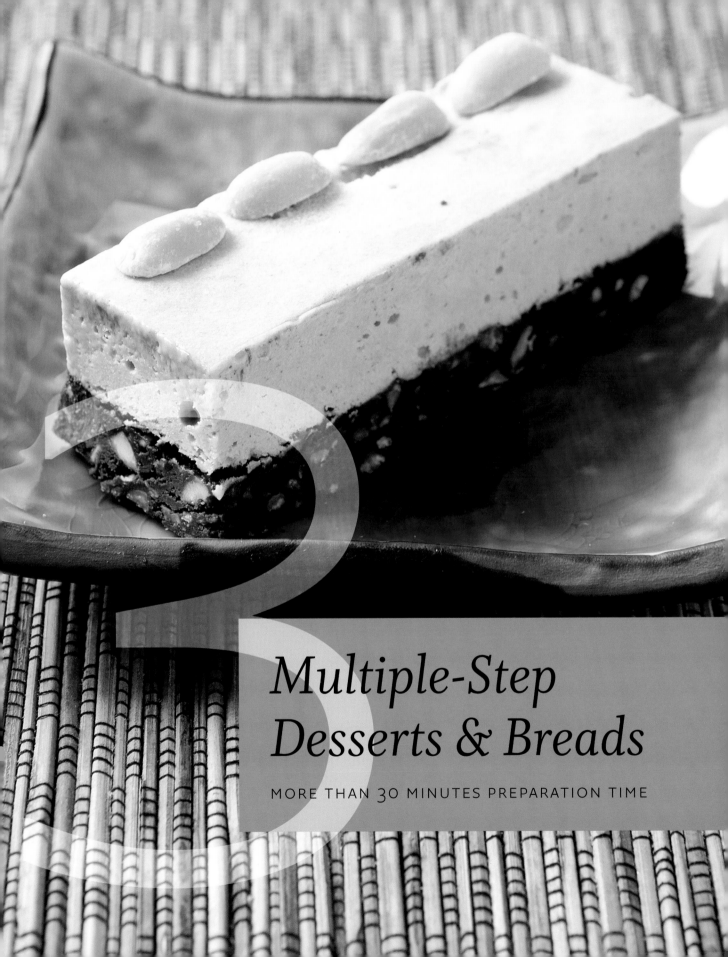

Multiple-Step Desserts & Breads

MORE THAN 30 MINUTES PREPARATION TIME

I am sure you've never thought that multiple-step desserts would be possible for someone with a busy lifestyle to pull off. This part will show you that you can fit more complex desserts into your schedule. You *do* have to plan, but kosher cooks are used to planning—we have Shabbat every week and holidays pop up all year.

Some of the desserts in this part are actually easy to make; they simply take time. Others are more challenging as well as being more time-consuming. The beauty of these desserts is that many of the steps take less than thirty minutes and some even require less than ten. You can mix a one-bowl cake in five minutes, bake it, cool it, and freeze it. Several days later you can spend fifteen minutes or less to prepare a filling for it and refrigerate that. A day or two later, you can spend fifteen to twenty minutes assembling the final dessert. Each step does not require you to stand in the kitchen for hours. With careful planning, you can spread the

work out over days or longer. It will *look* like you slaved all day, and only you will know that you didn't.

Many of the desserts in this chapter are not typically parve desserts, so you can try some new things. Some desserts require special skills and equipment that may be new to you; be patient. In this part, you will learn how to make several kinds of cookies and pastry doughs, fancy layer cakes, French tarts and pastries, and individual plated desserts and mousses. I teach you how to assemble layer cakes for celebrations, how to use a pastry bag with success, and even fill éclairs. Anyone can master a new skill by doing it a few times.

In this part, I have tried to offer you contemporary desserts served in restaurants and fancy bakeries. Although they cannot be made at the last minute, all of them are worth your time and effort.

This part of the book also includes a section on baking challah. Most Jews have access to decent store-bought challah, but in many parts of the world, the only way to have challah for Shabbat and holidays is to bake it yourself. If you have never baked challah before, start with the Classic Challah, the one I bake every week. All challah bakers have a favorite recipe, but I hope you will enjoy trying some new recipes and ways to flavor and shape challah as much as I did writing this section of the book.

Cracked-Top Chocolate Cookies

MAKES 6 TO 7 DOZEN

STORAGE

To freeze the cookie dough in balls, freeze them for one hour on a cookie sheet and then remove to an airtight container or freezer bag and freeze up to three months. Store baked cookies covered with plastic or in an airtight container at room temperature for five days or freeze for up to three months.

These cookies can be baked two ways: with or without a coating of confectioners' sugar. I like to bake half the dough one way and half the other as I like the way the two kinds look on a platter. You can freeze the cookie-dough balls and bake the cookies when you want, or freeze the cookies already baked. As for the baking time, you decide if you want them very soft and chewy (12 to 14 minutes) or crunchy on the outside and chewy inside (14 to 16 minutes), which I like.

⅔ cup canola or vegetable oil

2 cups sugar

1 cup parve unsweetened cocoa

4 large eggs

2 teaspoons pure vanilla extract

2 cups all-purpose flour

2 teaspoons baking powder

½ teaspoon salt

½ cup confectioners' sugar, for coating cookies (optional)

1 In a large bowl, whisk together the oil, sugar, and cocoa. Add the eggs, one at a time, and whisk well after each addition. Add the vanilla and whisk again. Add the flour, baking powder, and salt and mix well with a wooden spoon or silicone spatula.

2 Place the dough in the refrigerator for 1 hour.

3 Line three baking sheets with parchment, or bake in batches. Use a tablespoon to

scoop up the dough and roll into balls about 1 inch in diameter. If you'd like to coat the cookies in confectioners' sugar, place the confectioners' sugar in a small bowl. Roll the cookie balls in the confectioners' sugar until they are heavily coated with sugar. Place the cookie-dough balls on the prepared baking sheets about 1½ inches apart. Place the sheets in the freezer for at least 15 minutes. You can freeze them longer and bake when you want fresh-baked cookies.

4 Preheat the oven to 350°F. Bake the cookies for 12 to 16 minutes, depending on how chewy or crunchy you like your cookies. Either way, they will appear soft when baked. The cookies will spread and crack on top when they are almost done. Slide the parchment onto cooling racks and let cool.

Almond Tuilles

MAKES ABOUT 30 COOKIES

STORAGE

Store covered with plastic or in an airtight container at room temperature for five days or freeze for up to three months.

These are thin, very crispy, curved cookies. Whenever I teach them in a class, my students complain that it takes too much effort to spread the batter on the cookie sheets. Once they taste the first batch, they are sold on them, decide that they are definitely worth the trouble, and want to bake as many as possible. Once the cookies are baked, they can be shaped into bowls, tacos, or cannolis, as well as the curved round cookies I describe below, and filled with any mousse or cream.

2 large egg whites

½ cup sugar

2½ tablespoons all-purpose flour

2 tablespoons parve margarine

1 teaspoon orange zest (grated outer peel) (from 1 orange)

⅔ cup sliced almonds (with or without skin)

Other options: pine nuts or pistachios, or lemon or lime zest

1 In a bowl, whisk together the egg whites, sugar, and flour. Heat the margarine in the microwave for about 30 seconds or until melted. Add to the bowl with the egg

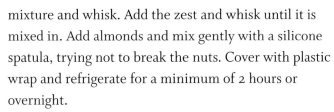

mixture and whisk. Add the zest and whisk until it is mixed in. Add almonds and mix gently with a silicone spatula, trying not to break the nuts. Cover with plastic wrap and refrigerate for a minimum of 2 hours or overnight.

2   When you're ready to bake the cookies, preheat the oven to 400°F. Use a Teflon baking sheet or grease and flour a regular cookie sheet. Drop teaspoons of batter onto the sheet, 3 to 4 inches apart. Do not spread batter for more than 10 cookies at a time on that cookie sheet; you need to bake in batches so you only have to shape 10 cookies at a time. If you bake too many at a time, some cookies will get too hard and get stuck to the cookie sheet after baking because you will not be able to remove them from the sheets quickly enough. With a fork dipped in water, flatten the batter, spreading gently and separating the nut slices, until the circles are about 3 inches round. This takes time and the more patient you are, the thinner and crisper the cookies become. Once one sheet is in the oven, repeat spreading the batter on a second cookie sheet and bake.

3   Bake for 7 to 8 minutes, or until the edges are brown and center is golden brown. Remove from oven and let cookies sit about 15 seconds. Use a flat-blade metal spatula or other metal spatula to scrape up each cookie and place onto a curved mold or around a rolling pin so that the cookies bend on their underside and the almond side is on top. Let cool.

To make these tuilles for Passover, simply substitute cake meal for the flour.

Rugelach Three Ways

MAKES 60 TO 70 PIECES

STORAGE

Store covered with plastic or in an airtight container at room temperature for five days or freeze for up to three months.

I am a big fan of rugelach made with cream cheese, so I used soy cream cheese to make these. There are so many different fillings for rugelach; my favorite is apricot jam or chocolate. It is fun to make different flavors so that when you place them on a platter, you see rows of different color swirls. In my baking classes, I give the students a buffet of choices so they can create their own combinations. Here I've given you three fillings to choose from. If you prefer to make one type, simply double one of the filling recipes (each filling amount is enough for half the dough). Or you can divide the dough into four and make four types—any flavor of jam, coconut, raisins, currants, or any kind of chopped nuts make great fillings.

---

1 cup (2 sticks) parve margarine

8 ounces parve cream cheese, softened

2 cups plus 2 tablespoons all-purpose flour, plus extra
   for sprinkling

1 tablespoon confectioners' sugar

Filling(s) of your choice (see pages 148–49)

---

1 To make the dough: Place the margarine, cream cheese, flour, and confectioners' sugar in the bowl of a mixer or food processor fitted with a metal blade or stand mixer with a paddle and mix just until the dough comes together. You can also mix the dough together by hand with a wooden spoon in a large bowl.

2 Divide the dough in half and wrap each ball in plastic and flatten. Freeze 1½ hours or overnight and then remove from freezer half an hour before using. The dough is ready to be rolled when you can press gently into it. If it gets too soft, put it back in the freezer to firm up.

3 Preheat the oven to 350°F.

4 To roll out the rugelach, place a large sheet of parchment on the counter. Sprinkle some flour on the parchment, place one of the dough discs on the parchment, sprinkle again with flour, and then top with a second sheet of parchment. Rolling on top of the parchment, roll out the dough to 13 x 10 inches. Peel back the top parchment once or twice while rolling and sprinkle some more flour on the dough. Remove the top parchment but reserve for re-use. This portion of dough is now ready to be filled with one of the three fillings, or another filling of your choice.

5 After filling the dough, fold the right and left sides (the short sides) of the dough ½ inch in toward the center to keep the filling inside. Using the parchment to help you, roll the long side from the top toward you, working slowly and rolling as tightly as you can.

6 Place the parchment you used on top of the dough when rolling it to line a cookie sheet. Place the loaf on the cookie sheet with the seam on the bottom and flatten slightly.

7 Bake for 35 to 40 minutes, or until the top begins to brown. Let cool and then slice into 1-inch pieces. These can be frozen. I prefer to freeze the baked loaves and then slice them when ready to serve.

Chocolate Filling

4 ounces parve chocolate chips
6 tablespoons parve whipping cream
¼ cup pecan halves (optional)

Melt the chocolate chips on the stovetop or in the microwave, following the "Melting chocolate" instructions (see Foolproof Tips and Techniques), mixing often until the chocolate is smooth. Remove from heat, add cream, and mix well. If using pecans, place them in a plastic bag and crush with a rolling pin. Spread the chocolate mixture evenly on the dough all the way to the edges and then sprinkle with pecan pieces.

Apricot and Cinnamon Filling

½ cup apricot jam or preserves

2 tablespoons sugar

1 teaspoon ground cinnamon

Spread the apricot jam or preserves evenly on the dough. Combine sugar and cinnamon in a small bowl and then sprinkle on top of the jam.

Orange and Pine Nut Filling

½ cup sweet orange marmalade

⅓ cup pine nuts

Spread the orange marmalade over the dough and sprinkle on the pine nuts.

Cinnamon Horns

MAKES 80 HORNS

STORAGE

Store covered in plastic at room temperature or freeze in an airtight container or freezer bag for up to three months.

My friend Howard Jacobson's mother is known for her butterhorns. Howard gave me the recipe to see if I could make them parve. They came out great on the first try and my husband Andy and I ate twenty of them right out of the oven. I froze some so Howard could taste them at his son's *sheva berachot* (post wedding) dinner at my house. He said they tasted really good, but nothing like his mother's.

¼ ounce (1 envelope) active dry yeast

2 tablespoons warm water

1 cup parve sour cream

3 large egg yolks

1 cup (2 sticks) parve margarine, at room temperature

3 cups all-purpose flour, divided

¼ teaspoon salt

1 cup sugar

2½ tablespoons ground cinnamon

1⅓ cups slivered almonds

1 In a large bowl, dissolve the yeast in the warm water. Add the sour cream and mix. Add the eggs and margarine and beat well. Add 2 cups of the flour and the salt and beat with an electric mixer on medium speed. Add the last cup of flour by hand and knead to form a smooth dough. Flour your hands and divide the dough into 10 balls. Place on a cookie sheet and cover with plastic. Chill in the refrigerator for 8 hours or overnight.

2 When you're ready to bake the cookies, preheat the oven to 450°F. Line 2 cookie sheets with parchment.

3 In a small bowl, mix together the sugar and cinnamon. Place the slivered almonds in the bowl of a food processor fitted with a metal blade and chop into very small pieces. You can also place the nuts in a plastic bag and bang them with a rolling pin. Place in a small bowl.

4 Remove the dough balls from the refrigerator. Sprinkle 2 tablespoons of the cinnamon-sugar on the counter or on a large cutting board and spread to about a 6-inch circle. Place a dough ball on top of the cinnamon-sugar and use a rolling pin to roll the dough into a circle about 6 inches in diameter. You may need to add a little flour to your rolling pin so the dough does not stick.

5 Sprinkle another tablespoon of the cinnamon-sugar on top of the dough and then 2 tablespoons of almond pieces. Use your hands to press the nuts into the dough. Cut the circle into 8 pie wedges, then roll up each triangle from the wide end to the point and curve into a crescent shape. Place on the prepared cookie sheets, about 1 inch apart. Repeat with the other dough circles. You may need to bake in batches if you cannot fit all the horns on 2 sheets.

6 Bake for 10 to 13 minutes, until the top is golden and the bottom is browned.

Brownie Pops

MAKES FORTY-EIGHT 1½-INCH SQUARE POPS
STORAGE

Store standing in cups, flat on waxed paper, or place into a large airtight container in the refrigerator for up to five days or freeze for up to three months.

I was once at a bar mitzvah where all the desserts were served on sticks, which gave me the idea for these Brownie Pops. You can sprinkle any type of nut, coconut, sprinkles or colored sugars on the wet chocolate for a more festive look. I like to make different shapes and use many different decorations. You can sprinkle the decorations on all or part of the shapes.

Parve margarine, for greasing pan

16 ounces parve semisweet or bittersweet chocolate, divided

⅓ cup canola or vegetable oil

1 cup sugar

¼ cup parve plain soy milk

2 large eggs

1 teaspoon pure vanilla extract

¼ teaspoon salt

½ teaspoon baking powder

¼ cup parve unsweetened cocoa

1 cup all-purpose flour

¼ to ½ cup finely ground nuts of your choice, shredded coconut, sprinkles or colored sugar, for sprinkling on brownies

48 lollipop sticks

1 Preheat the oven to 350°F. Line an 8-inch square baking pan with foil, allowing some to extend up and over the sides. Grease the bottom and sides with some margarine.

2 Break 6 ounces of the chocolate into small pieces and melt either on the stovetop or in the microwave,

following the "Melting chocolate" instructions (see Foolproof Tips and Techniques).

3 When the chocolate is melted, add the oil and sugar and whisk well. Add the soy milk, eggs, and vanilla and whisk again. Add the salt, baking powder, and cocoa and whisk again. Finally, add the flour and mix well with a silicone spatula. Pour into the pan and spread evenly. Bake for 30 minutes, or until the top looks dry. Let cool for a half hour and then place in the freezer for a minimum of 1 hour.

4 Melt the remaining 10 ounces of chocolate. Remove the brownie from the freezer and peel off the foil. Place on a cutting board. Trim off the sides to make them even. (Feel free to eat the trimmings.) Cut the brownie into 1½-inch strips and then into small squares. You can also cut 2-inch squares and then each square into two triangles. (I have also used cookie cutters to cut interesting shapes but to do this you will need to thin out the baked brownie by first cutting squares the size of your cookie cutters and then slicing each square into two layers—the cookie cutters can't go through a thick brownie. You can then use the cookie cutters to cut shapes out of the pieces).

5 Place a lollipop stick in the bottom of each shape and dip into the melted chocolate, covering all sides and the bottom of the shape around the stick. Hold the brownie over the bowl to drip off the excess chocolate. Sprinkle finely ground almonds, pistachios or other nuts, shredded coconut, sprinkles, or colored sugar on the wet chocolate. Place the sticks standing up into a cup to set. Serve on a platter on their sides or stand them up in a cup, bowl, or small vase filled with sugar.

◇ *Cinnamon, Vanilla, & Raspberry Macaroons*

MAKES 25 TO 30 MACAROONS

STORAGE

> *Store in an airtight container at room temperature for up to two days.*

These are the famous colorful cookies that you will see all over France, where they are known as macarons. I have designed this recipe to make three different macaroons: vanilla, cinnamon, and a pretty pink raspberry version. You can mix and match these macaroons with three fillings—vanilla or cinnamon buttercream, or raspberry jam—or with a decadent chocolate ganache filling. On occasion, I have filled the vanilla macaroons with Caramel Filling (page 216).

---

1 cup almond flour (see "Making almond flour," page xxvii)

1¾ cups confectioners' sugar

4 large egg whites, at room temperature (set out at least 1 hour)

¼ cup sugar

Seeds scraped from 1½ vanilla beans, for vanilla macaroons

1½ teaspoons ground cinnamon, for cinnamon macaroons

Few drops brown food coloring, for cinnamon macaroons

Few drops red food coloring, for pink macaroons

Filling(s) of your choice (see pages 155–56)

---

1   Line 2 cookie sheets with parchment.

2   To make the macaroon batter: Place the almond flour and confectioners' sugar in a food processor fitted with a metal blade. Process for 3 minutes. Sift into another bowl, discarding the large pieces.

3   In a large bowl, beat the egg whites with a stand or hand-held electric mixer on high speed until stiff. Turn the speed to low, add the sugar slowly and then turn up the speed to high for another 3 minutes. Add the almond and sugar mixture and mix lightly with a silicone spatula.

4   To make vanilla-flavored macaroons: Add the scraped vanilla bean seeds to the batter and mix well. To make the cinnamon-flavored macaroons: Add the cinnamon and the brown food coloring to the bowl and mix well. To make the pink

macaroons: Add the red food coloring to the bowl and mix well, adding more color if necessary to achieve a bright pink color.

5 Place the batter into a pastry bag fitted with a ¼-inch round tip. Squeeze out circles onto the parchment-lined sheets until they are about 1½ inches in diameter. Leave 2 inches of space between each circle. Let sit at room temperature for 1 hour.

6 Preheat the oven to 300°F. Bake for 20 to 22 minutes, switching the cookie sheets halfway through baking. Do not let the tops brown. Let cool and then use a metal flat-blade spatula to remove from the parchment. Place on a rack to cool.

7 To fill cookies, make pairs of them that look about the same size. Place about 1 to 1½ teaspoons of the filling of your choice (see below) in the center of the bottom of one cookie, place the other on it so the tops face outside, and then press gently so you can see the filling from the sides.

Chocolate Ganache Filling (for 25 to 30 cookies)

4 ounces parve semisweet or bittersweet chocolate, finely chopped

⅓ cup parve whipping cream

Place the chocolate pieces in a heatproof bowl. Heat the cream in a saucepan until boiling and then pour over the chocolate. Let sit for 30 seconds and then whisk until smooth. Place in the refrigerator for 15 minutes to harden up a bit.

Vanilla or Cinnamon Buttercream Fillings (for 25 to 30 cookies)

2 cups sugar

½ cup water

4 large eggs

26 tablespoons parve margarine, at room temperature (set out at least 1 hour)

1½ teaspoons pure vanilla extract

Seeds scraped from 1 vanilla bean, for vanilla buttercream filling

¾ teaspoon ground cinnamon, for cinnamon buttercream filling

1 Place the sugar and water in a small heavy saucepan and cook over high heat, stirring to dissolve the sugar. Meanwhile, place the eggs in the bowl of a stand mixer fitted with a whisk or in a large bowl if using a hand mixer. Insert a candy thermometer into the saucepan. Dip a pastry brush in cold water and brush the sides of the saucepan to dissolve any sugar crystals that form above the sugar mixture.

2 Watch the thermometer closely. When it reaches 230°F, turn the stand mixer on to medium speed to beat the eggs. When the thermometer goes up another 5 degrees to 235°F, turn off the heat. Turn the speed of the mixer down to low and then slowly pour the cooked sugar into the bowl, down the side of the bowl, not directly onto the wire whisk. If using a hand-held mixer, when the sugar reaches 230°F, beat the eggs for 1 minute, turn off the mixer, and then bring the sugar over to your bowl when it reaches 235°F and pour in as explained above. When all of the syrup has been poured in, turn the mixer up to high speed and beat for a full 10 minutes, or until the bowl is completely cool to the touch. The mixture will start out very yellow, but over time will turn a light yellow to beige color. Do not rush the mixing; it is very important to make sure the mixture is completely cool before adding the margarine.

3 Turn the speed to low and use a spoon to add the very soft margarine in clumps to the bowl. When all the margarine has been added, turn up the speed to medium-high and beat for 2 minutes more, until the mixture is light and creamy. Add the vanilla extract and turn the speed up to high for 20 seconds.

4 To make the vanilla buttercream filling: Add the vanilla bean seeds to the buttercream and mix vigorously. To make the cinnamon buttercream filling: Add the cinnamon to the buttercream and mix well. Place in the refrigerator for 30 minutes to harden up a bit.

Raspberry Filling (for 25 to 30 cookies)

1⅓ cups raspberry jam

To prepare the raspberry filling, place the jam into a bowl and whisk to make it easier to spread.

Chocolate, Coconut, & Macadamia Nut Candy

MAKES 25 TO 30 CANDIES

STORAGE

Store covered in plastic in the refrigerator for up to five days or freeze up to three months.

This dessert started out as a large tart, but my family and I decided that it was too rich to eat an entire slice. Next I made it into tartlets and we decided it was still too rich to eat that much. I finally settled on a candy—one or two of these is satisfying enough. I suggest adding Sabra liqueur to the chocolate. Sabra is an Israeli liqueur uniquely flavored with bittersweet chocolate and orange that can be found in liquor stores or kosher supermarkets. If you like the combination of chocolate and orange flavors, it's worth tracking down. This recipe calls for dry coconut flakes, not the moist, shredded coconut sold in bags.

CRUST

½ cup whole, dry roasted macadamia nuts

½ cup (1 stick) parve margarine, cut into tablespoons

⅓ cup sugar

1 cup all-purpose flour, plus extra for rolling out dough

2 tablespoons confectioners' sugar

FILLING

½ cup dry coconut flakes

14 ounces parve semisweet or bittersweet chocolate

½ cup parve whipping cream

2 tablespoons corn syrup

2 tablespoons parve margarine, softened

½ to 1 teaspoon Sabra (orange-flavored) liqueur (optional)

1 To make the crust: Place the macadamia nuts into the bowl of a food processor fitted with a metal blade and process until the nuts are completely ground and the mixture starts to look like peanut butter. You will need to scrape down the sides of the bowl. Add the margarine, sugar, flour, and confectioners' sugar and process until the dough comes together. Wrap in plastic, flatten, and place in the refrigerator 8 hours or overnight.

2   When you're ready to bake the candies, preheat the oven to 350°F. Place a sheet of parchment on the counter and sprinkle it with some flour. Place the chilled dough on the parchment, sprinkle again with flour, and then top with a second sheet of parchment. Roll on top of the parchment until you have a square a little larger than 8 inches on each side. Remove the top parchment. Place an 8-inch square baking pan on top of the dough and trim the dough around the pan, so the dough is the same size as the pan. Lift up the parchment and dough and place it parchment-side down in the baking pan.

3   Use a fork to prick the dough all over. Cover the dough with the parchment you placed on top of the dough when rolling it. Cover the top parchment with pie weights or beans. Bake for 25 minutes. Remove the parchment and weights and then bake another 6 to 8 minutes to dry out the crust. Remove from oven and let cool in the pan. Leave the oven on to toast the coconut.

4   To make the filling: Line a jelly roll pan with parchment and spread the coconut on the pan. Bake for 5 minutes, or until the coconut turns golden. Let cool for 15 minutes.

5   Break the chocolate into pieces and melt either on the stovetop or in the microwave, following the "Melting chocolate" instructions (see Foolproof Tips and Techniques).

6   In a small saucepan, bring the cream and corn syrup to a boil, stirring constantly. Add to the melted chocolate and mix with a whisk until the mixture is smooth. Add the margarine and whisk well. Add the toasted coconut (reserving 1 tablespoon to decorate the tops of the candies later) and liqueur, if using, and mix well.

7   Pour the chocolate coconut mixture over the baked crust, reserving a few tablespoons to decorate the top of the candies later. Spread evenly. Place in the refrigerator to set for at least 1 hour.

8   To serve, lift the parchment and candy out of the pan. Cut into about 1½-inch squares. Place the reserved chocolate mixture in a pastry bag with a star tip and pipe a star on top of each square. Sprinkle a little of the toasted coconut on top of the chocolate cream.

◇ Chocolate Truffles

MAKES ABOUT 35 TRUFFLES

STORAGE

Store in an airtight container in the refrigerator for five days or freeze up to three months.

People are always excited about homemade truffles and they really are easy to make. You can experiment with different brands of parve chocolates to see which you prefer. I like using the Swiss brand.

---

10 ounces parve semisweet or bittersweet chocolate

½ cup parve whipping cream

2 tablespoons parve unsweetened cocoa

---

1. Line a jelly roll pan with parchment or waxed paper. Set aside.
2. Break or chop the chocolate into small pieces and melt either on the stovetop or in the microwave, following the "Melting chocolate" instructions (see Foolproof Tips and Techniques).
3. Heat the cream until very hot, not boiling. Whisk into the melted chocolate until combined.
4. Spread the chocolate onto prepared pan. Place in the freezer for 25 minutes.
5. Slide the parchment or waxed paper off the pan. Line the pan with a new sheet of parchment or waxed paper. Scoop up teaspoons of the chocolate and roll into balls. It is helpful to wear plastic gloves for this. Place the balls onto the newly lined pan and freeze for 10 minutes.
6. Place the cocoa in a shallow bowl and roll the truffles in the cocoa. Place the truffles into a colander or sieve to shake off the extra cocoa. Place into the refrigerator.

◇ CHOCOLATE AMARETTO TRUFFLES

1. Preheat the oven to 325°F. Line a large jelly roll pan with parchment. Spread ⅔ cup of slivered almonds on the pan and toast for 20 minutes, stirring the nuts after 10 minutes. When the almonds are toasted, slide the parchment off the pan and let cool for 5 minutes.
2. Place the toasted almonds in the bowl of a food processor fitted with a metal blade. Process until the nuts are ground.

3 Complete Steps 2 and 3 for Chocolate Truffles (page 159). After whisking in the cream, add the ground toasted almonds and 2 teaspoons of almond-flavored liqueur and mix well. Complete Steps 4 and 5 for Chocolate Truffles.

4 You may dust the truffles in cocoa, following Step 6 for Chocolate Truffles, or you may roll them in additional ground toasted almonds.

◇ Chocolate Pistachio Candies

MAKES ABOUT 80 CANDIES

STORAGE

Store loaf in the freezer for up to three months and slice as needed.

These taste like truffles, just without the rolling. The recipe makes a large loaf, so I keep it in the freezer and slice pieces as needed.

---

21 ounces parve semisweet or bittersweet chocolate

1 teaspoon pure vanilla extract

1½ cups parve whipping cream

2 tablespoons sugar

1 cup whole, shelled, raw, unsalted pistachio nuts (see tip below)
(about ⅔ pound of nuts in their shells)

If you buy the nuts in their shells, pry the nuts out of their shells and then rub them between your hands to remove as much of the outer papery skins as you can.

1 Place a piece of plastic wrap, about 13 inches long, on the counter and smooth out the creases. Tear off another piece of plastic the same size and place on top of the first to form a T-shape. Try hard to make sure each piece of plastic is smooth. Place the "T" of plastic inside a loaf pan and press the plastic into all the sides and corners. Wrap the hanging plastic around the outside of your pan.

2 Break the chocolate into pieces and melt either on the stovetop or in the microwave, following the "Melting chocolate" instructions (see Foolproof Tips and Techniques).

3 When the chocolate is melted, whisk in the vanilla.

4 In a small saucepan, or in a bowl in the microwave, heat the cream and sugar until it boils. Stir the cream. Don't worry if it is lumpy.

5 Add the cream to the melted chocolate in 4 parts, whisking vigorously after each addition until the mixture is completely smooth. Stir in the pistachio nuts. Let cool for 5 minutes. Pour the mixture into the prepared loaf pan and smooth the top with a silicone spatula. Cover the top with a new piece of plastic and place in the freezer for 2 hours or overnight.

6 To serve, unwrap the loaf and use a sharp knife to cut it into 1-inch slices and then cut each slice into 1-inch squares.

◇ Dried Fruit Truffles

MAKES ABOUT 32 TRUFFLES

STORAGE

Store in an airtight container at room temperature for up to five days.

This recipe was supposed to be a filling for hamentaschen that didn't come out as I expected; when baked, they came out too hard. I had a lot of leftover filling and so I rolled it into balls. After I ate the whole plate, I realized that I had created a candy with no added sugar. Serve them in little round paper cups on a platter.

⅓ cup whole, raw almonds

10 dried apricots

10 pitted dates

1 teaspoon orange blossom water (optional)

1 Place the almonds, apricots, and dates in the bowl of a food processor fitted with a metal blade. Process until the mixture comes together. Add the orange blossom water, if using, and pulse a few times.

2 Scoop up 1 teaspoon of the mixture at a time and roll into balls. Let sit on a plate for at least 2 hours to dry and then store in an airtight container.

Cakes, Pastries, & Dessert Breads

Black & White Layer Cake

MAKES ONE 8- OR 9-INCH SIX-LAYER CAKE, 12 TO 16 SERVINGS
STORAGE

> *Store in the refrigerator until serving. If you want to freeze the cake after it has been assembled, place it on a cardboard circle or cookie sheet and freeze for 2 hours. Remove from freezer, wrap the entire cake in plastic, and return to the freezer and freeze for up to three months. Thaw 1 hour before serving.*

I served this cake on my son Sam's birthday and ended up cutting 22 thin slices out of it. You can make either or both cakes in advance and freeze, wrapped in plastic, or assemble the whole cake and then freeze it.

CHOCOLATE CAKE

Spray oil containing flour or spray oil plus 2 tablespoons flour
    for greasing and flouring pans
1½ cups all-purpose flour
½ cup parve unsweetened cocoa
½ teaspoon baking soda
½ teaspoon baking powder
½ teaspoon salt
1¼ cups sugar
2 large eggs
⅓ cup canola or vegetable oil
½ teaspoon pure vanilla extract
½ cup water
½ cup parve plain soy milk

VANILLA CAKE

1 large egg plus 3 whites

1 cup canola or vegetable oil

½ cup parve plain soy milk

1 cup sugar

1¼ cups all-purpose flour

1 teaspoon baking powder

1 teaspoon pure vanilla extract

⅛ teaspoon cream of tartar

SUGAR SYRUP

½ cup water

⅔ cup sugar

CHOCOLATE GANACHE

20 ounces parve semisweet or bittersweet chocolate, chopped or
broken into 1-inch pieces

2 teaspoons pure vanilla extract

1¼ cups parve plain soy milk

4 tablespoons parve margarine

1 Preheat the oven to 350°F. Grease and flour two 8- or 9-inch round pans.

2 To make the chocolate cake: In a large bowl, mix together the flour, cocoa, baking soda, baking powder, salt, and sugar. Add the eggs, oil, vanilla, water, and soy milk. Beat by hand with a whisk or with an electric mixer on medium speed until combined, about 1 minute, scraping down the sides of the bowl as necessary. Place the batter in one of the prepared pans. Bake for 45 minutes, or until a skewer inserted in the cake comes out clean. Let cool for 10 minutes, and then remove from the pan to a rack to cool completely.

3 To make the vanilla cake: Separate the whole egg and place the yolk in a medium bowl and the 4 whites in another medium bowl. Into the bowl with the egg yolk, add the oil, soy milk, sugar, flour, baking powder, and vanilla. Beat by hand with a whisk or with a hand-held or stand electric mixer on medium-high speed for 1 minute.

4 Add the cream of tartar to the bowl with the egg whites and beat with an electric mixer on high speed, or with a whisk, until stiff. Fold half the whites into the vanilla cake batter and when almost mixed in, fold in the rest of the whites and mix

gently until combined. Place in the other prepared pan and bake for 35 minutes, or until a skewer inserted into the cake comes out clean. You may bake both cakes at the same time. Let cool for 10 minutes, and then remove from the pan to a rack to cool completely.

5   While the cakes are baking, prepare the sugar syrup. Place water and sugar in a small heavy saucepan over medium heat. Stir to dissolve the sugar and bring to a rolling boil. Remove from heat. Let sit at room temperature until you are ready to use. Place in a bowl and cover if you are not using within a few hours.

6   To make the ganache: Melt the chocolate on the stovetop or in the microwave, following the "Melting chocolate" instructions (see Foolproof Tips and Techniques).

7   When the chocolate is melted, whisk in the vanilla. Heat the soy milk in the microwave until hot, not boiling, about 1½ minutes. Add to the chocolate mixture a little at a time and whisk well after each addition. Finally add the margarine and mix until very smooth. Cover with plastic and place in the refrigerator for 15 minutes.

8   Take each cake and trim the top and sides to make the cake even (be sure to eat the trimmings; this is where you get rewarded for your efforts before the layer cake is done). Following the instructions in "Slicing cake layers" (see Foolproof Tips and Techniques), slice each cake into three pieces so that you will have six layers. Set aside the bottom of the vanilla cake to use as the top layer of the cake.

9   Place one slice of the chocolate cake on a serving plate and put some pieces of waxed paper under the cake to catch the drippings. Take a pastry brush, dip into the sugar syrup, and brush the top of the cake to moisten it. Use a metal or silicone spatula to spread a thin layer (about ⅓ cup) of the ganache evenly on that layer of cake; just use enough ganache to cover the layer. Place a slice of vanilla cake on top, moisten with the syrup, and spread another ⅓ cup of ganache. Repeat alternating flavors of cake until you reach the top, where you will place the vanilla bottom, bottom-side up. As you assemble the cake, try to make it even by looking at the cake from the side and gently pressing down on any sides that are too tall.

10 Use your silicone or metal flat-blade spatula to spread the ganache on the top and sides of the cake so that the layers are no longer visible. Try to reserve 1 to 2 tablespoons of ganache for decorating the cake. Heat a long, metal flat-blade spatula in very hot or boiling water, wipe lightly with a paper towel, and then immediately slide around the sides and top of the cake to make the ganache completely smooth; you may need to reheat the blade and do this a few times.

11 Place any leftover ganache in a pastry bag and use to make any flowers, dots, or swirls that you like on top of the cake. Or, you can scrape additional chocolate with a vegetable peeler on top of the cake.

Toasted Almond Layer Cake

MAKES ONE 9-INCH TRIPLE-LAYER CAKE, 12 TO 16 SERVINGS

STORAGE

Store in the refrigerator for up to four days. If you want to freeze the cake after it has been assembled, place it on a cardboard circle or cookie sheet and freeze for 2 hours. Remove from freezer, wrap the entire cake in plastic, and return to the freezer and freeze for up to three months. Thaw 1 hour before serving.

I invented this cake when I had a catering business in Switzerland and people ordered it to use as a birthday cake. Although the recipe has several parts, you do not have to make them at one time. I usually make the sponge layer and syrup a day or two ahead and then the buttercream just before I assemble the cake. Don't be scared of the multiple steps; each one is not difficult and you will be rewarded with a unique cake.

ALMOND SPONGE CAKE

Spray oil containing flour or spray oil plus 2 tablespoons flour
    for greasing and flouring pan
4 egg whites plus 4 large eggs
2 tablespoons sugar
1 cup confectioners' sugar
1 cup almond flour (see "Making almond flour," page xxvii)
½ cup all-purpose flour
1 tablespoon canola or vegetable oil
¾ cup sliced almonds

AMARETTO SYRUP

½ cup sugar
½ cup water
1 tablespoon amaretto (almond-flavored liqueur)

ALMOND BUTTERCREAM ICING

1½ cups sugar

¼ cup water

3 large eggs

2½ sticks (1¼ cups) parve margarine, at room
   temperature (set out for at least 1 hour)

4 teaspoons almond extract

1 Preheat the oven to 350°F. Take a 9-inch round baking
   pan, trace the bottom onto a piece of parchment, and
   cut out the circle. Grease the round pan, place the
   parchment circle in the pan, and then grease the top of
   the parchment.

2 To make the almond sponge cake: In a medium bowl,
   beat the 4 egg whites with an electric mixer on high
   speed until stiff. Turn the speed down to low, add the
   2 tablespoons of sugar and then beat on medium speed
   another 30 seconds. Transfer the beaten whites into a
   bowl. Into the bowl that you have just used to beat the
   whites, place the confectioners' sugar, almond flour,

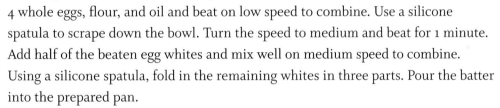

   4 whole eggs, flour, and oil and beat on low speed to combine. Use a silicone
   spatula to scrape down the bowl. Turn the speed to medium and beat for 1 minute.
   Add half of the beaten egg whites and mix well on medium speed to combine.
   Using a silicone spatula, fold in the remaining whites in three parts. Pour the batter
   into the prepared pan.

3 Bake for 30 minutes, or until a skewer inserted in the center comes out clean.
   Let cool in the pan for 10 minutes and then turn the cake out onto a rack to cool
   completely. Peel off the parchment circle. As the cake is cooling, move the cake
   around the rack so that it does not stick. If you are not assembling the cake right
   away, wrap it in plastic wrap once it has cooled.

4 Raise the oven temperature to 375°F. Place the sliced almonds on a jelly roll pan.
   Shake a little so the nuts are in one layer. Bake for 10 minutes, stirring once, to
   toast the almonds. Set aside.

5 To make the amaretto syrup: In a small heavy saucepan, bring the sugar and
   water to a boil over high heat, stirring occasionally, to dissolve the sugar. Once

the mixture boils, turn off the heat, add the almond liqueur, and stir. This can be made up to 2 days in advance and stored, covered in a bowl or container at room temperature.

6 To make the almond buttercream icing: Place the sugar and water in a small heavy saucepan over high heat, stirring to dissolve the sugar. Meanwhile, place the eggs in the bowl of a stand mixer fitted with a wire whisk. If using a hand-held mixer, place the eggs into a medium bowl. Insert a candy thermometer into the saucepan. Dip a pastry brush in cold water and brush the sides of the saucepan to dissolve any sugar crystals that form above the sugar mixture. Watch the thermometer closely. When it reaches 230°F, turn the stand mixer on to medium speed to beat the eggs. When the thermometer goes up another 5 degrees to 235°F, turn off the heat and bring the saucepan over to the mixer. If using a hand-held mixer, when the sugar reaches 230°F, beat the eggs for 1 minute, turn off the mixer, and then bring the sugar over to your bowl when it reaches 235°F and pour in as explained below.

7 Turn the speed of the mixer down to low and then slowly pour the cooked sugar into the bowl, down the side of the bowl, not directly onto the wire whisk. When all of the syrup has been poured in, turn the mixer up to high speed and beat for a full 10 minutes, or until the bowl is completely cool to the touch. The mixture will start out very yellow, but over time will turn a light yellow to beige color. Do not rush the mixing; it is very important to make sure the mixture is completely cool before adding the margarine to the cream.

8 Turn the speed to low and use a dull knife or spoon to add the very soft margarine in clumps to the bowl. When all the margarine has been added, turn up the mixer speed to medium-high and beat for 2 minutes more, or until the mixture is light and creamy. Add the almond extract and beat on high speed for 20 seconds. Place the cream in the refrigerator until you're ready to use it. This can be made up to 3 days in advance.

9 To assemble the cake, use a sharp knife to trim the top and sides of the cake so that they are even. Following the instructions in "Slicing cake layers" (see Foolproof Tips and Techniques), slice the cake into three pieces so that you will have three layers.

10 Place the top of the cake top-side down on a cardboard circle on a small cookie sheet or serving plate. Using a pastry brush, soak the cake all over with some of the amaretto syrup. Use a spatula to spread about one-quarter of the almond cream evenly on top of the cake. Sprinkle some of the toasted almonds on top. Place the

middle piece of cake on top of the cream. Once again, soak with syrup, spread with one-quarter of the cream, and then sprinkle on some almonds (reserve some almonds to place on the sides of the cake).

11 Take the last piece of cake and brush the inner side (or cut side), with syrup, then place the syrup-soaked side down on top of the last layer of cream and nuts (so that the bottom of the baked cake becomes the top of the assembled cake). Spread part of the remaining cream over the top and sides of the cake, leaving some cream for another layer and to decorate the top.

12 Heat a metal spatula by running it under boiling water and dry slightly. Slide the spatula around the sides and top of the cake to smooth them. Place in the freezer for 10 minutes and place the extra cream in the refrigerator. Remove from the freezer and spread some more cream on the top and the sides and smooth again with a heated metal spatula. Save a little cream to decorate (store in the refrigerator). Place the cake back in the freezer for 2 hours. Move the cake to the refrigerator about 2 hours prior to serving.

13 When you're ready to serve, press the remaining toasted nuts on the sides of the cake. Use a pastry bag with a star tip to decorate the top of the cake however you like with the remaining cream.

Dark Chocolate Mousse Layer Cake

MAKES ONE 12-INCH CAKE, 18 SERVINGS

STORAGE

Store in the refrigerator until serving. If you want to freeze the cake after it has been assembled, place it on a cookie sheet and freeze for 2 hours. Remove from freezer, wrap the entire cake in plastic, and return to the freezer and freeze for up to three months. Thaw a half hour in the fridge before serving.

My mother was visiting for Rosh Hashanah and the first night was her birthday. My mother has always loved chocolate; she used to hide Entenmann's Chocolate Fudge Cake in her bedroom closet so my brothers and I would not eat it. (Of course, we always knew her hiding place.) I invented this for her. After everyone was served, there was one piece left. She asked me to hide it for her for the next day; no one was getting seconds but her.

Spray oil containing flour or spray oil plus 2 tablespoons flour
for greasing and flouring pan

2 cups all-purpose flour

¾ teaspoon baking soda

¾ teaspoon baking powder

1½ cups sugar

¾ teaspoon salt

½ cup parve unsweetened cocoa

¾ teaspoon pure vanilla extract

½ cup canola or vegetable oil

⅔ cup parve plain soy milk

2 teaspoons instant coffee granules dissolved into ⅔ cup boiling water
or ⅔ cup coffee/espresso

2 large eggs plus 1 egg white

MOUSSE

10½ ounces parve semisweet or bittersweet chocolate, chopped or
broken into 1-inch pieces

1½ cups parve whipping cream, divided

2 tablespoons sugar, divided

2 large eggs, separated

1 ounce parve semisweet or bittersweet chocolate, for decorating
(optional)

1 Preheat the oven to 350°F. Grease and flour a 12-inch loaf pan.

2 In a large bowl, mix together the flour, baking soda, baking powder, sugar, salt, and cocoa. Add the vanilla, oil, soy milk, coffee dissolved in water, eggs and egg white, and mix well. Pour into the prepared loaf pan. Bake for 50 to 55 minutes, until a skewer inserted into the cake comes out clean. Let cool for 10 minutes and then remove from the pan and let cool on a wire rack.

3 To make the mousse: Melt the chocolate either on the stovetop or in the microwave, following the "Melting chocolate" instructions (see Foolproof Tips and Techniques). Place into a large bowl.

4   Place ¼ cup of the whipping cream and 1 tablespoon of the sugar in a small saucepan over low heat. Once the cream is hot and the sugar has dissolved, add to the melted chocolate and whisk well. Add the egg yolks and whisk vigorously until creamy.

5   Beat the egg whites with an electric mixer on high speed until stiff. Turn the speed to low, add the remaining 1 tablespoon of sugar and turn the speed up to high and beat another 30 seconds. Fold the stiff egg whites into the chocolate mixture. Using the same bowl and whisk attachment, whip the remaining 1¼ cups of whipping cream until stiff. Fold into the chocolate and egg white mixture and mix well. Place the mousse in the refrigerator 20 minutes.

6   When the cake is completely cool, trim the top so that it is completely flat. You can also trim the sides of the cake so that they are completely straight. Slice the loaf across into 3 long layers. Line the loaf pan that you used to bake the cake with waxed paper, making sure some hangs over the sides. Place one layer of cake into the pan on top of the wax paper. Cover with one-fourth of the mousse. Place the second cake layer on top of the mousse and cover with another fourth of the mousse. Add the top layer of cake and then cover the top with mousse. You should have one-fourth of the mousse left; cover and place in the refrigerator. Place the loaf pan with the mousse cake in the freezer for 1 hour.

7   Remove cake from the freezer and use the wax paper to carefully lift the cake out of the loaf pan, peel off the wax paper and place the cake on a long serving dish. Use the remaining mousse to cover the top and sides of the cake. Heat a long metal flat-blade spatula with boiling water, dry slightly with a towel, and use to smooth the top and sides of the cake. Place the serving plate with the cake back in the freezer. Transfer to the refrigerator ½ hour before serving.

8   If you like, you may decorate the cake with chocolate ribbons by taking 1 ounce of semisweet or bittersweet chocolate and using a vegetable peeler or grater to shave some chocolate onto the top and sides of the cake.

Sorbet Cake

MAKES ONE 9-INCH TRIPLE-LAYER CAKE, 12 TO 16 SERVINGS

STORAGE

*Store cake in the freezer for up to three months and the sauces
in the refrigerator for up to 6 days.*

This is an easy, beautiful, and refreshing summer dessert. I like to serve it with both sauces but you can make just one or even serve it by itself. You can use other flavors of sorbet.

Spray oil containing flour or spray oil plus 2 tablespoons flour
for greasing and flouring pan

1 large egg plus 3 whites

1 cup canola or vegetable oil

½ cup parve plain soy milk

1 cup sugar

1¼ cups all-purpose flour

1 teaspoon baking powder

1 teaspoon pure vanilla extract

⅛ teaspoon cream of tartar

1 cup mango sorbet (from 1 pint container)

1 cup raspberry sorbet (from 1 pint container)

---

1 recipe Mango Sauce (page 293)

1 recipe Strawberry Sauce (page 294)

---

1 Preheat the oven to 350°F. Grease and flour a 9-inch round baking pan.

2 Separate the whole egg and place the yolk in one medium bowl and the 4 whites into another. Into the bowl with the egg yolk, add the oil, soy milk, sugar, flour, baking powder, and vanilla. Beat with a hand-held or stand electric mixer on medium-high speed or whisk by hand for 1 minute.

3 With an electric mixer on high speed, beat the egg whites with the cream of tartar until stiff peaks form. Use a silicone spatula to fold half the whites into the batter and, when almost mixed in, add the rest of the whites and mix until combined and you don't see any more egg-white clumps. Place in the prepared baking pan and bake for 35 minutes, or until a skewer inserted into the cake comes out clean. Let cool for 10 minutes, and then turn the cake out of the pan onto a rack and let cool completely.

4 When the cake is cool, take the sorbet pints out of the freezer and let sit for 15 minutes to soften. You can also place the sorbet containers into the microwave for 15 seconds or until it feels soft when you squeeze the container. Don't let it melt.

5 Following the instructions in "Slicing cake layers" (see Foolproof Tips and Techniques), slice the cake into three pieces so that you will have three layers.

6 Place the bottom slice on a serving plate. Place the 1 cup of mango sorbet in the center of the cake. Use a spatula to spread it out to the sides as evenly as you can, moving the spatula back and forth. Place the middle slice of cake on top of the mango sorbet. Place the 1 cup of raspberry sorbet in the center of that cake and spread an even layer. Place the third, top piece of cake, on top.

7 Place in the freezer for 8 hours or overnight and keep in the freezer until you serve the cake. It can survive outside the freezer no longer than 30 minutes and then it will start melting.

8 Make the Mango Sauce and Strawberry Sauce.

9 To serve the cake, place the Mango Sauce on one half of a dessert plate and the Strawberry Sauce on the other half. Place a cake slice in the middle of the plate.

Coconut Cake with Lime Filling

MAKES ONE 9-INCH 3-LAYER CAKE, 16 TO 20 SERVINGS

STORAGE

Store in the refrigerator until serving. If you want to freeze the cake after it has been assembled, place it on a cardboard circle or cookie sheet and freeze for 2 hours. Remove from freezer, wrap the entire cake in plastic, and return to the freezer and freeze for up to three months. Thaw 1 hour before serving.

I usually do not like coconut desserts, but I have to admit I really like this one. This is a *giant* cake that fed everyone who walked into my house over an entire weekend. You can decorate it many ways. Below I describe using shredded coconut and lime zest. Last time I made this cake, instead of decorating the cake with coconut and lime zest, I took out my blowtorch—a huge thrill for my three sons—and browned the top. The icing tastes like marshmallow so the torched part tastes like toasted marshmallows.

CAKE

Spray oil containing flour or spray oil plus 2 tablespoons flour
for greasing and flouring pans
2 whole eggs plus 4 whites
2 cups canola or vegetable oil
1 cup coconut milk

2 cups sugar

2½ cups all-purpose flour

2 teaspoons baking powder

2 teaspoons pure vanilla extract

¾ cup shredded coconut

¼ teaspoon cream of tartar

LIME CREAM FILLING

3 eggs plus 2 egg yolks

1 cup sugar

5 tablespoons fresh lime juice (from 3 limes)

Zest (grated outer peel) of 1½ limes

5 tablespoons parve margarine

1 drop green food coloring (optional)

⅓ cup parve whipping cream

SEVEN-MINUTE FROSTING

1½ cups sugar

⅓ cup warm water

3 large egg whites, at room temperature

1 tablespoon light corn syrup

Dash of salt

1 teaspoon pure vanilla extract

OPTIONAL DECORATIONS

½ cup shredded coconut

Zest (grated outer peel) from ½ lime

1 Preheat the oven to 350°F. Grease and flour two 9-inch round baking pans.

2 To make the cake: Separate the eggs and place the yolks in one large bowl and all the 6 whites into another. Into the bowl with the egg yolks, add the oil, coconut milk, sugar, flour, baking powder, vanilla, and shredded coconut. Beat with a whisk or an electric mixer on medium-high speed for 1 minute.

3 Add the cream of tartar to the bowl with the egg whites and beat with an electric mixer on high speed until stiff peaks form. Fold the whites in three parts into the batter and, when almost mixed in, fold in the rest of the whites and mix until combined. Evenly pour the batter into the 2 prepared baking pans and bake for

50 minutes, or until a skewer inserted into the cakes comes out clean. Let cool for 10 minutes, remove from the pans to a rack and let cool completely.

4 To make the lime cream: In the top of a double boiler, or a heatproof bowl that can be fitted over a saucepan without falling in, combine the eggs, yolks, and sugar. Add the lime juice and zest and stir. Place a few inches of water in the bottom of the double boiler or saucepan, place the top portion of the double boiler or heatproof bowl on top and set over simmering water. Cook the lime cream, uncovered, stirring occasionally, until a thick mixture is formed. This takes approximately 25 minutes. Be patient and do not stir too much. If the water boils too fast, turn down the heat. Remove the bowl from the heat and whisk in the 5 tablespoons of margarine in small pieces. Add 1 drop of green food coloring, if using, and whisk in to color evenly. Cool for 5 minutes and then cover with plastic and refrigerate overnight. To use that day, place the bowl of lime cream over a larger bowl filled with ice and a little water (make sure it is below the level of the cream bowl) for 15 to 20 minutes until the cream is chilled. In a medium bowl, with an electric mixer on high speed, beat the whipping cream until stiff and fold into the lime cream. Set aside.

5 To assemble the cake, take each cake and, if necessary, trim the top to make it flat. For a more professional look, place the 2 cakes on top of each other and use a knife to trim the sides all around to make them even. Following the instructions in "Slicing cake layers" (see Foolproof Tips and Techniques), slice each cake in half to create four layers. Set aside one of the bottom cake slices to use as the top of the cake.

6 Place one layer on a serving plate. Spread with one-third of the lime cream. Add a second layer. Add another third of the cream and spread evenly. Repeat for the third layer, using the rest of the cream, and then place the reserved cake bottom, bottom-side up, on top of the lime cream. Place in the refrigerator for 20 minutes.

7 Meanwhile, prepare the seven-minute frosting. Pour a few inches of water into the bottom of a double boiler or a medium saucepan and bring to a boil, then reduce the heat to medium. Off heat, place the sugar and ⅓ cup warm water in the top of the double boiler or in a metal or other heatproof bowl that can sit on top of the saucepan without falling in. Whisk to dissolve the sugar. Add the egg whites, corn syrup, and salt and beat for 1 minute with an electric mixer on medium-high speed. Place over the gently boiling water and beat with an electric mixer on high speed for a full 7 minutes. If the water starts to bubble too much, turn the heat down.

Remove from heat, add vanilla, and beat until the frosting is thick and has soft peaks, another 30 seconds.

8   Spread the frosting all around the sides of the cake and then cover the top of the cake. Heat a long flat metal spatula and use to smooth the top and sides, if desired. Sprinkle the top with the shredded coconut and lime zest, if desired.

Classic Cheesecake

MAKES ONE 9- OR 10-INCH CAKE, 12 TO 16 SERVINGS

STORAGE

Store covered in plastic in the refrigerator for up to five days or freeze up to three months.

After perfecting my dairy cheesecake to demonstrate at a Chabad cooking event in northern Virginia to celebrate the Jewish holiday of Shavuot (on which Jews traditionally eat only dairy), I used that recipe as the model for this one. It can be served with Shiny Chocolate Sauce (page 295) or Strawberry Sauce (page 294).

8 tablespoons parve margarine, plus 1 tablespoon to grease pan

2 cups parve graham cracker crumbs or thirty-two 2 x 2-inch graham crackers crushed in a food processor

1¼ cups plus 4 tablespoons sugar, divided

2 pounds parve cream cheese, at room temperature (set out at least 1 hour)

5 large eggs

1 teaspoon lemon zest (grated outer peel) (from 1 lemon)

2 teaspoons pure vanilla extract

1   Preheat the oven to 325°F.

2   Take a 9- or 10-inch springform pan, trace the bottom onto a piece of parchment, and cut out. Cover the top of the pan bottom with aluminum foil, and then wrap the excess foil under the bottom. Attach the pan sides to the bottom, lock in place, and then unwrap the foil and wrap up around the exterior sides of the pan. Rub 1 tablespoon of margarine around the bottom and sides of the pan. Place the parchment circle in the bottom of the pan and grease with some margarine.

3 Place the 8 tablespoons of the margarine in a large microwave-safe bowl and melt. Add the graham cracker crumbs and 4 tablespoons of the sugar and mix to combine. Spoon into the prepared pan. Use your fingers to press in the crumb mixture so that it covers the bottom and about ¼-inch up the sides of the pan.

4 In the bowl of a stand mixer, or in a large bowl if using a hand-held mixer, beat the cream cheese until smooth. Add the eggs, one at a time, and scrape down the bowl after each egg is added to make sure all the cream cheese and eggs are combined and the mixture looks creamy. There should be no lumps in the batter. Add the remaining 1¼ cups of sugar, lemon zest, and vanilla and beat on medium speed for 30 seconds, or until everything is combined.

5 Pour the batter on top of the graham cracker crust in the pan. Place the pan in a large roasting pan with sides higher than 2 inches. Place the roasting pan and cake on the middle rack of the oven. Bring over a kettle and pour boiling water into the roasting pan, around the cheesecake pan, until the water reaches a third to halfway up the sides of the cheesecake pan.

6 Bake for 1 hour and 10 minutes. Turn off the oven and prop the oven door open with a wooden spoon. Leave the cake in the oven for another hour. Remove the cake pan from the roasting pan and set on a rack until the cake is completely cooled. Place in the refrigerator 8 hours or overnight. Remove the sides of the pan. Use a wide knife or long metal spatula to separate the parchment circle from the foil and slide the cheesecake onto a serving platter.

◇ Chocolate Mousse Truffle Cake

MAKES ONE 9- OR 10-INCH CAKE, 12 TO 16 SERVINGS
STORAGE

Store covered in plastic in the refrigerator for up to three days or freeze up to three months.

This cake consists of a dense flourless chocolate cake bottom and an airy chocolate mousse top.

¾ cup (1½ sticks) parve margarine

16 ounces parve semisweet chocolate, roughly chopped

6 large eggs, separated

1 teaspoon parve unsweetened cocoa

½ cup sugar

⅓ cup parve whipping cream

---

1   Preheat the oven to 350°F. Take a 9- to 10-inch springform pan, trace the bottom onto a piece of parchment, and cut out. Cover the top of the pan bottom with aluminum foil, and then wrap the excess foil under the bottom. Attach the pan sides to the bottom, lock in place, and then unwrap the foil and wrap it up and around the exterior sides of the pan. Rub 1 tablespoon of the margarine around the bottom and sides of the pan. Place the parchment circle in the bottom of the pan and grease with some of the margarine. Grease the sides of the pan as well.

2   Place the chocolate and remaining margarine in a heatproof bowl over simmering water (or use a double boiler) and stir often until melted. Remove from heat, add the egg yolks and cocoa, and beat with an electric mixer for 1 minute until thick.

3   In a separate bowl, beat the egg whites with a hand-held or stand electric mixer on high speed until stiff. Turn the speed down to low, add the sugar a little at a time and, once all the sugar is added, turn the speed up to high for 1 minute. Fold the stiff egg whites into the chocolate mixture. Pour two-thirds of this batter into the prepared pan (reserve the other one-third for the mousse). Place the pan in a large roasting pan with sides higher than 2 inches. Place the roasting pan and cake on the middle rack of the oven. Pour boiling water into the roasting pan, around the cake pan, to reach halfway up the sides of the cake pan.

4   Bake for 40 minutes. Remove the cake pan from the water bath (leaving the roasting pan with water in the oven to cool safely) and let the cake cool in the pan.

5   While the cake is baking, prepare the mousse. In a bowl, whip the cream with an electric mixer on high speed until stiff and fold into the reserved batter. Mix well. Place in the refrigerator until the cake cools.

6   When the cake has cooled, spoon the mousse on top of the cake layer and try to smooth the top as much as possible with a silicone spatula. Place in the refrigerator 8 hours or overnight.

7   To remove the sides of the cake pan, heat a sharp knife and run it all around the cake. Open the spring and remove the sides of the pan. Use a spatula to separate the parchment circle from the foil and slide the parchment and cake onto a serving plate. Store the cake in the refrigerator and then place in the freezer 1 hour before serving to help you cut perfect slices.

Jelly Doughnuts

MAKES ABOUT TWENTY-FIVE 3-INCH DOUGHNUTS

STORAGE

Store covered at room temperature for up to one day.

Homemade doughnuts are really special. I did the final testing of these while we were having work done on the house. Imagine the looks on the faces of the contractors when I brought them a plate of these to taste.

¼ ounce (1 envelope) active dry yeast

¼ cup warm water

¾ cup plus 1 teaspoon sugar, divided

¾ cup parve plain soy milk

4 tablespoons parve margarine

2 large eggs

1 teaspoon salt

1 teaspoon pure vanilla extract

3½ to 4 cups all-purpose flour, plus extra for dusting pans and
    work surface

4 to 5 cups canola or vegetable oil, for deep-frying

½ to 1 cup raspberry or strawberry jam

1 In a large bowl, place the yeast, ¼ cup warm water, and 1 teaspoon of the sugar and stir. Let sit 10 minutes.

2 Add ½ cup of the sugar, the soy milk, margarine, eggs, salt, vanilla and 3 cups of the flour to the bowl with the yeast mixture and mix either with a wooden spoon or with a dough hook in a stand mixer. Add between ½ cup and 1 cup more flour, a little at a time, and mix until the dough is smooth and not sticky, scraping down the sides of the bowl and mixing in well before you add more flour. Cover with a clean dish towel and let rise for 1 hour in a warm place. I use a warming drawer on a low setting, or you can turn your oven to its lowest setting, place the bowl in the oven, and then turn off the oven after 5 minutes.

3 Punch down the dough, then shape back into a ball and let it rest, covered with the towel, for 10 minutes. Take 2 cookie sheets and sprinkle some flour on them.

4 Sprinkle some flour on the counter and roll the dough out to about ⅓-inch thick. Using a 3-inch round cookie cutter or drinking glass, cut out circles and place them on the prepared cookie sheets. Re-roll any scraps and cut out more circles. Place the cookie sheets back in the warm place. Let rise another 45 minutes.

5 Heat about 2 inches of oil in a medium saucepan to 360°F. Use a candy thermometer to see when the oil stays at 360°F for a few minutes and adjust the flame to keep the oil at that temperature.

6 Take out another cookie sheet and line it with foil. Place a wire rack on top of the cookie sheet and set near the stovetop. Add the doughnuts top-side down in the oil and cook 1½ minutes. Use tongs or chopsticks to turn the doughnuts over and cook another 1½ minutes. Lift with a slotted spoon and place on the wire rack to cool. Repeat with all the doughnuts.

7 Use a knife or skewer to puncture a hole in the side of each doughnut, moving the knife or skewer around inside to make a space for the jam. Place ½ cup of the jam in a pastry bag fitted with a small, round tip (about ¼-inch) and squeeze some jam into the hole; you will feel the doughnut get heavier. Add more jam into the pastry bag as needed. Roll each filled doughnut in the remaining ¼ cup of sugar and serve. These taste best the day they are made.

Cinnamon Buns

MAKES ABOUT 20 BUNS

STORAGE

Store covered in plastic at room temperature for up to four days or freeze
up to three months.

I felt like a real hero when my four kids returned home from school one day and I presented these buns. They asked, "Where did you buy these?" You may bake these buns two ways: tightly nestled in a pan or separately to look like round pastries. The pan-baked buns are softer, the individual buns a little crunchier on the outside. Or, if you can't decide, you can also bake one-half of the recipe in a greased 8-inch square pan and the other half as individual buns on a cookie sheet.

DOUGH

1 cup parve plain soy milk

½ ounce (2 envelopes) active dry yeast

⅓ cup plus 1 teaspoon sugar, divided

4¼ cups all-purpose flour, plus extra for dusting work surface

2 large eggs, lightly beaten

4 tablespoons (½ stick) parve margarine, softened, plus extra to grease
   pan (if pan-baking buns)

½ cup canola or vegetable oil

FILLING

1 cup (2 sticks) parve margarine, softened

1½ cups light brown sugar

2 tablespoons ground cinnamon

GLAZE

1 cup confectioners' sugar

2 to 3 tablespoons boiling water

½ teaspoon pure vanilla extract

1 To make the dough: Heat the soy milk until lukewarm. Pour into a large bowl and add the yeast and 1 teaspoon of the sugar and let sit for 10 minutes. Add the flour, eggs, remaining ⅓ cup of sugar, margarine, and oil and mix well. Knead using either a dough hook in a stand mixer for 2 to 3 minutes or by hand until the dough comes together into a ball. Cover with plastic and let rise 1 hour.

2 In the meantime, prepare the filling. Place the margarine, brown sugar, and cinnamon in a medium bowl and mix with a whisk or beat with an electric mixer until smooth. Set aside.

3 Preheat the oven to 350°F. Take a piece of parchment about 2-feet long and place on the counter. Sprinkle with some flour. Place the dough on the floured parchment, sprinkle with some more flour, and roll it into a 15 x 24-inch rectangle. Spread the cinnamon filling all over the dough, all the way to the edges.

4 Roll up the dough beginning with the long side of the rectangle, so you end up with a log about 24 inches long. Use a sharp knife to cut the roll into 1-inch slices. You can bake these two ways.

5 To make soft, pan-baked buns, grease a 9 x 13-inch pan with some margarine. Place the buns in the pan with the cinnamon swirl–side up. Bake for 40 minutes, or until browned on the outside edges.

6 To make individually baked buns with a slightly crunchy exterior, line 2 cookie sheets with parchment. Place the sliced buns cinnamon swirl–side up on the pans 3 inches apart. Bake for 30 minutes, or until golden-brown.

7 Let cool for 5 minutes in the pan (or on the cookie sheets) and prepare the glaze. Place the confectioners' sugar in a medium bowl. Whisk in 1 tablespoon of the boiling water and the vanilla. Whisk in another tablespoon of boiling water and see if you have a thick, pourable glaze. If you think it is too thick, add another tablespoon of boiling water and whisk to combine. If you accidentally make it too thin, just add some more confectioners' sugar. Use the whisk to drizzle the glaze over the cinnamon buns and enjoy.

Chocolate Babka

MAKES TWO 12-INCH LOAVES, 25 SERVINGS

STORAGE

*Store wrapped in foil at room temperature. If you will not eat it within
24 hours, freeze it for up to three months. Thaw at room temperature for
4 hours before serving.*

This is the most popular dessert I teach in my classes, and it is the dessert for which I am most famous. I bring this to people when they have babies, when someone dies, or when I just need to put a smile on someone's face. The recipe on which the following is based came from my friend Limor's mom, Aliza Cohen, who used to bake them for me when I was in high school. I did a demonstration of babka at a bridal shower for my friend Katie Wexler because she and her husband had met when he brought a store-bought babka to a singles brunch. Katie opened the door, saw the babka and said "You brought a babka! You are my new best friend."

½ cup warm water

½ ounce (2 envelopes) active dry yeast

2½ cups plus 1 teaspoon sugar, divided

5 cups all-purpose flour, plus extra for sprinkling

3 cups (6 sticks) parve margarine, softened, divided

2 large eggs plus 1 white (reserve yolk for glazing)

½ cup parve unsweetened cocoa

Spray oil, for greasing pans

½ cup parve mini or regular chocolate chips

1 Place the ½ cup warm water, yeast, and 1 teaspoon of the sugar in a large mixing bowl and let sit 10 minutes, until the mixture bubbles. Add ½ cup of the sugar, the flour, 2 sticks of the margarine, and the 2 whole eggs and egg white. Combine by hand with a wooden spoon or with a dough hook in a stand mixer until all the ingredients are mixed in. Cover the bowl with plastic and let rise 2 to 4 hours, until the dough has increased in size.

2 Meanwhile, make the filling. In a medium bowl, combine the remaining 2 cups of the sugar with the cocoa. Add the remaining 4 sticks margarine and mix well with a hand-held or stand mixer or by hand with a whisk. You can let the filling sit out covered while the dough is rising.

3 Preheat the oven to 375°F. Grease two 12-inch-long loaf pans with spray oil.

4 Divide the dough into four pieces. On a large piece of parchment sprinkled with a little flour, roll each piece into a 10 x 7-inch rectangle. Spread one-fourth of the filling on one of the rectangles and then sprinkle on one-fourth of the chocolate chips. Roll up the dough beginning with the long side of the rectangle. Repeat with the next dough rectangle. When you have two rolls, twist them around each other, trying to keep the seams on the bottom. Tuck the ends under and place into one of the loaf pans. Do the same with the other two pieces of dough. Brush the tops of the loaves with the reserved egg yolk mixed with a little water.

5 Bake for 45 minutes, or until very brown on top. Cool for 20 minutes in the pan. Run a knife around the babka, then remove from the pans and let cool.

CINNAMON BABKA

Replace the cocoa and chocolate chips with 3½ tablespoons ground cinnamon.

Babkas freeze extremely well. I brought one to the bris of my friend Abby Cherner's son. Abby didn't want to share it with her guests so she hid it in the freezer. Well, she found it around her son Noah's first birthday—and still ate it. She said, "No way was I wasting a perfectly good babka."

Cinnamon Apricot Pull-Apart Babka

SERVES 10 TO 12

STORAGE

Store covered in plastic at room temperature for up to four days or freeze up to three months.

My late Aunt Lillian was a great cook and baker. One of my favorites of hers was what she called a "conversation cake." She took little challah dough balls, dipped them in margarine and sugar, and then baked them in a pan, placing candied fruit between the balls. As an extra surprise, she would often hide some pennies in the cake for us kids to find. It was exciting to be the person to find them (without swallowing them, of course). This recipe is a tribute to her, though the filling idea came from my friend Jonathan Javitt's mom while we were sitting at Jonathan's pool on July 4th in Annapolis. The assembly is rather messy and takes time, but you will like the result. Do not turn the babka onto a rack right out of the oven; the balls will fall apart. Let the babka cool first in the pan.

DOUGH

½ cup lukewarm water

½ ounce (2 envelopes) active dry yeast

½ cup plus 1 teaspoon sugar, divided

5 cups all-purpose flour, plus extra for rolling out the dough

1 cup (2 sticks) parve margarine, softened

3 large eggs

FILLING

1½ cups sugar

4 tablespoons ground cinnamon

½ cup apricot preserves

½ cup (1 stick) parve margarine

Spray oil, for greasing pan

1 To make the dough: Place the warm water, yeast, and 1 teaspoon of the sugar in a large mixing bowl and let sit 10 minutes, until the mixture bubbles. Add the remaining ½ cup of sugar, flour, margarine, and eggs. Combine by hand with a wooden spoon or by using a dough hook in a stand mixer until all the ingredients are mixed in. Cover bowl with plastic and let rise 3 to 4 hours, until the dough has increased in size.

2 Meanwhile, for the filling, combine the 1½ cups of sugar and cinnamon in a bowl.

3 Place the remaining stick of margarine in a heatproof bowl and heat in the microwave until melted. Set aside.

4 Preheat the oven to 375°F. Grease a large Bundt pan with spray oil.

5 Divide the dough into 4 parts. Place a large piece of parchment on the counter and sprinkle generously with flour. Place one part of the dough on the parchment and roll out as thin as you can, less than ¼-inch thick. Use a cookie cutter or glass, about 2 inches in diameter, to cut circles of the dough as close to each other as possible. Reroll all the scraps and cut out more circles. Place ¼ teaspoon of apricot preserves in the center of each circle and sprinkle on ¼ teaspoon of the cinnamon-sugar. Close the dough around the filling and squeeze with your hand to form a ball. Do not worry if some jam squeezes out. When you have all the balls made, dip each into the melted margarine and roll in the cinnamon-sugar. Place around the bottom of the Bundt pan. Repeat with the other three pieces of dough and place the balls evenly around the pan.

6 Bake for 45 minutes or until golden on top. Let cool for 30 minutes in the pan and then turn onto a rack. To serve, I turn it back over onto a serving a plate so it looks like a crown. To eat, each person pulls off some pieces.

You should always proof yeast in water with a little sugar. If the mixture does not bubble, the yeast is dead and you need to dump it and try again with fresher yeast.

Babka Cupcakes with Crumb Topping

MAKES 14 TO 15 CUPCAKES

STORAGE

Store covered in plastic at room temperature for up to four days or freeze up to three months.

Claire Shoyer, these are for you.

BABKA CUPCAKES

¼ cup warm water

½ ounce (2 envelopes) active dry yeast

1¼ cups plus 1 teaspoon sugar, divided

2½ cups all-purpose flour, plus extra for sprinkling

1½ cups (3 sticks) parve margarine, softened, divided, plus extra
   for greasing muffin pan

1 large egg plus 1 white

¼ cup parve unsweetened cocoa

⅓ cup parve mini or regular-size chocolate chips

CRUMB TOPPING

¼ cup sugar

1 tablespoon flour

4 teaspoons canola or vegetable oil

¼ teaspoon ground cinnamon

1 Place the warm water, yeast, and 1 teaspoon of the sugar in a large mixing bowl and let sit 10 minutes, or until the mixture bubbles. Add ¼ cup of sugar, the flour, 1 stick of the margarine, and the eggs. Combine by hand with a wooden spoon or with a dough hook in a stand mixer until all the ingredients are mixed in. Cover bowl with plastic and let rise 2 to 4 hours, until the dough has increased in size.

2 Meanwhile, for the chocolate filling, combine the remaining 1 cup of sugar with the cocoa in a medium bowl. Add the remaining 2 sticks of margarine and mix well with a hand-held or stand electric mixer, or by hand with a whisk. You can let the filling sit out covered while the dough is rising.

3 To make the crumb topping: In a small bowl, place the sugar, flour, oil, and cinnamon and mix with a silicone spatula.

4 Preheat the oven to 375°F. Grease 14 to 15 cups of a muffin pan or pans.

5 Divide dough into four pieces. On a large piece of parchment sprinkled with flour, roll each piece into a rectangle, as thin as you can. Spread one-fourth of the cocoa and sugar mixture on one of the dough rectangles and then sprinkle on one-fourth of the chocolate chips. Roll up the dough beginning with the long side of the rectangle to create long, thin rolls.

6 Slice each roll into ¾-inch slices. Place 4 slices into each muffin cup, arranging the first 2 at angles in the bottom and then the second 2 on top, also at angles, none with the chocolate swirls facing straight up. Use your fingers to sprinkle some of the crumb topping on top of each babka cupcake; use up all the topping.

7 Bake for 25 to 30 minutes, or until browned on top. Cool for 20 minutes in the pan. Run a knife around the babkas, then remove from the pan and let cool.

Mini Éclairs

MAKES ABOUT FORTY 3-INCH ÉCLAIRS

STORAGE

Store the éclairs in the refrigerator for up to four days or freeze in an airtight container for up to three months.

A good éclair is something very special. Lucky for you, the éclair pastry and the vanilla cream recipes work perfectly substituting soy milk for milk. I really can't tell the difference between my dairy and parve éclairs. Éclairs are made with French "choux pastry," a dough used in many French desserts that is light and crisp on the outside yet airy on the inside. The pastry was named "choux," meaning cabbage, because the inside of the baked pastries looks like layers of cabbage leaves.

CHOUX PASTRY

½ cup parve plain soy milk

½ cup water

½ cup (1 stick) parve margarine, cut into tablespoons

½ teaspoon salt

1 cup all-purpose flour, sifted after measuring

6 large eggs, divided

1 cup parve plain soy milk

½ vanilla bean, split and the seeds scraped, or 1 teaspoon vanilla extract

2 tablespoons parve margarine

5 tablespoons sugar

3 large egg yolks

3½ tablespoons all-purpose flour, sifted after measuring

SHINY CHOCOLATE SAUCE

1 cup water

1⅓ cups sugar

6 ounces parve semisweet or bittersweet chocolate, chopped or
   broken into 1-inch pieces

1 Preheat the oven to 475°F. Line 2 cookie sheets with parchment.

2 To make the choux pastry: Place the soy milk, water, margarine, and salt in a
   medium saucepan and bring to a boil over medium heat. Remove from the heat
   and, with a wooden spoon, mix in the sifted flour. Place the saucepan over low
   heat and cook for 1 minute more, stirring constantly to dry out the dough.
   Remove from the heat.

3 Place the dough in a medium bowl and add 5 of the eggs, one at a time, mixing
   thoroughly with a wooden spoon after the addition of each egg. Be patient, this
   takes time.

4 Place the dough in a pastry bag with a ¼- to ½-inch round tip. Pipe out lines 1 x 3
   inches long on the prepared cookie sheets. Place the lines 2 inches apart. You can
   do this by holding the bag at an angle ¼ inch above the baking sheet, squeezing out
   the dough and holding the pastry bag in place until the amount you have squeezed
   out is about an inch wide, and then slowly moving the bag along as you squeeze out
   more dough. When your line is 3 inches long, slowly lift up the tip up and over the
   line you squeezed out; the end will stay rounded. You will get the hang of it after a
   few lines.

5 Beat the sixth egg in a small bowl and brush each line gently with some of the
   beaten egg to smooth out the top.

6 Place the baking sheets in the oven and turn off the oven. After 15 minutes,
   turn the oven on again to 350°F. Bake the pastries another 15 to 20 minutes. They
   are done when the cracks on the top are the same color as the rest of the pastry.

Remove to rack and let cool. If you are filling the pastries that day, leave uncovered on the cookie sheet. If you do not plan to fill them that day, store in an airtight container at room temperature.

7   To make the pastry cream: In a heavy saucepan, bring the soy milk, scraped seeds and vanilla bean or vanilla extract, margarine, and 2 tablespoons of the sugar to boil. Meanwhile, use a whisk to beat the egg yolks and the remaining sugar in a medium bowl. Add the flour and use a silicone spatula to gently mix into the eggs. Strain half the soy milk mixture into the egg bowl and whisk. Strain the other half of the soy milk into the egg mixture and mix well.

8   Return mixture to the saucepan and cook on low heat for 2 minutes, whisking constantly. You will need a silicone spatula to mix the cream in the corners of the pot so it does not burn. Remove from heat and place in a bowl. Let sit 5 minutes and then cover with plastic and place in refrigerator until chilled, 4 hours or overnight. To use sooner, place the bowl of pastry cream over a larger bowl filled with ice and a little water (below the level of the bowl with the cream) for 15 to 20 minutes, or until cream is chilled. Mix occasionally. This can be made 2 to 3 days in advance and stored at room temperature.

9   Place the pastry cream in a pastry bag with a small tip, about ⅛ inch in diameter. Each éclair will have a flat side and rounded side. Hold the pastry so the rounded side faces you. Using the pastry bag tip, or a skewer, make two holes in the rounded side of the pastry (not the flat side that sat on the cookie sheet), about 1 inch apart. Squeeze the cream into the pastry through the holes, one at a time, tilting the nozzle to get the cream in the entire pastry, until you feel the pastry get heavier or the cream starts coming out one of the holes.

10 When the éclairs are filled, make the shiny chocolate sauce. To make this sauce, you will first make a simple sugar syrup. Place the water and sugar in a small heavy saucepan over medium heat. Stir to dissolve the sugar and bring to a rolling boil. Remove from the heat. This portion of the syrup can be made 2 to 3 days in advance and stored at room temperature.

11 Melt the chocolate either on the stovetop or in the microwave, following the "Melting chocolate" instructions (see Foolproof Tips and Techniques). Whisk until smooth. Add the sugar syrup a tablespoon at a time and whisk until you get a consistency you can drizzle. If the sauce starts to harden, just add a little more sugar syrup and whisk until you get a thick, pourable consistency. Store the chocolate sauce covered at room temperature and reheat in a microwave and whisk when needed.

12 Take each éclair and dip the flat side (without the pastry cream holes) into the chocolate, allowing the excess to drip off. Repeat with all the other éclairs.

Chocolate Rolls

MAKES ABOUT 4 DOZEN SLICES

STORAGE

Store the rolls covered at room temperature for up to five days or freeze up to three months.

When I first tasted Lisa Silverman's signature dessert, the dairy version of these rolls, these slices of chocolate just melted in my mouth. I like to think my parve version is just as good. For the best texture, I like to make these the day before I plan to eat them.

DOUGH

1 cup (2 sticks) parve margarine, at room temperature

8 ounces parve cream cheese, at room temperature

2 cups plus 2 tablespoons all-purpose flour, plus extra for sprinkling

1 tablespoon confectioners' sugar

FILLING

One 12-ounce bag parve semisweet chocolate chips

1½ cups pecan halves

⅓ cup parve whipping cream

1 In a large bowl, with an electric mixer or by hand with a whisk, beat the margarine and cream cheese together until smooth. Scrape down the bowl with a silicone spatula. Add the flour and confectioners' sugar and mix just until the dough comes together. Divide into two pieces, wrap each ball in plastic, and then flatten. Place in freezer for 1½ hours or overnight. If you freeze the dough overnight, you will need to let it thaw until it is malleable before rolling.

2 Preheat the oven to 350°F. Line a cookie sheet with parchment.

3 To make the chocolate filling, melt the chocolate chips either on the stovetop or in the microwave, following the "Melting chocolate" instructions (see Foolproof Tips and Techniques).

4 Meanwhile, place the pecan halves in a freezer bag and bang with a rolling pin to break them into small pieces. When the chocolate is melted, remove from the heat and stir in the cream. Add the nuts and stir to mix in.

5 Place a large piece of plastic wrap, about 15 inches long, on the counter and sprinkle flour on it. Sprinkle some flour on both sides of one of the dough pieces and place on the floured plastic. Hit the dough a few times with the rolling pin to soften it. Place a piece of parchment the size of the plastic wrap on top of the dough and, rolling on top of the parchment, roll the dough into a rectangle, about 11 x 14 inches.

6 Spread half of the chocolate filling on the dough all the way to the edges. Fold all the edges in about ⅓ of an inch; this will keep the filling inside the roll. Using the plastic wrap to help you, roll up the long side of the dough, working slowly and rolling as tightly as you can. Place the roll on the prepared baking sheet, seam-side down, and flatten slightly. Repeat with the second piece of dough.

7 Bake for 40 minutes, or until the top is light but the bottom golden. Let cool and cut into ½-inch slices when serving.

Lemon Tart

SERVES 8

STORAGE

Store covered in the refrigerator for up to four days.

This is a popular French tart made of lemon curd in a sugar cookie crust. I sold many of these when I had a catering business in Geneva, Switzerland. You can turn it into a lemon meringue tart by topping it with the meringue from the recipe for Key Lime Pie (page 200) and then placing it in a 450°F oven for a few minutes to lightly brown the meringue. I like to decorate the top with thin lemon slices cut into quarters, placed as a border around the tart.

SWEET DOUGH CRUST

1 cup all-purpose flour, plus extra for sprinkling

⅔ cup confectioners' sugar

5 tablespoons parve margarine, frozen for 30 minutes and
    then cut into tablespoons

1 large egg yolk

2 tablespoons cold water

¼ teaspoon pure vanilla extract

LEMON CREAM

3 large eggs plus 2 egg yolks

1 cup sugar

5 tablespoons fresh lemon juice (from 3 lemons)

Zest (grated outer peel) of 1 lemon

5½ tablespoons parve margarine, plus extra to grease pan

Paper thin lemon slices, for decoration (optional)

1 To make the crust: Place the flour, confectioners' sugar, and margarine in the bowl of a food processor fitted with a metal blade. Process for 10 seconds, or until the mixture resembles sand. You can do this by hand by cutting the margarine into the dry ingredients using two knives or a pastry cutter. Add the egg yolk, cold water, and vanilla and process or hand mix with a silicone spatula or wooden spoon until the dough comes together into a ball. Place the dough on a large piece of plastic wrap. Gather into a ball, cover with the plastic, and then flatten. Chill 1 hour in the freezer or overnight in the refrigerator.

2 To make the lemon cream: Place the eggs, yolks, and sugar in a heatproof bowl and set over a medium saucepan with simmering water (or use a double boiler). Add the lemon juice and zest to the bowl and whisk. Cook the lemon cream, uncovered, whisking occasionally, until a thick mixture is formed. This takes approximately 25 minutes. Be patient and do not stir too much. Don't leave the whisk in the bowl with the lemon mixture while it cooks; it may get too hot to touch. If the water in the saucepan boils too fast, turn down the heat.

3 Remove the bowl from the heat and whisk in the margarine a tablespoon at a time. Cool for 10 minutes and then cover with plastic and refrigerate 8 hours or overnight. To use that day, place the bowl of lemon cream in a larger bowl of ice water (below the level of the bowl with the lemon cream) for 15 to 20 minutes, or until the cream is chilled.

4 Preheat the oven to 350°F. Grease an 8-inch tart ring, with or without a removable bottom, with a little margarine and place on parchment on a cookie sheet.

5 Remove the dough from the freezer or refrigerator and let sit at room temperature just until you can press it gently. Place a piece of plastic wrap larger than the tart ring on the counter and sprinkle with flour. Place the dough on top. Sprinkle with a little more flour and cover with a piece of parchment. Roll on top of the parchment to roll out the dough until it is at least 1 inch larger than the tart ring. Remove the parchment. Place your hand under the plastic, lift the dough up and turn it over into the tart ring, using your fingers to gently press the dough into the corners. Remove the plastic and use a rolling pin to roll over the top to trim off the excess dough.

6 Freeze 10 minutes. Cover the dough with foil or parchment and fill with beans or pie weights. Bake for 20 minutes. Remove the foil or parchment and weights and bake another 5 minutes. Remove the ring and allow to cool. This can be made in advance, wrapped in plastic, and frozen until ready to fill. Be careful with the crust—it is delicate.

7 Preheat the oven to 450°F. Scoop the lemon cream into the baked tart shell and spread evenly. Bake for 5 minutes to set the cream. Allow to cool and then chill at least 4 hours before serving. The tart is best when chilled several hours or a day before serving.

8 To serve, you can decorate the top with the slices of lemon.

◇ Key Lime Pie

SERVES 8

STORAGE

Store in the refrigerator for up to four days.

Though this pie is a classic American dessert, it is not a typical parve dessert, and in developing this recipe I learned why. The filling is generally cooked on the stove with condensed milk for which there is no parve substitute. I tried cooking several lime fillings with bad results, so I turned to my favorite lime curd and thickened it up a little. I made this with regular limes, but if you can find the small, round key limes, use those, just double the amount as the ones I have seen are very small. As there is no flour anywhere in this recipe, you can enjoy it on Passover too.

CRUST

4 tablespoons parve margarine

2 cups ground walnuts (from 4 cups walnut halves)
   (see "Making ground walnuts," page xxviii)

3 tablespoons light brown sugar

FILLING

5 large eggs plus 3 yolks

1½ cups sugar

7 limes or 14 key limes

½ cup (1 stick) parve margarine

1 drop green food coloring (optional)

MERINGUE TOPPING

⅔ cup sugar

¼ cup water

2 large egg whites

1 Preheat the oven to 350°F. You will need an 8- or 9-inch pie pan for this dessert.

2 To make the crust: Place the margarine in a medium microwave-safe bowl and heat for 45 seconds, or until melted. Add the walnuts and brown sugar and mix until combined. Place this mixture into the pie pan and press to cover the bottom and about 1 inch up the sides. Place in the oven for 15 minutes. Remove from oven and set aside. Leave the oven on.

3 To make the lime cream: Place the eggs, yolks, and sugar in a heatproof bowl and set over a medium saucepan with simmering water (or use a double boiler). Zest 3 of the limes (or 6 key limes) and add to the bowl. Stir to combine. Juice the 3 zested limes plus the remaining 4 limes (or 8 key limes) to obtain about ½ cup juice, then stir it into the egg and sugar mixture. Cook uncovered over simmering water for about 25 minutes, stirring occasionally, until a thick mixture is formed. Be patient and do not stir too much. If the water in the double boiler boils too fast, turn down the heat. Remove the bowl from the heat and whisk in the margarine in small pieces until the cream is smooth. Add the green food coloring, if using, and stir.

4 Pour the cream into the prepared crust and smooth. Place the pie on a cookie sheet and bake for 20 minutes, or until the outside edges of the cream are set (the inside can remain a little wobbly). Let cool and then place in the refrigerator for at least 2 hours.

5 To make the meringue topping: In a small heavy saucepan, bring the sugar and water to a boil, stirring to dissolve the sugar. Continue to cook the sugar until it reaches 230°F (use a candy thermometer to check the temperature). You can dip a pastry brush in water and wipe down the sides of the pot if any sugar crystals appear on the sides. While the sugar is cooking, in a medium bowl, beat the egg whites with an electric mixer on high speed until stiff. When the sugar is ready, turn the mixer speed to low and then slowly pour the cooked sugar into the bowl, down the side of the bowl, not directly onto the wire whisk. When all of the sugar has been poured in, turn the mixer up to medium-high and beat for 1 minute until the meringue is thick and shiny.

6 Use a silicone spatula to spread the meringue all over the top of the pie. You can use a blowtorch to lightly brown the top or place it in a 450°F oven for a few minutes, watching the entire time, until the top browns.

Pear & Almond Tart

SERVES 8

STORAGE

Store in the refrigerator for up to three days.

In this classic French dessert, poached pears are baked in an almond cream in a cookie crust. Don't worry about the three parts: you can make the dough in advance and freeze it, make the almond cream three days before, and prepare the pears two days before. You can then assemble it all on the day you will serve the tart. I learned how to make a dairy version of this tart in cooking school in Paris.

SWEET DOUGH CRUST

1 cup all-purpose flour, plus extra for sprinkling

⅔ cup confectioners' sugar

5 tablespoons parve margarine, frozen for 30 minutes and cut in pieces

1 large egg yolk

2 tablespoons cold water

¼ teaspoon pure vanilla extract

POACHED PEARS

7 cups water

1 cup sugar

1 tablespoon pure vanilla extract

Juice from 1 lemon

3 firm pears

ALMOND CREAM

5 tablespoons parve margarine, plus extra to grease pan

⅓ cup sugar

½ cup almond flour (see "Making almond flour," page xxvii)

1 tablespoon all-purpose flour

1 large egg

1 teaspoon pure vanilla extract

1 teaspoon rum (optional)

2 tablespoons apricot jam, for glazing pears

2 tablespoons confectioners' sugar, for sprinkling on tart

1 To make the crust: Place the flour, confectioners' sugar, and margarine in the bowl of a food processor fitted with a metal blade. Process for 10 seconds, or until the mixture resembles sand. You can do this by hand by cutting the margarine into the dry ingredients using two knives or a pastry cutter. Add the egg yolk, cold water, and vanilla and process or hand mix with a silicone spatula or wooden spoon until the dough comes together into a ball. Place the dough on a large piece of plastic wrap. Gather into a ball, cover with the plastic, and then flatten. Chill 1 hour in the freezer or overnight in the refrigerator.

2 To make the poached pears: In a medium saucepan, bring water, sugar, and vanilla to a boil. Meanwhile, place the lemon juice in a shallow bowl. Slice the very bottom and very top off of each pear and peel, making sure to keep the pear shape. Halve the pears from stem to bottom. With a ½-teaspoon measuring spoon or melon baller, starting at the top of a pear half, gently scoop out the thin vein that runs from top to the bottom and the core and seeds of the pear. You want to keep the shape of the pear.

3 As each half is prepared, place in the lemon juice and turn to coat. When the poaching syrup has boiled, add the pears to the pot and cook uncovered for approximately 15 minutes on medium heat so the pears simmer, or until the tip of a sharp knife slides easily into the inside of one of the pear halves; do not cut through.

4 Once the pears are cooked, remove the pan from the heat and let the pears cool in the syrup. Transfer the pears to a bowl or container, ladle some of the cooking liquid on top, and cover. The pears may be chilled for 2 days.

5 To make the almond cream: With an electric mixer on high speed or a whisk, beat the margarine until soft. Add the sugar, almond flour, and flour and beat or whisk again. Add the egg, vanilla, and rum, if using. Turn up the speed of the mixer to high and whip until the mixture is light and airy, about 1 minute. The cream may be made 3 days in advance and stored covered in the refrigerator.

6 When you're ready to assemble and bake the tart, preheat the oven to 425°F. Place the pear halves on paper towels to dry. Grease an 8- or 9-inch tart ring, with or without a removable bottom, with a little margarine and place on a parchment-lined cookie sheet.

7 Remove the dough from the freezer or refrigerator and let sit at room temperature just until you can press

it gently. Place a piece of plastic wrap larger than the tart ring on the counter and sprinkle with flour. Place the dough on top. Sprinkle with a little more flour. Cover with a piece of parchment and roll on top of the parchment to roll out the dough until it is at least 1 inch larger than the tart ring. Remove the parchment.

8   Place your hand under the plastic, lift the dough, and turn it over into the tart ring, using your fingers to gently press the dough into the corners. Remove the plastic and use a rolling pin to roll over the top to trim off the excess dough.

9   Use a silicone spatula to spread the almond cream evenly on the bottom of the dough, all the way to the edges. Take each pear half, place on a small cutting board and, using a small sharp knife, make thin crosswise (not top to bottom) slices into the pears all the way through, being careful to keep each slice in place to retain the shape of the pear.

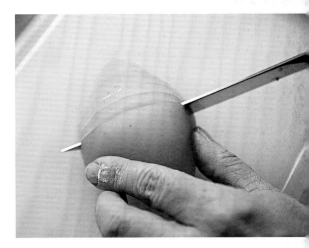

10 Using a metal flat-blade spatula, carefully pick up the entire sliced pear half and place on the cream, stem side facing the center. Repeat for the next pear half and place across from the first, the stem sides facing each other. Carefully place the remaining halves in the ring, spacing them evenly. With your fingers, gently fan each pear from the center to the ring.

11 Bake for 30 for 35 minutes, or until golden-brown. Slide the parchment and the tart onto a rack to cool.

12 To serve, warm the apricot jam in the microwave for 15 seconds and stir. Sift the confectioners' sugar over the baked almond cream and then brush the pears with the jam. If the tart will not be served the same day, it must be refrigerated.

Pistachio & Raspberry Tart

MAKES 8 SLICES OR 9 SQUARES IF USING A SQUARE PAN

STORAGE

Store covered at room temperature for up to three days.

I saw this in a pastry shop in Paris and asked the owner what was in it and she told me. It was made in a square tart pan, which was becoming a new trend in Parisian pastry shops. I did not taste it because it was my third pastry shop that day and I just could not ingest any more sugar. My daughter Emily got a picture of it before she got yelled at to stop. I came home and created this.

SWEET DOUGH CRUST

1 cup all-purpose flour, plus extra for sprinkling

⅔ cup confectioners' sugar

5 tablespoons parve margarine, frozen for 30 minutes and
     cut into pieces, plus extra for greasing pan

1 large egg yolk

2 tablespoons cold water

¼ teaspoon pure vanilla extract

PISTACHIO CREAM

5 tablespoons parve margarine

⅓ cup sugar

½ cup shelled and ground pistachio nuts (from about ⅔ cup shelled)
     (about ½ pound of nuts in their shells)

1 tablespoon all-purpose flour

1 large egg

1 teaspoon pure vanilla extract

RASPBERRY FILLING

1 cup fresh raspberries

2 teaspoons sugar

4 teaspoons hot water

1 To make the crust: Place the flour, confectioners' sugar, and margarine in the bowl of a food processor fitted with a metal blade. Process for 10 seconds, or until the mixture resembles sand. You can do this by hand by cutting the margarine into the dry ingredients using two knives or a pastry cutter. Add the egg yolk, cold water, and vanilla and process or hand mix with a silicone spatula or wooden spoon until the dough comes together into a ball. Place the dough on a large piece of plastic wrap. Gather into a ball, cover with the plastic, and then flatten. Chill 1 hour in the freezer or overnight in the refrigerator.

2 Beat the margarine in a mixer with a wire whisk. Add the sugar, ground pistachios, and flour and mix well, scraping down the bowl as needed. Add the egg and vanilla and mix again until combined. Turn up the speed of the mixer to high and whip until the mixture is light and airy, about 1 minute. Cover cream with plastic and refrigerate. The cream may be made 3 days in advance.

3 While the dough is chilling, prepare the raspberry filling. Place the raspberries into the bowl of a food processor fitted with a metal blade or a blender. Add the sugar and water and process until completely puréed. Strain to remove the seeds and set aside.

4 When you're ready to assemble and bake the tart, preheat the oven to 350°F. Remove the dough from the freezer or refrigerator and let sit at room temperature just until you can press it gently. Grease an 8- or 9-inch tart ring, with or without a removable bottom, with a little margarine and place on a cookie sheet covered with parchment. Place a piece of plastic wrap larger than the tart ring on the counter and sprinkle with flour. Place the dough on top. Sprinkle with a little more flour. Cover with a piece of parchment and roll on top of the parchment to roll out the dough until it is at least 1 inch larger than the tart ring. Remove the top parchment. Place your hand under the plastic, lift the dough, and turn it over into the tart ring, using your fingers to gently press the dough into the corners. Remove plastic and use a rolling pin to roll over the top to trim off the excess dough.

5 Spread the pistachio cream evenly on top of the dough. Use a small spoon to spoon the raspberry purée on top of the cream, trying to make it look like ink splotches. Do not spread the purée all over; you will want to see some green.

6 Bake for 40 minutes, or until the pistachio cream starts to brown.

Caramelized Nut Tart

SERVES 8

STORAGE

Store covered in the refrigerator for up to five days and let sit out 20 minutes before serving.

During a trip to Israel, my brother's mother-in-law, Varda Dascal, took me to her favorite bakery in Jaffa, Piece of Cake. I met the owner, Moshe, who took me on a tour and let me taste everything. He gave me these mini nut tarts to taste and I just loved them. If you like nuts and sweet desserts, this tart is for you. All Moshe said was to toast the nuts, cook them in caramel, and bake them in a tart shell. I added almond extract to the basic crust that is used in other recipes to emphasize the nut flavor. These tarts are now a regular addition to my Thanksgiving dessert buffet.

SWEET DOUGH CRUST

1 cup all-purpose flour, plus extra for sprinkling

⅔ cup confectioners' sugar

5 tablespoons parve margarine, frozen for 30 minutes and
   then cut in pieces, plus extra for greasing pan

1 large egg yolk

2 tablespoons cold water

¼ teaspoon pure vanilla extract

¼ teaspoon almond extract

FILLING

1 cup whole almonds

1 cup walnut halves

1 cup whole hazelnuts (filberts)

½ cup pecan halves

½ cup raw, unsalted cashews

1 cup sugar

¼ cup water

⅔ cup parve whipping cream

3 tablespoons parve margarine

1 tablespoon honey

1 teaspoon pure vanilla extract

1 teaspoon almond flavored liqueur

1 To make the crust: Place the flour, confectioners' sugar, and margarine in the bowl of a food processor fitted with a metal blade. Process for 10 seconds, or until the mixture resembles sand. You can do this by hand by cutting the margarine into the dry ingredients using two knives or a pastry cutter. Add the egg yolk, cold water, and the vanilla and almond extracts and process or hand mix with a silicone spatula or wooden spoon until the dough comes together into a ball. Place the dough on a large piece of plastic wrap. Gather into a ball, cover with the plastic, and then flatten. Chill 1 hour in the freezer or overnight in the refrigerator.

2 Preheat the oven to 350°F. Place all of the nuts on a jelly roll pan. Toast the nuts for 20 minutes, stirring twice. Set aside.

3 Remove the dough from the freezer or refrigerator and let sit at room temperature just until you can press it gently. Preheat the oven to 350°F. Grease an 8-inch tart ring, with or without a removable bottom, with a little margarine and place on parchment on a cookie sheet. Place a piece of plastic wrap larger than the tart ring on the counter and sprinkle with flour. Place the dough on top. Sprinkle with a little more flour. Cover with a piece of parchment and roll on top of the parchment to roll out the dough until it is at least 1 inch larger than the tart ring. You will want to peel back the parchment and sprinkle some more flour on the dough 2 to 3 times while you are rolling. Remove the top parchment. Place your hand under the plastic, lift the dough, and turn it over into the tart ring, using your fingers to gently press the dough into the corners. Remove plastic and use a rolling pin to roll over the top to trim off the excess dough.

4 Freeze 10 minutes. Line dough with foil or parchment and fill with beans or pie weights. Bake for 20 minutes. Lift up the edges of the foil or parchment to remove it and the weights and bake the shell another 5 minutes. Remove from oven and remove ring. Leave the oven on.

5 Place the sugar and water in a heavy saucepan and heat over low heat, stirring to dissolve the sugar. Turn the heat up to medium and let boil, without stirring, until the mixture turns amber, swirling the pot once or twice. This takes about 10 to 12 minutes; be patient. Turn the heat to low, add the whipping cream, and stir until the caramel is smooth. Whisk in the margarine, honey, vanilla and almond liqueur. Add the toasted nuts and use a silicone spatula to mix well. Remove from heat. Place the nut mixture and any caramel left in the saucepan into the tart shell and spread evenly. Bake for 20 minutes.

6 Let cool for ½ hour and then serve at room temperature.

Fruit Tart

SERVES 8

STORAGE

Store in the refrigerator for up to two days.

As you can see, this can be a very colorful tart and you get to design it. To plan out my design, after I have baked the tart shell, I place the empty tart ring on top of waxed paper on a cookie sheet. You can have sections of different fruits as shown here or place sliced fruit in concentric circles (see photo of the tart in the chocolate crust on page 213). You can use only one type of fruit too. After I design the fruit in the ring, I place the cookie sheet in the refrigerator and, when I am ready to serve, I fill the tart shell with the pastry cream and then carefully move the fruit one piece at a time on top of the cream. If I use fruit that has pits, such as cherries, I remove the fruit just before slicing the tart and divide it among the plates.

SWEET DOUGH CRUST

    1 cup all-purpose flour, plus extra for sprinkling

    ⅔ cup confectioners' sugar

    5 tablespoons parve margarine, frozen for 30 minutes and then
        cut into tablespoons, plus extra for greasing pan

    1 large egg yolk

    2 tablespoons cold water

    ¼ teaspoon pure vanilla extract

PASTRY CREAM

    1 cup parve plain soy milk

    ½ vanilla bean, split and scraped, or 1 teaspoon vanilla extract

    5 tablespoons sugar

    2 tablespoons parve margarine

    4 large egg yolks

    3 tablespoons flour, sifted after measuring

    6 to 8 cups fruit: strawberries, raspberries, blackberries, blueberries,
        sliced kiwi, mango, halved kumquats, cherries, star fruit, etc.

1 To make the crust: Place the flour, confectioners' sugar, and margarine into the bowl of a food processor fitted with a metal blade. Process or mix for 10 seconds, until the mixture resembles sand. You can make this by hand by cutting the margarine into the dry ingredients with two knives or a pastry cutter. Add the egg yolk, water, and vanilla and process or mix by hand until the dough comes together into a ball. Place dough on a large piece of plastic wrap. Gather into a ball, cover with the plastic and then flatten. Chill 1 hour in the freezer or overnight in the refrigerator.

2 Remove the dough from the freezer or refrigerator and let sit at room temperature just until you can press it gently. Preheat the oven to 350°F. Grease an 8-inch tart ring, with or without a removable bottom, with a little margarine and place on parchment on a cookie sheet. Place a piece of plastic wrap larger than the tart ring on the counter and sprinkle with flour. Place the dough on top. Sprinkle with a little more flour. Cover with a piece of parchment and roll on top of the parchment to roll out the dough until it is at least 1 inch larger than the tart ring. You will want to peel back the parchment and sprinkle some more flour on the dough 2 to 3 times while you are rolling. Remove the top parchment. Place your hand under the plastic, lift the dough, and turn it over into the tart ring, using your fingers to gently press the dough into the corners. Remove plastic and use a rolling pin to roll over the top to trim off the excess dough.

3 Freeze 10 minutes. Line dough with foil or parchment and fill with beans or pie weights. Bake for 20 minutes. Lift up the edges of the foil or parchment to remove it and the weights and bake the shell another 5 minutes or until the dough begins to brown in center. Remove from the oven and let cool.

4 To make the pastry cream: In a heavy saucepan, bring the soy milk, scraped seeds and vanilla bean or vanilla extract, margarine, and 2 tablespoons of the sugar to boil. Meanwhile, use a whisk to beat the egg yolks and the remaining sugar in a medium bowl. Add the flour and use a silicone spatula to gently mix into the eggs. Strain half the soy milk mixture into the egg bowl and whisk. Strain the other half of the soy milk mixture into the egg mixture and mix well.

5 Return mixture to the saucepan and cook on low heat for 2 minutes, whisking constantly. You will need a silicone spatula to mix the cream in the corners of the pot so it does not burn. Remove from heat and place in a bowl. Let sit 5 minutes and then cover with plastic and place in refrigerator until chilled, 4 hours or overnight. To use sooner, place the bowl of pastry cream over a larger bowl filled with ice and a little water (below the level of the bowl with the cream) for 15

to 20 minutes, or until cream is chilled. Mix occasionally. This can be made 2 to 3 days in advance and stored at room temperature.

6 To serve, whisk the cream and use a silicone spatula to scoop up the cream and spread in the baked crust. Smooth the top. Place the fruit on top as close to serving time as possible.

Fresh Fruit Tart with a Chocolate Crust

8 SLICES

STORAGE

Store in the refrigerator up to one day.

You can get as creative as you want and use kiwi slices, blueberries, or mango slices instead of or in addition to the raspberries and strawberries. This tart is fragile—it really must be eaten within a few hours of assembly and does not hold up well the next day.

CHOCOLATE CRUST

¾ cup all-purpose flour, plus extra for sprinkling

¼ cup parve unsweetened cocoa

⅔ cup confectioners' sugar

½ cup (1 stick) parve margarine placed in the freezer for 30 minutes, cut into 10 pieces, plus extra for greasing pan

PASTRY CREAM

1 cup parve plain soy milk

½ vanilla bean, split and scraped, or 1 teaspoon vanilla extract

5 tablespoons sugar

2 tablespoons parve margarine

4 large egg yolks

3 tablespoons flour, sifted after measuring

---

8 ounces fresh raspberries

8 ounces fresh strawberries

1 To make the crust: Place the flour, cocoa, and confectioners' sugar into the bowl of a food processor fitted with a metal blade. Process a few seconds to mix. Add the margarine pieces and process until the mixture comes together. You can make by hand by cutting the margarine into the dry ingredients with two knives or a pastry cutter and then squeezing with your hands until the dough comes together. Gather into a ball, flatten and wrap in plastic. Place in the freezer for 20 minutes or overnight in the refrigerator.

2 Preheat the oven to 350°F. Remove dough from the freezer or refrigerator and let sit just until it softens a little so it can be rolled. Grease an 8-inch tart ring, with or without a removable bottom, with a little margarine and place on parchment on a cookie sheet. Place a large piece of plastic wrap on the counter and sprinkle with flour. Place the dough on top, sprinkle with some more flour and cover with a piece of parchment. Roll on top of the parchment to roll out the dough until it is at least 1 inch larger than the tart ring. You will want to peel back the parchment and sprinkle some more flour on the dough 2 to 3 times while you are rolling.

3 Place your hand under the plastic, lift the dough, and turn over into the tart ring, using your fingers to gently press the dough into the corners. Remove plastic and use a rolling pin to roll over the top to trim off the excess dough.

4 Freeze 10 minutes. Line ring with foil or parchment and fill with beans or pie weights. Bake for 20 minutes. Lift up the edges of the foil or parchment to remove it and the weights and bake the shell another 5 minutes. This can be made in advance and frozen, wrapped in plastic.

5   To make the pastry cream: In a heavy saucepan, bring the soy milk, scraped seeds and vanilla bean or vanilla extract, margarine, and 2 tablespoons of the sugar to boil. Meanwhile, use a whisk to beat the egg yolks and the remaining sugar in a medium bowl. Add the flour and use a silicone spatula to gently mix into the eggs. Strain half the soy milk mixture into the egg bowl and whisk. Strain the other half of the soy milk mixture into the egg mixture and mix well.

6   Return mixture to the saucepan and cook on low heat for 2 minutes, whisking constantly. You will need a silicone spatula to mix the cream in the corners of the pot so it does not burn. Remove from heat and place in a bowl. Let sit 5 minutes and then cover with plastic and place in the refrigerator until chilled, 4 hours or overnight. To use sooner, place the bowl of pastry cream over a larger bowl filled with ice and a little water (below the level of the bowl with the cream) for 15 to 20 minutes, or until cream is chilled. Mix occasionally. This can be made 2 to 3 days in advance and stored at room temperature.

7   To assemble the tart, whisk the pastry cream until smooth and then use a silicone spatula to spread evenly in the bottom of the chocolate tart shell. Clean and dry the strawberries and slice thinly. Place the larger strawberry pieces in a circle just inside the tart ring. Add a row of raspberries and keep alternating until you have covered the cream. Serve within 4 hours.

Salted Chocolate Caramel Tartlets

MAKES EIGHT 3-INCH TARTLETS

STORAGE

Store in the refrigerator for up to five days.

When I went to a food writers' conference in 2008, there was someone there promoting different flavors of salt to flavor both savory and sweet dishes. I had never seen so many colors and textures of salt. He even sent some samples to the participants after the conference. In this dessert, the salt helps balance the very sweet caramel.

SWEET DOUGH CRUST

1 cup all-purpose flour, plus extra for sprinkling

⅔ cup confectioners' sugar

5 tablespoons parve margarine, frozen for 30 minutes and then
    cut into tablespoons, plus extra for greasing pans

1 large egg yolk

2 tablespoons cold water

¼ teaspoon pure vanilla extract

CARAMEL FILLING

¾ cup sugar

¼ cup parve whipping cream

3 tablespoons parve margarine

¼ teaspoon salt

¼ teaspoon pure vanilla extract

CHOCOLATE TOP

2 ounces parve bittersweet or semisweet chocolate, chopped into
    very small pieces

½ cup parve whipping cream

1 teaspoon coarse salt

1   To make the crust: Place the flour, confectioners' sugar, and margarine in the bowl of a food processor fitted with a metal blade. Process for 10 seconds, or until the mixture resembles sand. You can do this by hand by cutting the margarine into the dry ingredients using two knives or a pastry cutter. Add the egg yolk, cold water, and vanilla and process or hand mix with a silicone spatula or wooden spoon until the dough comes together into a ball. Place the dough on a large piece of plastic wrap. Gather into a ball, cover with the plastic, and then flatten. Chill 1 hour in the freezer or overnight in the refrigerator.

2   Preheat the oven to 350°F. Grease eight 3-inch tart pans with a little margarine and place close to each other on parchment on a cookie sheet.

3   Remove the dough from the freezer or refrigerator and let sit at room temperature just until you can press it gently. Place a large piece of plastic wrap on the counter and sprinkle with flour. Place the dough on top, sprinkle with some more flour and cover with a piece of parchment. Roll on top of the parchment to roll out the

dough until it is about ¼-inch thick. The dough needs to be large enough to cover all the tart pans. You will want to peel back the parchment and sprinkle some more flour on the dough 2 to 3 times while you are rolling.

4   Peel off the parchment, place your hand under the plastic wrap, lift up the dough, and turn it over on top of the tart pans. Use your fingers to press the dough into the pans. Remove the plastic wrap and use your fingers to gently press the dough into the corners of the pans. If you have any holes, just take pieces of dough and patch them up. Roll the rolling pin over the top of the tart pans to trim off the dough and remove the excess dough. Once again, make sure the dough is in the corners of the pans. Prick the dough with a fork all over. Freeze 10 minutes.

5   Line each tart pan with a piece of foil about an inch large than the pan and fill with dried beans or pie weights. Bake for 20 minutes. Remove foil and bake another 8 to 10 minutes, or until the dough begins to brown in the center. Let cool. These crusts can be made up to 4 days in advance and stored in an airtight container at room temperature or stored longer in the freezer.

6   To make the caramel filling: Place the sugar in a heavy saucepan over medium-low heat. Stir to dissolve the sugar. When it is melted, turn the heat to high to boil until the caramel turns golden and all the sugar clumps have dissolved, stirring often.

7   Meanwhile heat the cream until hot, not boiling. Remove the saucepan with the sugar from the heat and add the cream, margarine, salt, and vanilla and whisk together; the mixture will boil up. Return to heat and cook for 5 minutes on medium-low heat, whisking often. Place in a bowl and place in the refrigerator for 1 hour, whisking every 15 minutes.

8   Place a tablespoon of caramel filling into each tart shell and place in the refrigerator for 1 hour.

9   To make the chocolate top: Place the chopped chocolate in a bowl. Boil the cream and then pour over the chocolate. Let sit 30 seconds and whisk until smooth. Spoon a tablespoon of chocolate over the caramel in each tart, tilting to cover the caramel, but not the crust. Place back into the refrigerator for 10 minutes. To serve, sprinkle a little salt over the chocolate.

Mini Lemon or Lime Tarts

MAKES THIRTY 1- TO 1½-INCH TARTS

STORAGE

The tart shells may be stored in an airtight container at room temperature for four days or frozen up to three months. Store the filled tarts in the refrigerator for up to one day.

You will need 60 mini tart pans, 1 to 1½ inches wide, to make these. You can decorate the tops with any fruit. Assemble as close as you can to serving.

SWEET DOUGH CRUST

1 cup all-purpose flour, plus extra for sprinkling

⅔ cup confectioners' sugar

5 tablespoons parve margarine, frozen for 30 minutes and then
    cut into tablespoons, plus extra for greasing pans

1 large egg yolk

2 tablespoons cold water

¼ teaspoon pure vanilla extract

LEMON OR LIME CREAM

3 large eggs plus 2 egg yolks

1 cup sugar

Zest (grated outer peel) of 1 lemon or lime

5 tablespoons fresh lemon juice (3 lemons) or lime juice (5 limes)

5½ tablespoons parve margarine

Thin slices of lemon or lime, thin strips of lemon or lime peel,
    or fresh berries, for decoration

1 To make the crust: Place the flour, confectioners' sugar, and margarine in the bowl of a food processor fitted with a metal blade. Process for 10 seconds, or until the mixture resembles sand. You can do this by hand by cutting the margarine into the dry ingredients using two knives or a pastry cutter. Add the egg yolk, cold water, and vanilla and process or hand mix with a silicone spatula or wooden spoon until the dough comes together into a ball. Place the dough on a large piece of plastic wrap. Gather into a ball, cover with the plastic, and then

flatten. Chill 1 hour in the freezer or overnight in the refrigerator.

2 To make the lemon or lime cream: Place the eggs, yolks, and sugar in a heatproof bowl and set over a medium saucepan with simmering water (or use a double boiler). Add the lemon or lime juice and zest to the bowl and whisk. Cook the curd, uncovered, whisking occasionally until a thick mixture is formed. This takes approximately 25 minutes. Be patient and do not stir too much. Don't leave the whisk in the bowl with the lemon or lime mixture while it cooks; it may get too hot to touch. If the water in the saucepan boils too fast, turn down the heat.

3 Remove bowl from the heat and whisk in the margarine a tablespoon at a time. Cool for 10 minutes and then cover with plastic and refrigerate 8 hours or overnight. To use that day, place the bowl of cream over a larger bowl filled with ice and a little water (below the level of the cream bowl) for 15 to 20 minutes until cream is chilled. Mix occasionally.

4 Preheat the oven to 425°F. Grease 30 mini tart pans (1 to 1½ inches wide) with some margarine and place on a parchment-covered cookie sheet, close together.

5 Remove the dough from the freezer or refrigerator and let sit at room temperature just until you can press it gently. Place a large piece of plastic wrap on the counter and sprinkle with flour. Place the dough on top, sprinkle with some more flour and cover with a piece of parchment. Roll on top of the parchment to roll out the dough until it is about ¼-inch thick. The dough needs to be large enough to cover all the tart pans. You will want to peel back the parchment and sprinkle some more flour on the dough 2 to 3 times while you are rolling.

6 Peel off the top parchment, place your hand under the plastic wrap, lift up the dough, and turn it over on top of the tart pans. If there is dough not covering a pan and pans that do not have dough, place the empty pans under the extra dough.

7 Remove plastic wrap. Break off a small piece of dough that does not cover a pan and roll into a small ball. Dip the ball in flour and then use it to press the dough into the bottoms of the tart pans. Use more flour if the ball sticks to the dough. Roll your rolling pin over the tops of the tart pans. Remove excess dough and re-roll

as necessary to fill the 30 pans. Place another tart pan (ungreased) on top of each dough-lined pan and press gently.

8   Bake for 10 minutes. Let cool and carefully remove shells from pans, using your fingernail or the tip of a small sharp knife. Store in an airtight container. These may be made in advance and frozen.

9   To serve, use a pastry bag or a small spoon to place some cream into the tart shells. Garnish each with a slice of fresh lemon or lime, a berry or two, or pieces of lemon or lime zest. Serve within 4 hours.

MINI FRUIT TARTS

Complete Step 1 on page 218, for the Mini Lemon or Lime Tarts. Make one recipe of Pastry Cream (page 213), following Steps 5 and 6 on page 215. Complete Steps 4 through 8 for the Mini Lemon or Lime Tarts. To serve, use a pastry bag or small spoon to place some of the pastry cream inside each shell. Decorate with strawberries, raspberries, blackberries, kiwi, or mango pieces.

Apple Strudel

MAKES 4 ROLLS, 20 SERVINGS

STORAGE

Store in the refrigerator for up to four days.

This is the classic Jewish dessert made easy by the use of store-bought filo dough. You can dress it up by placing sauce on individual serving plates and then the slice of strudel. Try Cinnamon Crème Anglaise (page 296) or Caramel Sauce (page 295).

Juice of 1 lemon

7 Red Delicious apples

5 tablespoons sugar

1 teaspoon ground cinnamon

⅓ cup challah bread crumbs (see page 222), plain bread crumbs, or ground almonds

1 package filo dough, thawed according to package
    directions

½ cup (1 stick) parve margarine, melted

⅓ cup chopped nuts or raisins/currants (optional)

1 Preheat the oven to 350°F. Line a large jelly roll pan with parchment. Place the lemon juice in a bowl. Peel and core the apples. Chop them into 1-inch pieces and add to lemon juice. Add sugar, cinnamon, bread crumbs or ground almonds, and the optional nuts, raisins, or currants and toss lightly.

2 To make the strudel: Have ready a clean, damp (not dripping) kitchen towel. Place a piece of parchment the size of your baking pan on the counter. Take the filo out of its package and unroll. Separate one sheet and place on top of the parchment. Use a pastry brush to brush the filo sheet with the melted margarine. Place a second sheet on top and brush with more margarine. Repeat with 2 more sheets. Cover the remaining filo with the damp towel.

3 Place one-fourth of the filling along one long end of the filo, 2 inches from the edge. Fold the right and left sides (the short sides) in 1 inch. Starting from the side with the filling, roll up tightly until you have a long log. Place on the prepared pan. Repeat with additional filo dough and the rest of the filling to make three more logs.

4 Bake for 40 minutes or until filo looks crisp. Strudel is best served warm. You can refrigerate overnight and warm in a low 225°F oven for 30 minutes.

Molten Chocolate Cakes

MAKES 12 INDIVIDUAL CAKES

STORAGE

Store covered in the refrigerator for up to five days.

Molten chocolate cakes generally need to be eaten soon after they are taken out of the molds, which I initially thought would make them a bad choice to serve on Shabbat. One time when I made them, I had some left over and ate them a few hours after they were baked. Although the center was not as "molten," they were still gooey inside.

½ cup (1 stick) parve margarine

½ cup plus 1 tablespoon all-purpose flour

1 tablespoon parve unsweetened cocoa

7 ounces parve semisweet or bittersweet chocolate, chopped or
   broken into 1-inch pieces

2 large eggs plus 2 yolks

½ cup sugar

1 You will need twelve 3-inch fluted molds or small ramekins. Melt 1 tablespoon of the margarine and use a pastry brush to brush the inside of the 12 molds. Combine the 1 tablespoon of flour with the cocoa in a shallow bowl. Holding a mold over the bowl, spoon about 1 tablespoon of the flour and cocoa mixture into the mold. Tilt the mold all around and shake to cover all the sides. Tap the extra flour and cocoa back into the bowl. Repeat with the other 11 molds and place them on a jelly roll pan.

2 Place the chocolate and the remaining margarine in a heatproof bowl over boiling water to melt (or use a double boiler). While the chocolate and margarine are melting, mix the eggs, egg yolks, and sugar in a large bowl with an electric mixer on low speed until combined. Turn the speed up to high and beat for 5 minutes.

The mixture will look creamy. Add the remaining ½ cup of flour and beat on low speed until just combined. Gently whisk in the melted chocolate and margarine mixture until combined.

3 Divide the batter among the prepared molds, about ⅓ cup for each mold. Place in the refrigerator for ½ hour or up to 4 hours.

4 Preheat the oven to 350°F. Bake for 9 to 10 minutes; you just want the edges to look set; the center can still look unbaked. Let rest for 1 minute. Run a knife around the sides, and then turn over onto a plate to serve. Serve immediately, if possible.

Chocolate Peanut Butter Mousse Cakes

SERVES 16

STORAGE

Store covered in the freezer for up to three months.

This is a frozen, no-bake dessert that tastes like a candy bar. I put salted peanuts into the chocolate crust to give the dessert some crunch and balance the sweetness of the mousse. I use regular pre-sweetened and salted creamy peanut butter, not the natural kind. If you use the natural kind, add an additional 2 teaspoons of sugar to the egg whites.

CHOCOLATE PEANUT BOTTOM

2 tablespoons parve margarine, plus extra for greasing pan

10 ounces parve semisweet or bittersweet chocolate, chopped or
    broken into 1-inch pieces

⅔ cup parve plain soy milk

1 teaspoon pure vanilla extract

1 cup shelled, roasted and salted peanuts, chopped into ¼-inch pieces,
    plus 16 peanut halves for decoration

PEANUT BUTTER MOUSSE

¾ cup creamy peanut butter

⅓ cup boiling water

4 large eggs, separated

2 teaspoons sugar

¼ cup parve whipping cream

1 Take an 8-inch square baking pan, trace the bottom onto a piece of parchment, and cut out the square. Grease the pan, place the parchment square over the bottom, and grease again.

2 Melt the chocolate either on the stovetop or in the microwave, following the "Melting chocolate" instructions (see Foolproof Tips and Techniques).

3 Place the melted chocolate in a medium bowl. Heat the soy milk until hot, not boiling, and add to the melted chocolate in four parts, stirring well to incorporate the soy milk each time. Add the margarine and vanilla and whisk well. Add the chopped nuts and stir. Spread into the bottom of the prepared pan and smooth the top. Place in the freezer for a minimum of 10 minutes.

4 To make the peanut butter mousse: Place the peanut butter in a medium bowl. Add the boiling water, a little at a time, and whisk to dissolve the peanut butter. It will get very thick and then thin out as you add more water. Add the egg yolks and whisk well. In a separate bowl, beat the egg whites until stiff with an electric mixer on high speed. Turn the speed down to low, add the sugar, and then turn the speed up to high for 30 seconds. Add the beaten egg whites to the peanut-butter mixture and use a whisk to gently mix in.

5 In a small bowl with an electric mixer on high speed, whip the cream until stiff and add to peanut butter mixture. Whisk until smooth. Remove the chocolate bottom from the freezer. Scoop the mousse on top of the chocolate and use a silicone spatula to smooth the top. Cover with plastic wrap and freeze for a minimum of 2 hours.

6 To serve, remove from the freezer and let sit for 5 minutes at room temperature. Use a large heated knife to cut into 1 x 4-inch bars. I use a metal flat-blade spatula to lift them out and serve on individual plates. Place a peanut half or two on top of each bar.

Chocolate Crêpes

MAKES ABOUT SIXTEEN 7-INCH CRÊPES

STORAGE

*Cover the stack of crêpes with plastic and store in the refrigerator for
up to three days.*

Don't be afraid of this recipe. I taught my daughter Emily's French class to make them in
eighth grade and the kids made perfect crêpes. To serve them on Shabbat, fill with chocolate and fold the crêpes in advance and place them on a cookie sheet. Warm in a low
225°F oven. When you are planning a meal that includes this dessert and also includes
kids, do not use your favorite white tablecloth. It is very messy.

CRÊPE BATTER

3 tablespoons margarine
1 cup all-purpose flour
¼ teaspoon salt
3 tablespoons sugar
3 large eggs
2 tablespoons canola or vegetable oil
2 teaspoons pure vanilla extract
1¼ cups parve plain soy milk
¾ cup parve whipping cream

1 tablespoon margarine, melted, for frying crêpes
5 ounces parve semisweet chocolate, chopped or broken
    into 1-inch pieces
Sliced strawberries and/or other berries (optional)

1 Heat the 3 tablespoons margarine in a heatproof bowl in the microwave for
   30 seconds, or until melted. In a large bowl, whisk together the flour, salt, sugar,
   eggs, oil, vanilla, soy milk, whipping cream, and melted margarine. Use a sieve
   to strain the mixture into another bowl, whisking to get as much batter through the
   sieve as you can, and discard the gloppy stuff in the strainer. Cover the bowl and
   place in the refrigerator for a minimum of 2 hours or overnight.

2 When you're ready to make the crêpes, have the following out and in easy reach: a pie plate to hold the cooked crêpes; an 8-inch crêpe pan or small non-stick frying pan; parchment or waxed paper torn into 16 pieces about the size of your crêpe pan or small frying pan; and a long, silicone or metal flat-blade spatula. Whisk the crêpe batter.

3 Heat the crêpe pan or frying pan over medium-high heat. Brush some of the melted margarine around the pan. When the pan is hot, use an oven mitt to lift the pan off the stove and with your other hand scoop up about ¼ cup of the batter and pour into the top center of the pan, turning the pan clockwise 3 times to spread the batter so it evenly covers the bottom of the pan. Sometimes you may need to add a little more batter to cover the bottom or fill in holes. (By the third crêpe, you will know just how much batter covers the pan.) Return to the heat.

4 Cook for 1 minute, or until the edges of the crêpe are brown. The cooking time varies depending on how thick each crêpe is. Use a spatula to separate the edges from the pan and then lift up the crêpe and turn it over. Cook on the other side for 15 seconds and then flip onto the pie plate. If the crêpes are browning too quickly, turn down the heat. I usually turn down the heat after about 5 crêpes because the pan gets too hot. Set the cooked crêpes aside in the pie plate and place a piece of parchment or waxed paper between each crêpe. Brush the pan with more melted margarine every 3 to 4 crêpes.

5 Melt the chocolate either on the stovetop or in the microwave, following the "Melting chocolate" instructions (see Foolproof Tips and Techniques). Whisk until smooth.

6 To serve, place some melted chocolate in the center of a crêpe, fold the right and left sides in and drizzle some more chocolate on top. You can also add any fruit inside or on top of the crêpes.

Chocolate, Pistachio, & Raspberry Filo Packages

SERVES 10

STORAGE

Store in the refrigerator for up to two days.

About nineteen years ago, the weekend Andy and I got engaged, we had a great meal that featured a dessert like this. It stuck in my head for this long until I figured out how to make the pistachio part. You can serve this with Raspberry Sauce (page 294). This reheats well in a low oven.

½ cup whole, shelled, unsalted pistachio nuts, brown skin rubbed off (about ⅓ pound of nuts in their shells)

½ cup sugar

1 large egg white

1 package filo dough, thawed according to package directions

1 cup fresh raspberries

6 ounces parve chocolate chips

Spray oil, for spraying filo dough

2 teaspoons confectioners' sugar, for sprinkling

1 Preheat the oven to 375°F. Place the pistachio nuts in the bowl of a food processor fitted with a metal blade. Process until nuts are completely ground. Add sugar and process 30 seconds more. Add egg white and process until combined. Place in a small bowl and set aside, covered. This can be made 3 days in advance and stored in the refrigerator.

2 Line a cookie sheet with parchment.

3 Open up the package of filo dough and unroll with the longer side facing you. Cut the stack of sheets in half so you have 2 squares. Place 1 square on the counter and spray with the oil. Add a second sheet and spray again.

Add a third and spray. Place 1 tablespoon of the pistachio paste in the center of the square, 5 raspberries next to the pistachio paste, and then 2 tablespoons of chocolate chips next to the raspberries and pistachio paste. You will see 3 separate piles.

4   Grab the corners of the filo together with one hand and then with your other hand squeeze tightly around the top, shaping the filo into a beggar's purse. Twist the top gently. Repeat with the other squares of filo until you have 10 packages. Place packages on a parchment-covered baking sheet.

5   Lightly grease the outside of the packages with the spray oil and sprinkle with a little confectioners' sugar. Bake for 20 minutes, or until the filo is lightly browned. Serve warm. These can be reheated in a low 225°F oven for 20 minutes.

Profiteroles

STORAGE

Store covered in the freezer for up to three months.

Profiteroles are éclair puffs filled with ice cream and drizzled with chocolate sauce. You can assemble them before Shabbat and place them in the freezer.

CHOUX PASTRY DOUGH

½ cup parve plain soy milk

½ cup water

½ cup (1 stick) margarine, cut into 8 pieces

¼ teaspoon salt

1 cup all-purpose flour, sifted after measuring

6 large eggs, divided

SHINY CHOCOLATE SAUCE

1 cup water

1⅓ cups sugar

6 ounces parve semisweet or bittersweet chocolate, chopped or
   broken into 1-inch pieces

---

1 pint parve vanilla or other flavor ice cream

---

1 Preheat the oven to 475°F. Line 2 cookie sheets with parchment.

2 To make the choux pastry dough: In a medium saucepan, bring the soy milk, water, margarine, and salt to a boil over medium-low heat. Remove from the heat and, with a wooden spoon, mix in the sifted flour. Place the pan over low heat and cook for 1 minute more, stirring constantly to dry out the dough. Remove from the heat.

3 Place the dough in a bowl and add the 5 eggs, one at a time, mixing thoroughly after the addition of each egg. You will need to mix vigorously to completely incorporate the egg into the dough.

4 Place the dough in a pastry bag with a ½-inch round tip and pipe out circles of dough, about 2 inches in diameter, onto the parchment-lined cookie sheets, leaving an inch between each circle. It's easiest to hold the pastry bag vertically, tip down, squeezing slowly until you have the size you want, then lifting up the tip.

5 Beat the remaining egg in a small bowl. Brush the top and sides of each circle with the beaten egg and smooth out the little tip on the top.

6 Place the cookie sheets in the oven and immediately turn off the oven. After 15 minutes, turn the oven on again to 350°F. Bake the pastries for another 30 to 40 minutes, or until the cracks on the top are the same color as the rest of the pastry. Remove to rack and let cool. If you are filling the pastries that day, leave uncovered on the cookie sheet. If you do not plan to fill them that day, store in an airtight container at room temperature.

7 While the pastries are baking, make the chocolate sauce. To make this sauce, you will first make a simple sugar syrup. Place the water and sugar in a small heavy saucepan over medium heat. Stir to dissolve the sugar and bring to a rolling boil. Remove from the heat. This can be made 2 to 3 days in advance and stored at room temperature.

8 Melt the chocolate either on the stovetop or in the microwave, following the "Melting chocolate" instructions (see Foolproof Tips and Techniques). Whisk until smooth. Add the sugar syrup a tablespoon at a time and whisk until you get a consistency you can drizzle. If the sauce starts to harden, just add a little more sugar syrup and whisk until you get a thick, pourable consistency. Store the sauce covered at room temperature and reheat in a microwave and whisk when needed.

9 To serve, lift the top of the pastry part way off, leaving some part attached, spoon some ice cream in the middle, and then drizzle the top with the chocolate sauce. I usually serve three per plate.

Éclair Puffs with Caramel Sauce

MAKES 40 PUFFS, 10 SERVINGS

STORAGE

Store in the refrigerator until serving. These must be eaten within a day of assembling them.

This French birthday cake, known as *croquembouche*, consists of choux pastry puffs filled with vanilla pastry cream and dipped in caramel. It is assembled as a pyramid. To eat, just pull off the puffs and enjoy a tasty but sticky dessert.

CHOUX PASTRY

½ cup parve plain soy milk

½ cup water

½ cup (1 stick) margarine, cut into 8 pieces

¼ teaspoon salt

1 cup all-purpose flour, sifted

6 large eggs, divided

PASTRY CREAM

2 cups soy milk

1 vanilla bean, split lengthwise and scraped (reserve seeds),
  or 2 teaspoons vanilla extract

10 tablespoons sugar

4 tablespoons parve margarine

6 large egg yolks

7 tablespoons all-purpose flour, sifted after measuring

CARAMEL SAUCE

1 cup sugar

1 cup boiling water

1　Preheat the oven to 475°F. Line 2 cookie sheets with parchment.

2　To make the choux pastry dough: Place the soy milk, water, margarine, and salt in a medium saucepan and bring to a boil over medium-low heat. Remove from the heat and, with a wooden spoon, mix in the sifted flour. Place the pan over low heat and cook for 1 minute more, stirring constantly to dry out the dough. Remove from the heat.

3　Place the dough in a bowl and add 5 of the eggs, one at a time, mixing thoroughly after the addition of each egg. You will need to mix vigorously to completely incorporate the eggs into the dough.

4　Place the dough in a pastry bag with a ½-inch round tip and pipe out circles of dough, about 1½ inches in diameter, onto the prepared cookie sheets, leaving an inch between each one. It's easiest to hold the pastry bag vertically, tip down, squeezing slowly until you have the size you want, then lifting up the tip.

5　Beat the remaining egg in a small bowl. Brush the top and sides of each circle with the beaten egg and smooth out the little tip on the top.

6　Place the baking sheets in the oven and immediately turn off the oven. After

15 minutes, turn the oven on again to 350°F. Bake the pastries another 30 to 40 minutes, or until the cracks on the top are the same color as the rest of the pastry. Remove to a rack and let cool. If you are filling the pastries that day, leave uncovered on the cookie sheet. If you do not plan to fill them that day, store in an airtight container at room temperature for up to 2 days.

7   To make the pastry cream: In a heavy saucepan, bring the soy milk, scraped seeds and vanilla bean or vanilla extract, margarine, and 4 tablespoons of the sugar to boil. Meanwhile, use a whisk to beat the egg yolks and the remaining sugar in a medium bowl. Add the flour and use a silicone spatula to gently mix into the eggs. Strain half the soy milk mixture into the egg bowl and whisk. Strain the other half of the soy milk into the eggs and mix well.

8   Return mixture to the saucepan and cook on low heat for 2 minutes, whisking constantly. You will need a silicone spatula to mix the cream in the corners of the pot so it does not burn. Remove from heat and place in a bowl. Let sit 5 minutes and then cover with plastic and place in refrigerator until chilled, 4 hours or overnight. To use sooner, place the bowl of pastry cream over a larger bowl filled with ice and a little water (below the level of the bowl with the cream) for 15 to 20 minutes, or until cream is chilled. Mix occasionally.

9   Meanwhile, make the caramel sauce. Place the sugar in a heavy-bottomed saucepan over medium heat and cook, stirring often, until all of the sugar has melted and you have a deep amber-colored syrup. Remove from the heat and carefully add the boiling water. The mixture will boil up and you will see some balls of caramel in the pot. Return the pan to medium heat and cook at a rolling boil for 10 minutes. Stir often until all of the caramel pieces have melted and you have a smooth syrup. Let cool, cover with plastic, and store at room temperature. This can be made 3 days in advance.

10   Place the pastry cream in a pastry bag with a small round-tipped nozzle, about ¼-inch wide. Using the tip of the pastry bag, poke a hole in the center of the bottom of each puff and then squeeze in some cream until you feel the pastry get heavier or the cream starts coming out of the hole.

11   When you have filled all the puffs, dip the bottoms in the caramel sauce and place them on a dinner plate in concentric circles, covering the plate. When you have 1 layer, drizzle some caramel sauce on the tops of the puffs. Create the second layer, one circle smaller than the first. Drizzle the tops and repeat until you have a pyramid of puffs and caramel.

Strawberry Vanilla Verrines

MAKES 8 VERRINES

STORAGE

Store in the refrigerator for up to two days.

When I was in Paris in June 2008, every pastry shop had rows of *verrines*—individual desserts served in clear glass cups. It is basically an individual trifle, sometimes containing a cookie or cake, cream, and fruits in layers so you can see almost all of what is inside. This version is just fruit and cream—no carbs.

STRAWBERRY GEL

16 ounces fresh strawberries, washed, hulled, and halved

¼ cup sugar

2 tablespoons unflavored kosher gelatin powder

VANILLA BAVARIAN CREAM

1 cup parve plain soy milk

4 tablespoons sugar, divided

½ vanilla bean, split lengthwise and scraped (reserve seeds)

4 large egg yolks

2 tablespoons unflavored kosher gelatin powder

1¼ cups parve whipping cream

8 large mint leaves, for garnish

¼ cup additional fruit, such as raspberries or chopped mango or kiwi, for garnish (optional)

1 To make the strawberry gel: Remove 6 strawberries (12 halves) and set aside. Place the remaining strawberries in a food processor or blender and process or blend until completely puréed, scraping down the sides of the processor bowl or blender as needed. Place the strawberry purée in a small saucepan. Add the sugar and mix. Cook on medium-low heat for 3 minutes, stirring occasionally, until the sugar melts. Add the gelatin, mix, and then remove from the heat. Strain into a medium bowl and place in the refrigerator for a minimum of 1 hour or overnight.

2 To make the vanilla Bavarian cream: Place the soy milk, 2 tablespoons of the sugar, and the vanilla bean and seeds in a medium saucepan and bring to boil over medium heat. Meanwhile, in a separate medium bowl, using an electric mixer on medium speed, beat the egg yolks with the remaining 2 tablespoons of sugar. When the soy milk boils, strain half into the egg mixture and whisk well. Strain the rest into the bowl and whisk again. Pour this mixture back into the saucepan and place over low heat. Place a candy thermometer in the pan. Cook for 3 minutes, whisking constantly. When the mixture reaches 180°F, add the gelatin and whisk. Cook another 2 to 3 minutes, until the mixture reaches 200°F. It should bubble a little. Remove from the heat and pour the mixture into a bowl. Let cool, and place in the refrigerator for 4 hours or overnight, or place the bowl of cooked cream in a larger bowl filled with ice cubes and a little water, whisking occasionally, until the cream is cool to the touch.

3 Whip the cream until stiff and fold into the cooked cream.

4 To assemble the verrines, place 8 short drinking or brandy glasses on a jelly roll pan. Spoon or ladle the vanilla cream into each glass until about half full, using about three-fourths of the cream; you will not use up all the cream. Place the glasses in the refrigerator for 20 minutes.

5 Spoon about 2 tablespoons of the strawberry gel over the vanilla cream in each glass, as evenly as you can, to create an even red stripe. Place back in the refrigerator for another 20 minutes.

6 Remove from refrigerator and spoon more vanilla cream on top of the strawberry gel to create a small white stripe. Return to the refrigerator.

7 To serve, cut the remaining strawberries and any other fruit you'd like to use and place on top of the vanilla cream in each glass.

8 Cut the mint leaves into thin strips. Sprinkle on top of the fruit. Verrines may be made a day in advance and stored in the refrigerator.

Chocolate Mousse

SERVES 12 TO 15

STORAGE

Store covered in the refrigerator up to three days.

This recipe makes a big bowl of mousse. To divide the recipe in half, use 5 egg yolks. You will notice that the raw yolks are not actually cooked, but they are added to hot, melted chocolate. I have eaten this safely for over ten years, but you should caution pregnant women who may be more worried about eating uncooked eggs.

1 pound parve bittersweet chocolate, chopped or broken
   into 1-inch pieces
4½ cups parve whipping cream, divided
6 tablespoons sugar
9 large egg yolks

1 Melt the chocolate either on the stovetop or in the microwave, following the "Melting chocolate" instructions (see Foolproof Tips and Techniques).

2 While the chocolate is melting, heat ½ cup of the whipping cream and the sugar in a small saucepan on medium heat, stirring often, until the sugar melts and the cream starts to boil. You can also heat the cream and sugar in the microwave in a glass measuring cup until the sugar is dissolved, about 1 minute. Don't worry if the cream starts to looks gloppy.

3 When the chocolate is melted, whisk in the cream and sugar mixture until smooth. Add the egg yolks, one at a time, and whisk well until the mixture is very smooth.

4 Whip the remaining 4 cups of whipping cream with an electric mixer on high speed. Watch carefully and stop mixing when you see the top of the whipped cream forming ribbons or swirls.

5 Add one-third of the whipped cream to the chocolate mixture and whisk until well blended. Pour the chocolate into the bowl with the rest of the whipped cream and mix with an electric mixer on low speed until the chocolate and cream are combined. Pour into a serving bowl, cover with plastic and chill 8 hours or overnight. I like to serve the mousse with a bowl of mixed berries. For a buffet, I will decorate the top of the mousse by melting 3 to 4 ounces of chocolate and drizzling it on top of the mousse in the serving bowl.

◇ Strawberry Mousse

SERVES 8

STORAGE

Store covered in the refrigerator for up to three days.

I like to serve this in individual ramekins. You could also use wine or martini glasses.

16 ounces fresh strawberries

1 teaspoon rum or cognac

2 teaspoons confectioners' sugar

Juice of 1 lemon

6 tablespoons sugar

2 tablespoons unflavored kosher gelatin powder

1 cup parve whipping cream

1 Remove the stems from the strawberries. Select 6 strawberries, slice thinly, and place in a small bowl with the rum and confectioners' sugar. Mix to combine and then place in the refrigerator.

2 Cut the remaining strawberries in half and place in a blender or food processor fitted with a metal blade. Purée the strawberries completely, scraping down the sides of the processor bowl or blender so that all the strawberry pieces are puréed.

3 Place the strawberry purée in a small saucepan. Add the lemon juice and sugar and stir. Cook on medium-low heat for 5 minutes, stirring occasionally, until the sugar melts. Add the gelatin, whisk, and then remove from the heat. Strain into a medium bowl, pressing hard to get as much strawberry purée through as possible, and place in the refrigerator for 20 minutes, stirring twice during that time.

4 In a large bowl with an electric mixer on high speed, whip the whipping cream until stiff. Remove the strawberry purée from the refrigerator and fold in the whipped cream in four parts. Scoop the mousse evenly into the ramekins and smooth the tops with the back of a spoon. Cover with plastic and place in the refrigerator for at least 3 hours or overnight.

5 To serve, remove from the refrigerator and place a few of the rum-soaked strawberry slices on top.

Rice Pudding

SERVES 10

STORAGE

Store covered in the refrigerator for up to four days.

My grandmother made a delicious, creamy, albeit dairy, rice pudding that I can still remember from my childhood. Her recipe is the inspiration for mine, minus her addition of golden raisins, which I omitted.

1 cup long-grained white rice

2 cups water

3½ cups parve rice milk

½ cup parve whipping cream

1 cup light brown sugar

1 teaspoon pure vanilla extract

2 large egg yolks

½ teaspoon, or more, ground cinnamon, for sprinkling on top

1 Place the rice and water in a small saucepan, bring to a boil, and then simmer at medium-low heat, uncovered, for 15 minutes.

2 In a separate, larger, heavy saucepan, place the rice milk, whipping cream, brown sugar, and vanilla and bring to a simmer over medium-low heat, stirring to dissolve the sugar.

3 When the rice is cooked, transfer the rice to the pan with the rice milk mixture. Cook uncovered on medium-low heat for 25 minutes, stirring often. You want the mixture to bubble while it cooks.

4 Beat the egg yolks with a whisk in a separate bowl. Scoop up about 1 cup of the rice mixture and, using a silicone spatula, mix into the eggs. Pour this egg and rice mixture back into the saucepan with the rest of the rice and cook another 15 minutes on medium heat, stirring occasionally, until creamy.

5 Scoop into a serving dish and then sprinkle with the cinnamon, adding more if desired. Chill 4 hours and serve cold.

Vanilla Flan

SERVES 12

STORAGE

Store in the refrigerator for up to three days.

I had tried to bake this several times and could not achieve the right creamy texture. Then I went to Israel for Passover and ate delicious kosher for Passover flan at Danielle Lefkowitz's bat mitzvah at the Har Zion Hotel in Jerusalem. I was amazed because they could not even use soy milk on Passover. They used a non-dairy cream that behaves like milk that we do not have in the United States. I was inspired to try again and finally, success.

1¼ cups sugar, divided

½ vanilla bean, split lengthwise and scraped (reserve seeds)

2½ cups parve plain soy milk

½ cup parve whipping cream

½ teaspoon pure vanilla extract

4 large whole eggs plus 1 yolk

1 Preheat the oven to 325°F. Place an 8-inch soufflé dish in the oven to warm. Place ¾ cup of the sugar in a heavy saucepan on medium heat. When the sugar starts to melt, stir occasionally until the sugar becomes an amber caramel and starts to thicken. Remove from the stove. Use oven mitts to remove the soufflé dish from the oven and pour in the caramel, using oven mitts to hold the dish and tilt it so the caramel coats the bottom and the sides. Set aside.

2 Place the vanilla seeds and bean in a medium saucepan. Add the soy milk, whipping cream, and vanilla extract and set over medium heat. When the mixture is hot, but not yet boiling, remove from the heat.

3 Place the eggs and yolk and remaining ½ cup sugar in a bowl and beat with an electric mixer on medium-high speed or whisk for 2 minutes until thick. Slowly strain the hot soy milk and cream mixture into the eggs while whisking. Discard the vanilla bean. Pour this mixture into the soufflé dish on top of the caramel.

4 Place the soufflé dish in a larger roasting pan and then add enough boiling water to reach 2 inches up the sides of the soufflé dish. To do this, place the soufflé dish in

the roasting pan in the oven and then pour boiling water into the pan; it is too hard to move the roasting pan with the hot water into the oven.

5 Bake for 1 hour. Carefully remove the soufflé dish from the hot water and let cool to room temperature. (Leave the roasting pan with water in the oven until it cools and you can remove it safely.) Cover the soufflé dish with plastic and place in the refrigerator until chilled, 8 hours or overnight.

6 To serve, run a knife along the sides of the dish, place a serving plate that has a rim on top (like a glass pie plate) on top of the dish, and then turn the flan onto the serving dish along with the caramel. Cut into wedges and serve with the caramel sauce.

Crème Brûlée

MAKES EIGHT 3- TO 4-INCH RAMEKINS

STORAGE

Store in the refrigerator for up to three days.

This recipe was one of my biggest challenges because I thought I could get the texture as creamy as the dairy version. The result is indeed creamy, but just not *as* smooth. Although you can burn the sugar topping in the oven, it comes out much better with a blowtorch, which you can buy at kitchen supply stores.

2 cups parve coffee creamer (such as Coffee Rich)

1 cup parve plain soy milk

1 whole vanilla bean, split lengthwise and scraped (reserve seeds)

3 large whole eggs plus 3 yolks

½ cup sugar

½ teaspoon cornstarch

½ cup light brown sugar

1 Preheat the oven to 350°F. In a medium saucepan, bring the coffee creamer, soy milk, vanilla seeds and bean to a boil over medium heat.

2 Meanwhile, in a medium bowl, whisk together the eggs and yolks with the sugar. Whisk vigorously.

3 When the creamer and soy milk mixture boils, strain half into the egg mixture and

whisk. Strain the remaining liquid mixture into the eggs and whisk until smooth. Add the cornstarch and whisk well. Return this mixture to the saucepan and cook over low heat for 5 minutes, whisking the entire time. The custard will thicken slightly. Use a ladle to pour the custard into the ramekins. Place the ramekins in a large baking pan with 2-inch sides, large enough to fit them all. Place the pan on the middle rack of the oven and bring over a pot of boiling water. Pour water into the larger pan to come halfway up the ramekins.

4 Bake for 1 hour. Carefully remove the ramekins from the water bath and place on a jelly roll pan. Place in the refrigerator at least 8 hours or overnight.

5 To make the hard sugar top: Place 1 tablespoon of the brown sugar on top of each custard. Use your fingers to spread the sugar as evenly as you can. Use a blowtorch to completely melt the sugar. Let sit 5 minutes to let the sugar harden. Alternatively, you can burn the sugar in the oven. Place the custards on a jelly roll or roasting pan and fill the pan with ice cubes all around the ramekins. Place under a broiler no more than 3 minutes, watching the entire time, until the top is bubbling. When I use the broiler method, I like to put the crème brûlées back in the refrigerator for at least 1 hour to firm up the custard.

Tiramisu

SERVES 12 TO 16

STORAGE

Store covered in the refrigerator for up to three days.

I am a serious coffee drinker who loves anything flavored with coffee. I don't think this book would have been possible without the major role played by the two espresso machines sitting on my kitchen counter.

2 cups brewed espresso coffee or 2 cups water plus 3 tablespoons
   instant espresso or Turkish coffee powder

4 tablespoons sugar, divided

4 large eggs, separated

1 tablespoon Marsala wine

8 ounces parve cream cheese

½ cup parve whipping cream

1½ seven-ounce packages (10 ounces total) parve ladyfinger cookies

2 teaspoons parve unsweetened cocoa

1 If you are using brewed espresso, add 2 tablespoons of the sugar to the espresso while still hot and stir to dissolve. If not, bring the 2 cups water, instant espresso or Turkish coffee powder, and 2 tablespoons of sugar to a boil in a small saucepan, stirring to dissolve the sugar. Boil for 3 minutes. Pour the hot brewed or instant coffee in a shallow bowl to cool. Set aside.

2 In a medium saucepan, place about 2 inches of water and bring to a boil, then reduce to simmer. Place the egg yolks and remaining 2 tablespoons sugar in a heatproof bowl and place over the simmering water. Using a hand-held mixer or electric whisk, beat the eggs and sugar for 2 minutes, or until the mixture becomes thick. Remove the bowl from the heat. Add the Marsala wine to the egg yolk mixture and mix for 30 seconds. Rinse the electric beaters or whisk.

3 In a separate bowl, beat the cream cheese and whipping cream with the electric mixer on low speed to combine, about 30 seconds. Turn up the speed to high for 1 minute. Add the egg mixture to the cream cheese mixture and beat for another 30 seconds. In a separate bowl, beat the egg whites until stiff. Add the beaten egg

whites to the egg yolk and cream cheese mixture in two parts and mix on low speed until combined. Set aside.

4 To assemble, you will need an 8 x 8-inch glass pan or other similar-sized serving dish. Take the ladyfinger cookies and, one at a time, dip both sides of each cookie in the coffee for 3 seconds per side. (If you dip them too long, they start to fall apart.) Place the cookies in the bottom of the serving dish to cover the entire bottom, packing them tightly next to each other. Scoop half of the cream mixture onto the cookies and spread evenly.

5 Take the cocoa and a sieve and tap 1 teaspoon of the cocoa all over the top of the cream. Add another layer of cookies dipped in coffee, packed tightly, and then another layer of cream. Smooth the top of the cream and then sift the rest of the cocoa over the cream. Cover tightly with plastic wrap and chill for 6 hours or overnight.

Challah

About Challah

Challah is the braided egg bread Jews eat on Shabbat and holidays. According to Claudia Roden's *Book of Jewish Food*, the challah as we know it today originated in the Middle Ages in southern Germany and then traveled to Poland, Eastern Europe, and Russia as Jews migrated. The tradition is to make a blessing over two challahs to remind us of the double portion of manna G-d gave the Jews on Shabbat when they wandered the desert.

The word *challah* means portion; the Jews were commanded to separate a portion of their dough to give to the priests at the Temple. To recall this, after the destruction of the Temple, rabbis commanded that Jews tear off a portion of dough before braiding and burn it (wrap in foil and place in the oven) and say a blessing.* This law, called "hafrashat challah" applies depending on how much flour is used. If one uses more than 3½ cups (all challah recipes here) you are required to break off the piece of dough but not say the blessing. If you use more than 7½ cups of flour (if you double any of these recipes), you must break off a small piece of dough and say the blessing. Traditionally, this mitzvah (commandment) given to women has, through the ages, provided a unique and auspicious opportunity to beseech G-d for anything they might need as they do this sacred act. So as you break off your piece of challah, think about praying for someone who is sick or for something important you need in your life. This mitzvah, just like the laws of keeping kosher, elevates the act of cooking and baking to a spiritual level.

Braiding Challah

This braiding method is for making three-braided challah. To braid the dough, place the three strands in front of you vertically, about 3 to 4 inches apart. Gently press the top ends together. Start at one side and pull one outside strand into the center. Take the outside strand from the other side and place that between the other two strands. Go to the other side and pull that strand into the center of the other two. You want to pull the dough a little each time to braid tightly. Keep

*Baruch atah adonoi elohainu melech haolam, asher kidshanu b'mitzvotav vitzivanu l'hafrish challah.

Blessed are you Lord our G-d, King of the universe, who has sanctified us with his commandments and commanded us to separate out the challah.

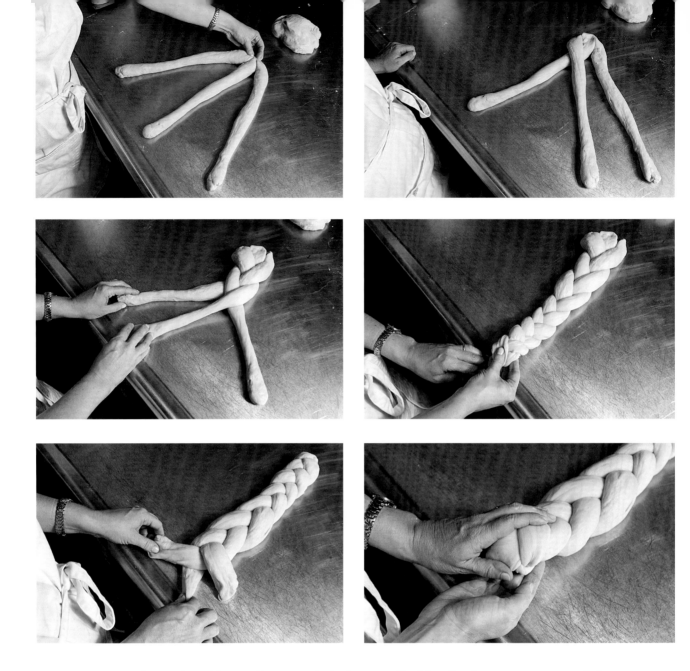

alternating sides until you reach the bottom. Braid as far down as you can and then press the ends of the strands together, tuck under the loaf, and press tightly.

Turn the loaf around. Undo the strands that you loosely pressed together when you started braiding. Now you will braid underneath: Take the outside strand that looks like it is on top of the other two and pull it under and in between the other two. Take the opposite outside strand and pull it under the other two. Repeat until you can braid no more, press the ends together and tuck underneath, pressing tightly.

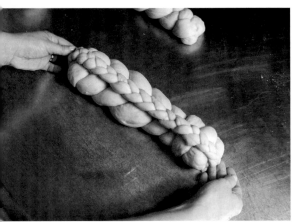

Making Challah with an Extra Braid

My friend Sue Stein suggested adding a long, thin braid on top of the three-braided challah for special occasions. Before you divide your dough into 3 parts, first break off a piece a little smaller than a tennis ball and set aside. Divide the rest of the dough into 3 equal balls and then roll strands and braid as described on page 245. Take the small piece of dough, divide into 3 and then braid a long, thin braid, about 2 feet long. Place on top of the larger challah and tuck the ends underneath. Bake on the lowest rack of the oven so the top does not burn.

Making Round Challah

The tradition is to serve round challahs on Rosh Hashanah, the New Year, to symbolize continuity. Some people knead raisins into the dough on this holiday.

To make a round challah, roll the dough into a very long strand, at least 3-feet long. Use one hand to hold one end of the strand, which will become the center, and, with your other hand, wrap the other end around the center to form a coil, pulling so that you can wrap tightly. Tuck the end into the side of the round loaf. Turn the whole loaf upside down and use your hands to press the sides to the counter. I find that round challahs hold their shape better if I make them this way. Note that round challahs bake a little longer than braided challahs because of their height and so should be placed on a low rack in the oven so the top does not burn.

Freezing Challahs

Some people like to braid the dough and then freeze it, wrapped in plastic. The loaves will need to sit at room temperature for several hours to rise before baking. I prefer to bake the challahs early in the week and freeze them baked; I simply have too many other dishes to prepare on Friday for Shabbat. A holiday coming up in a few weeks? Bake all the challahs in advance and you have one less thing to worry about baking. When freezing baked challah, I make sure they are not too brown and then wrap them in foil and freeze. I remove them from the freezer while my main course is cooking and tuck into the oven for ½ hour, wrapped in the foil. You can also warm them in a lower oven, at 250°F, for 45 minutes. I keep them wrapped as my crowd does not like the crust too hard. If you use the lower temperature, you can unwrap the challah and get a harder crust, if you like.

Challah Baking Tips

1 You may not always use all of the flour in a challah recipe. Just add until you can slide your hand across the dough. Err on the side of the dough being a little sticky rather than too dry.

2 Challahs will bake faster on darker cookie sheets, so keep an eye on them and move the cookie sheet up or down if the top or bottom of the challah starts to look too dark.

3 One way to test doneness is to put oven mitts on both hands, slide the challah out, and place top down into one hand. Take off the mitt on your free hand and tap the bottom with your fingers; if it sounds hollow, the challah is done.

4 Don't overbake the challah; many challahs taste dry because they are simply baked too long.

Classic Challah

MAKES 2 LARGE OR 3 MEDIUM BRAIDED CHALLAHS

When I started working on this chapter, I was thinking that I really just love my Classic Challah recipe, so why make anything else? After collecting and testing several recipes, I am glad I decided to include a variety of challahs. I really enjoyed tasting other challahs and my family loved the different flavors. My Classic Challah, like the other challahs in this chapter, is a three-braid challah, which I typically do in the interest of time. I learned during my research that many challah recipes have much longer rising times than my Classic Challah so it is a good choice if you have only 3 hours to spend baking challah.

½ cup plus 1 teaspoon canola or vegetable oil, divided

1 tablespoon salt

½ cup plus 2 tablespoons sugar

1 cup boiling water

½ cup cold water

½ ounce (2 envelopes) active dry yeast

1 teaspoon sugar, to activate the yeast

⅓ cup warm water

3 large eggs

7 cups bread flour

1 In a large bowl, whisk together ½ cup of the oil, the salt, and ½ cup plus 2 tablespoons of the sugar. Add the boiling water and whisk again to dissolve the salt and sugar. Add the cold water and mix again.

2 In a cup, dissolve the yeast in the warm water. Add the teaspoon of sugar and mix. Beat the eggs in a separate bowl and add to oil mixture, reserving 1 tablespoon to brush on the loaves. When the yeast bubbles, add the yeast mixture to the bowl and stir.

3 Add 6 cups of the flour 1 cup at a time, mixing the flour in completely after each addition. Place the dough on a floured surface and knead until smooth, adding a little flour at a time from the remaining cup of flour. The dough is done when you rub your palm across the dough and it feels smooth. Shape the dough into a ball.

4 Add the remaining 1 teaspoon of oil to the bowl and rub all around the bowl and on top of the dough. Place the dough into the oiled bowl and cover with plastic. Let rise 1 hour.

5 Divide the dough into 2 or 3 balls, depending whether you are making 2 or 3 loaves. Divide each ball into 3 pieces. Roll the pieces into strands of the same length and then braid, following the instructions on page 245.

6 Place on a parchment-lined cookie sheet and let rise 45 minutes. Preheat the oven to 375°F. Brush the tops and sides of the loaves with the reserved beaten egg mixed with a teaspoon of water. Bake for 35 minutes, or until browned.

Flavored Challahs

Each of the following variations flavors one challah, one-third of the dough from the Classic Challah recipe. Use the other two-thirds of the dough to make other flavors or braid and bake without flavoring. It is fun to present three flavors.

GARLIC CHALLAH

Crush 4 cloves of garlic and place in a small bowl with 3 tablespoons of extra virgin olive oil. Add salt and pepper to taste. Set aside. Complete Steps 1 through 4 for Classic Challah (opposite). Divide the dough into 3 balls. Select a ball to flavor and divide it into 3 pieces. Roll the pieces into long strands and place on parchment or waxed paper. Brush all sides generously with the garlic oil. Braid the strands, following the instructions on page 245. Complete Step 6 for Classic Challah, but brush once more with the garlic oil before brushing on the egg wash.

ZA'ATAR CHALLAH

Complete Steps 1 through 4 for Classic Challah (opposite). Divide the dough into 3 balls. Select a ball and divide into 3 pieces. Roll the pieces into long strands. Take a piece of parchment or waxed paper, and sprinkle 1 tablespoon of za'atar spice blend on top. Roll each strand in the za'atar to cover all sides. Braid the strands, following the instructions on page 245. Complete Step 6 for Classic Challah.

CHOCOLATE CHIP CHALLAH

Chop 3 ounces of chocolate into ¼- to ½-inch pieces. Complete Steps 1 through 4 for Classic Challah (opposite). Divide the dough into 3 balls. Select one ball and knead the chopped chocolate into the dough. Divide in 3 strands and braid, following the instructions on page 245. Complete Step 6 for Classic Challah.

If your yeast mixture does not bubble and thicken after 10 minutes, your yeast is dead. Dump the mixture out and start again with new yeast.

Sweet Honey & Saffron Challah

MAKES 2 LARGE CHALLAHS

The bris (circumcision) of my twins, Jake and Joey, was rather hectic. After Jake's turn, I was instructed by the mohel to take him upstairs and comfort him. That meant that I completely missed Joey's turn. I was starving and remembered that my friend Trudy Jacobson had brought me her challah. It has a unique sweetness from the honey, a very soft texture from the margarine, and I think the saffron performs some other magic to create a very tasty challah. The rising times are longer than my classic challah, but worth the time.

¼ teaspoon saffron threads

1 cup hot, not boiling, water

½ cup honey

¾ ounce (3 envelopes) active dry yeast

4½ to 5 cups bread flour, plus extra to dust work surface

¼ cup sugar

Dash of salt

½ cup (1 stick) parve margarine, at room temperature, plus extra to grease pan

3 large eggs, divided

1 teaspoon canola or vegetable oil

1 Place the saffron into the cup of hot water and stir to dissolve. Pour into a large bowl. Pour in the honey and whisk until dissolved. Add the yeast and stir again. Add 1½ cups of the flour and stir to mix everything together. Cover with a clean dishcloth and let sit for 30 minutes.

2 Meanwhile, in another bowl or the bowl of a stand mixer, place 2½ cups of the flour, the sugar, salt, and margarine. Using a whisk, an electric mixer, or the whisk attachment of a stand mixer, cut the margarine into the dry ingredients until it looks like sand and there are no big clumps of margarine.

3 After 30 minutes, the yeast mixture should have changed: It will either look thick, have bubbles, or have increased in size. If the mixture has not changed, your yeast may be dead and you should dump that mixture and make a new one with new yeast. Beat 2 of the eggs in a small bowl. Add the eggs to the yeast mixture and

mix using a wooden spoon or silicone spatula. Add the flour and margarine mixture in three parts, mixing well after each addition. With your hands or a dough hook on the stand mixer, knead the dough and add ¼ cup of the flour. If the dough remains sticky, add another ¼ cup of flour. Add more flour, a tablespoon at a time, until the dough is no longer sticky and feels smooth when you slide your hand across it. Remove the dough from the bowl.

4 Wash the bowl, dry it, and rub the oil around the bowl. Add the dough and rub the top with the oil on your hands. Cover with a dish towel and let rise 1½ hours.

5 Place the dough on a floured surface and punch it down to remove air pockets. Divide the dough into 2 balls. Divide each ball into 3 pieces. Roll the 3 pieces into strands the same length, shorter for a fatter challah, longer for a long and narrow challah. Braid the strands, following the instructions on page 245.

6 Place on a greased cookie sheet. Let rise another 1½ hours. Beat the remaining egg and brush the challahs with the egg.

7 Preheat the oven to 350°F. Bake for 30 to 35 minutes, or until the top is browned and when you lift the challah and tap on the bottom, it sounds hollow. Remove the challahs to a wire rack to cool.

FOUR- AND SIX-BRAIDED CHALLAH
If you have time, you can make a four- or six-braided challah using the recipes in this chapter. The best instructions and diagrams for making four- or six-braided challah are in the Lubavitch Women's book *Spice and Spirit: The Complete Jewish Cookbook.*

Whole-Wheat Challah

The inspiration for this recipe came from Lily Starr, a great baker and entertainer. She gave me the idea for what I call the "Crown Challah" for Rosh Hashanah. She breaks the dough into twelve balls and bakes them in a round pan (the number of dough balls symbolize the twelve tribes of Israel). The dough puffs up giving it the crown effect. You may add vital wheat gluten to the challah as well, which adds additional fiber to the bread. This recipe has three rising times, so plan accordingly.

PROOFING MIXTURE

> 1 tablespoon sugar
>
> 1 tablespoon bread flour
>
> ½ ounce (2 envelopes) active dry yeast
>
> 1 cup warm water

EGG MIXTURE

> 4 large eggs plus 1 egg yolk (reserve white)
>
> ¾ cup vegetable oil
>
> ½ cup sugar
>
> 1 tablespoon salt
>
> 1 tablespoon honey

FLOUR MIXTURE

> 7 cups (or more) bread flour, plus extra for greasing pan
>
> 1 cup whole-wheat flour
>
> ⅓ cup toasted wheat germ
>
> 2 tablespoons vital wheat gluten (optional)

> 1½ teaspoons canola or vegetable oil
>
> Spray oil containing flour, for greasing
>
> 1 tablespoon poppy seeds or sesame seeds, for sprinkling on top (optional)

1 To make the proofing mixture: Place the sugar, bread flour, yeast, and warm water in a medium bowl and whisk. Cover with plastic and let proof 10 minutes.

2 Meanwhile, make the egg mixture: In a large bowl, place the 4 whole eggs plus 1 yolk. Add the oil, sugar, salt, and honey and whisk. When the yeast mixture has bubbled, add it to the egg mixture. Add 1 cup of cold water to the bowl that contained the yeast mixture, swirl it around, dump into the egg mixture and whisk well.

On Rosh Hashanah when I am serving 30 people, I find it easier to give each person their own challah roll. I break off small balls of dough, roll a long strand and then tie in a knot so you have a little ball at the top. Bake for 20 to 35 minutes, depending on the size, watch carefully, and remove when they are golden brown.

3 To make the flour mixture: In a medium bowl, whisk together the bread flour, whole-wheat flour, wheat germ, and vital wheat gluten, if using. Add half of the dry-ingredient mixture to the egg mixture. Mix with whisk. Add the remaining dry ingredients and mix by hand or with a dough hook in a stand mixer until you have a soft dough. Knead by hand for 2 minutes, adding a little more bread flour if the dough is still a little sticky. The dough is done when you rub your palm across the dough and it feels smooth. Shape into a ball. Place 1 teaspoon of the oil in a large bowl and rub all around. Add the dough and rub the top with the oil on your hands. Cover with plastic and let rise 2 hours or until doubled.

4 Remove from the bowl, punch down, and knead a few times. Add the remaining ½ teaspoon of oil to the bowl. Shape dough into a ball, place in the bowl, cover with plastic wrap, and let rise 1 hour or until doubled.

5 Punch down again. To make 2 three-braid challahs: Divide into 6 pieces. Cover the pieces with plastic wrap and let rest for 10 minutes. To make 2 challah crowns: Divide the dough in half and use a knife to cut each half into 12 pieces. Cover with plastic and let rest 10 minutes.

6 Preheat the oven to 375°F.

7 To make braided challahs: Line a cookie sheet with parchment. Roll the 6 pieces into strands the same length, shorter for a fatter challah, longer for a long and narrow challah. Braid the challahs loosely, following the instructions on page 245, and place on the prepared sheets. Cover with plastic and let rise for 1 hour.

8 To make challah crowns: Take a 9-inch round pan and trace the bottom on parchment. Cut out the circle. Using spray oil containing flour, spray the bottom and sides of the pan. Place the parchment circle on the bottom. Cut a 4 x 12-inch strip of parchment and place as a band inside the sides of the pan. Grease the bottom and side parchment pieces with spray oil containing flour. Don't worry if the sides cave in now; they will stay in place when the dough is placed in the pan.

9 Take the 12 dough pieces and, one at a time, flatten with your hands into a circle, roll the circle up to create a cylinder, and then tuck the ends under, sealing them completely, almost creating a bubble of dough. The top should be smooth. Place

11 of them, seam-side down, in a circle around the pan, inside the parchment band. Place the last ball in the center. You can also place 9 around the perimeter and 3 in the center. Repeat for the other half of the dough. Cover with plastic and let rise 1 hour.

10 Beat the reserved egg white with 1 teaspoon water and brush on the braided challah or challah crowns. Sprinkle with poppy or sesame seeds, if desired.

11 Bake for 40 minutes, or until outside is browned. Let cool for 10 minutes. If you've made the crowns, let cool in the pan before gently tipping out onto a rack.

Harvest Challah

MAKES 2 LARGE OR 3 MEDIUM BRAIDED CHALLAHS

This challah contains part rye and part whole-wheat flour.

½ cup plus 2 teaspoons canola or vegetable oil, divided

1 tablespoon salt

½ cup plus 1 teaspoon sugar

1 cup boiling water

½ cup cold water

½ ounce (2 envelopes) active dry yeast

⅓ cup warm water

4 large eggs

2 tablespoons caraway seeds

½ cup sunflower seeds

½ cup pumpkin seeds

1 cup whole-wheat flour

1 cup dark rye flour

5 cups (or more) bread flour, plus extra to dust work surface

1 cup dried cranberries

1 In a large bowl, whisk together ½ cup of the oil, the salt, and ½ cup of the sugar. Add the boiling water and mix again to dissolve the salt and sugar. Add the cold water and mix again.

2 In a cup, dissolve the yeast in the warm water and add the remaining teaspoon of sugar. Beat the eggs in a separate bowl and add to oil mixture, reserving 1 tablespoon to brush on the loaves. Add the yeast mixture to the bowl and stir.

3 Add the caraway seeds, sunflower seeds, pumpkin seeds, whole-wheat and rye flours and mix. Add the bread flour 1 cup at a time and mix well until all the ingredients are mixed in.

4 Place the dough on a floured surface and knead until smooth. Add a little more bread flour if the dough feels sticky. The dough is done when it feels smooth as you rub your palm across it. Add the cranberries and knead in to evenly distribute throughout the dough. Add the remaining 2 teaspoons of oil to the bowl and rub all around the bowl and on top of the dough. Place the dough in the oiled bowl and cover with plastic. Let rise 1½ hours.

5 Divide the dough into 2 or 3 balls, depending on whether you are making 2 or 3 loaves. Divide each ball into 3 pieces. Roll the pieces into strands the same length, shorter for a fatter challah, longer for a long and narrow challah. Braid the strands, following the instructions on page 245.

6 Place on a parchment-lined cookie sheet and let rise 1 hour.

7 Preheat the oven to 375°F. Brush the tops and sides of the loaves with the reserved beaten egg mixed with a teaspoon of water. Bake for 35 minutes, or until browned. Remove to rack to cool.

Passover & Other
Special Diets

In this part I show you how to make
delicious desserts for Passover and how
to make virtually sugar-free desserts for
friends and family with special dietary
needs. You may find that you add these
desserts to your regular rotation.

On Passover, Jews are not permitted
to eat leavened bread for eight days.
For baking, Passover means that we
cannot use flour or yeast. No worries—
kosher bakers have learned to work
around those restrictions for years.
The Passover food industry has grown
tremendously since I was young and
now there are great baking products
you can use. There is even kosher for
Passover baking powder. You just have
to think creatively to get around flour. I
learned at cooking school in Paris how
to use nut flours with great results.

Passover is a major holiday for
entertaining and, as a result, you need
some beautiful desserts for your guests.
You also need simpler desserts to snack
on to get you through the week. The
Passover chapter contains desserts

that have uniquely Passover ingredients. In addition to the Passover recipes in this part, there are more than a dozen recipes sprinkled throughout other chapters in the book that can be eaten on Passover with no or minor substitutions. (Look for the "◇" when flipping through the book or see the Passover entry in the index.) Enjoy these recipes. I am sure you will appreciate eating something far tastier than canned coconut macaroons.

———

The chapter on no-sugar-added desserts is dedicated to my father, Reubin Marcus, a man who truly loves desserts, but is a diabetic. He believes that he does not have to suffer without desserts and all I hear from him are complaints about parve sugar-free desserts sold at kosher bakeries and in stores. I wanted to include this chapter so that everyone in the Jewish community would be able to find desserts they could eat. In addition, for those watching their weight, I wanted to give some healthier choices for desserts.

I am not claiming that this section is entirely sugar-free, I just did not add any sugar to any of these desserts. Some ingredients in these recipes—including readymade pie crust, parve whipping cream, and dried fruit—contain small amounts of sugar. You should always consult your doctor about how much dried fruit or white flour you should be eating. You will notice that I use granulated sugar substitutes sparingly. I find they have an aftertaste I don't like and prefer to use fruit and other natural ingredients to flavor a dessert. Additional sugar-free recipes in this book are Dried Fruit Truffles, Summer Fruit Triangles, Fruit Soup with Triple Sorbet Garnish (omit honey), and Strawberry Gazpacho (omit sugar).

Chocolate Chip Hazelnut Biscotti

MAKES 2 TO 3 DOZEN

STORAGE

*Place in an airtight container or freezer bags and store at room temperature
for up to five days or freeze up to three months.*

I grew up on Passover cake mixes. As my mother was a good cook, but not a baker, it was the only time each year when we had homemade cakes. Unfortunately, there were no kosher for Passover cookie mixes so the only cookies we got were packaged from the store. Now I just bake my own.

½ cup (1 stick) parve margarine, at room temperature

1 cup plus ½ teaspoon sugar, divided

2 large eggs

1⅓ cups matzoh cake meal

⅓ cup potato starch

¾ cup ground hazelnuts (filberts)

¾ cup parve chocolate chips

2 ounces parve semisweet chocolate, grated on the large holes
   of a box grater

---

1 Preheat the oven to 350°F. Line a cookie sheet with parchment.

2 In a large bowl, by hand or with an electric mixer on medium-high speed, beat the margarine and 1 cup of the sugar until creamy. Add the eggs and mix well. Add the cake meal, potato starch, and ground hazelnuts and mix again. Add the chocolate chips and grated chocolate and mix in.

3 Divide the dough in half and shape each into a loaf, about 3 x 7 inches. Place on the prepared cookie sheet, leaving a few inches between the logs. Sprinkle the remaining ½ teaspoon of sugar on top of the loaves.

4 Bake for 35 minutes. Slide the parchment and logs onto a cutting board to cool for 5 minutes. Place a new piece of parchment on the cookie sheet. Cut the loaves

across into ½- to ¾-inch slices and place back on the cookie sheet, cut-side down. Bake for 5 minutes more. Remove from oven and slide the parchment onto a rack to let cool.

Thin Farfel Cookies

MAKES ABOUT 10 DOZEN

STORAGE

Place in an airtight container or freezer bags and store at room temperature for up to five days or freeze up to three months.

For Passover, I always bake big batches of cookies so we have something to snack on during the holiday. These are very crispy. (*Note*: Matzoh farfel is simply little pieces of matzoh that people use to prepare various Passover dishes.)

---

2 cups matzoh farfel

½ cup (1 stick) parve margarine

1¾ cups sugar

2 large eggs

2 teaspoons vanilla extract

2 tablespoons matzoh cake meal

1 cup ground almonds

½ teaspoon salt

½ cup parve mini chocolate chips

---

1 Preheat the oven to 350°F. Line a cookie sheet with parchment. Add the farfel and spread out. Bake for 20 minutes on the middle rack of the oven. Remove from oven, slide the parchment off the sheet, and let cool.

2 Place the margarine in a large heatproof bowl and melt in the microwave. Add the sugar and stir. Add the eggs and vanilla and stir again. Add the toasted farfel, cake meal, ground almonds, and salt and mix. Add the chocolate chips and mix in to evenly distribute. Place the dough in the refrigerator for 20 minutes.

3 You will need to bake these in batches. Line 2 to 4 cookie sheets with parchment. Drop teaspoons of dough onto the parchment, 2 inches apart.

4 Bake for 10 to 12 minutes, or until the cookies begin to brown on the edges.

Chocolate Brownie Cookies

MAKES 6 TO 7 DOZEN

STORAGE

Place in an airtight container or freezer bags and store at room temperature for up to five days or freeze up to three months.

This recipe is based on one I got from Limor Decter who got it from Tsippy Nussbaum, who was her camper at Camp Tagola about thirty years ago. Tsippy loves Passover and has collected piles of Passover recipes that she loves to share. You will want to make these cookies all year round. They are the perfect gluten-free cookie.

---

15 ounces parve bittersweet chocolate, broken into 1-inch pieces

4 large eggs

1½ cups sugar

¼ cup vegetable oil

1 tablespoon strong brewed coffee (or dissolve 3 teaspoons instant coffee in ¼ cup hot water and use a tablespoon of that)

1 teaspoon vanilla extract

¼ teaspoon salt

½ cup potato starch

4½ cups ground almonds

---

1 Preheat the oven to 350°F. Line 2 to 3 cookie sheets with parchment or bake in batches.

2 Melt the chocolate either on the stovetop or in the microwave, following the "Melting chocolate" instructions (see Foolproof Tips and Techniques).

3 When the chocolate is melted, add the eggs, sugar, oil, coffee, and vanilla and mix well. Add the salt, potato starch, and ground almonds and mix until the dough comes together.

4 Using a teaspoon, scoop up a walnut-size amount of dough (1 to 1½ inches in diameter) and roll into a ball. Place on the prepared cookie sheets 1½ inches apart. Bake for 12 to 15 minutes, or until the cookies hold together and start to crack on top.

Marble Chocolate Matzoh

SERVES 12

STORAGE

Store in the refrigerator for six days or freeze for up to three months.

Marcy Goldman's Caramel Matzoh Crunch remains one of the best Passover creations ever. Her recipe inspired me to create this Passover confection. Once I learned that there were parve white chocolate chips on the market, and they were also kosher for Passover, I was determined to find a way to use them. I like the crunch of the toasted almonds but you can omit the nuts if desired. You can easily double this recipe for a crowd.

⅓ cup slivered almonds

10 ounces parve dark bittersweet chocolate, chopped or broken into 1-inch pieces

⅓ cup parve white chocolate chips

3 large or 4 small pieces of matzoh

1 Preheat the oven to 325°F. Line a jelly roll pan with parchment. Spread the almonds on the pan and toast for 15 minutes, stirring the nuts after 10 minutes. When the almonds are toasted, remove the pan from the oven and slide the parchment off the cookie sheet.

2 While the nuts are toasting, melt the dark chocolate in one heatproof bowl and the white chocolate in another. You can do this either on the stovetop or in the microwave, following the "Melting chocolate" instructions (see Foolproof Tips and Techniques). If you use the microwave method, be especially careful with the white chocolate chips so they do not burn.

3 When the almonds are toasted, use a large knife to roughly chop them into pieces about one-third of their original size. Mix the nuts into the melted dark chocolate.

4   Line 1 large or 2 smaller cookie sheets with waxed paper and place the matzohs on top of the waxed paper. Spread the dark chocolate and nut mixture all over the matzoh slices to cover them entirely on one side with the chocolate.

5   Drop clumps of the melted white chocolate randomly on top of the dark chocolate. Use a toothpick to swirl the chocolates to create a marble effect. Place in the refrigerator to set for 1 hour and then break into pieces to serve.

Chocolate Chiffon Cake

SERVES 16

STORAGE

Store covered in plastic at room temperature for up to five days or freeze wrapped in plastic for up to three months.

My friend Denyse Tannenbaum generously gave me this recipe for this book. I brought the cake to my friend Maria's for dessert after Shabbat lunch and surprised Denyse by presenting this cake. The smile that came to her face, seeing her family recipe in front of her, melted my heart.

———————

1 cup matzoh cake meal

½ cup potato starch

1 tablespoon baking powder

1 teaspoon salt

1½ cups sugar, divided

½ cup vegetable oil

8 large eggs, separated

¾ cup water

1 tablespoon rum extract

1 teaspoon fresh lemon juice

4 ounces parve bittersweet chocolate, chopped into ¼-inch chunks

———————

1   Preheat the oven to 350°F. In a large bowl, sift together the cake meal, potato starch, baking powder, salt, and ¾ cup of the sugar. Add the oil, egg yolks, water, and rum extract and beat until smooth.

2 In a separate bowl, use an electric mixer on high speed to beat the egg whites with the lemon juice until stiff. Turn the speed to low and gradually add the remaining ¾ cup of sugar. Turn the speed up to high and then beat until the whites are very stiff and shiny, about 1 minute more.

3 Use a silicone spatula to fold the egg-yolk mixture into the whites and then fold in the chopped chocolate.

4 Pour the batter into an ungreased 10-inch Bundt or tube pan. Bake for 1 hour. Let cool in the pan. When cool, use a knife to loosen the edges of the cake and turn onto a serving plate.

Mocha Matzoh Napoleon

SERVES 20

STORAGE

Store covered in the refrigerator for up to three days or in the freezer for up to two months.

The matzoh layers are soaked in coffee and, though softened, they dry out when chilled and hold the dessert together. The first version of the recipe was made in a loaf pan and served ten but I quickly realized that, on Passover, the crowds are bigger. To serve ten, just halve the recipe and prepare in a 12-inch loaf pan.

10 large matzohs

1 cup strong brewed coffee (or 6 tablespoons instant coffee granules dissolved in 1 cup of hot water), cooled

MOUSSE

23 ounces parve bittersweet chocolate, divided

8 large eggs, separated

1 cup sugar, divided

1 cup (2 sticks) margarine, at room temperature

1 Line a 9 x 13-inch pan with 2 pieces of plastic wrap that are large enough to drape over the sides.

2 Break the matzoh pieces in half. Pour the coffee into a shallow pan and add the matzoh pieces, turning them over so that each piece becomes soaked with the coffee. Set aside.

3 To make the mousse: Break 21 ounces of the chocolate into small pieces and melt either on the stovetop or in the microwave, following the "Melting chocolate" instructions (see Foolproof Tips and Techniques).

4 Meanwhile, in a large bowl, beat the egg yolks with ¾ cup of the sugar. Add the very soft margarine and beat with an electric mixer on medium-high speed or vigorously by hand with a whisk until combined. Add the melted chocolate and beat again.

5 In a separate bowl, with an electric mixer on high speed, beat the egg whites until they start to stiffen. Turn the speed to low, add the remaining ¼ cup of sugar, and then turn the speed back to high and beat until very stiff, about 1 minute more. Mix the whites in 5 parts into the chocolate mixture at low speed.

6 Spoon about one-fifth of the mousse into the prepared pan to cover the bottom. Add 3 to 4 matzoh halves to cover the mousse in 1 layer. Add another one-fifth of the mousse to cover the matzoh and then another layer of matzoh. Repeat until you have used all the matzoh. There should be 4 to 5 layers, depending on the size of your matzoh pieces. The last layer should be the mousse. Cover with plastic.

7 Place in the freezer for a minimum of 3 hours or overnight. Place in the refrigerator 1 hour before serving.

8 To serve, unmold the pan onto a large platter and peel off the plastic wrap. Use a grater or vegetable peeler to shave the remaining 2 ounces of chocolate on top of the mousse. Cut into 20 pieces.

Orange Cigarette Cookies

MAKES 30 COOKIES

STORAGE

Place in an airtight container and store at room temperature for up to five days or freeze up to three months.

After course after course of Seder foods and the main course, it is nice to offer your family and friends a small bite of something sweet for dessert. I made these cookies into several shapes. After working his way through a pile of cookies in the shape of cones, cups, bowls, and circles, my son Sam was certain that the cigarette shape tasted best. If you do not have the time to spread the batter, try just dropping spoonfuls of batter about 1½ inch in diameter and bake. Both shapes are great to stand up in a bowl of sorbet.

2 large egg whites

2½ tablespoons matzoh cake meal,
   plus extra for sprinkling on pan if
   not using Teflon

½ cup sugar

1 teaspoon orange zest (grated outer peel)

2 tablespoons parve margarine, plus extra for
   greasing pan if not using Teflon

1 In a bowl, whisk together egg whites, cake meal, and sugar. Add orange zest and mix. Heat the margarine in the microwave until melted and add to the bowl. Whisk well. Cover with plastic wrap and refrigerate for a minimum of 2 hours or overnight.

2 Preheat the oven to 400°F. Use a Teflon cookie sheet or grease and sprinkle cake meal on a regular cookie sheet. Stir the batter. Drop teaspoons of batter onto the sheet, 3 inches apart. With the back of a spoon, flatten the batter until the circle is about 2½ to 3 inches in diameter. This takes time; the more patient you are, the thinner and crisper the cookies become. I like to bake only 9 cookies at a time so that it is easier to roll the

cookies as soon as they are baked—they will dry flat if they sit on your cookie sheet too long and you may need an ice pick to get them off. (Of course, you get to eat the broken crumbs.)

3 Bake for 7 to 8 minutes, or until golden. Using a flat-blade spatula, carefully scrape up each cookie and place top-side down onto the counter. Place the handle of a wooden spoon on one end of the cookie and quickly wrap the cookie around the wooden handle to form a cigarette. Quickly repeat for the other cookies.

4 You can also place each cookie in a small rounded dish or bowl and let them cool, then use them as bowls for sorbet or fruit.

Strawberry Shortcake

MAKES ONE 8-INCH CAKE, 12 SERVINGS

STORAGE

Store in the refrigerator for up to two days.

This impressive-looking cake is very easy to make. Because the filling has fresh fruit, it does not have a long shelf life. I made it in the morning and we ate it that night. It was also fine the next day, but the berries were not as fresh. Do not decorate the top or sides with any fruit until just before serving as the fruit juices may bleed onto the cake. If you have another five minutes to spare, serve with fresh Strawberry Sauce (page 294).

Parve margarine or spray oil, for greasing pan

4 large eggs, separated

1 teaspoon vanilla extract, divided

½ cup sugar

½ cup matzoh cake meal

1 tablespoon potato starch

1 cup parve whipping cream

10 to 12 strawberries for filling, plus more for garnish

---

1 Preheat the oven to 425°F. Place an 8-inch round baking pan on top of a piece of parchment and trace a circle around the pan. Cut out the circle. Grease the bottom of the pan with some margarine or spray oil, place the parchment circle in the bottom of the pan, and then grease the circle and the sides of the pan.

2　To make the cake batter: In a small bowl, mix together the egg yolks and ½ teaspoon of the vanilla. Set aside. Place the whites in a mixing bowl and beat with a hand-held or stand electric mixer on high speed until stiff. Turn off the mixer, add the sugar, and mix on low speed until incorporated. Turn up the speed to high and mix 1 minute more. Add the yolk mixture and mix on low speed until combined. Add the cake meal and potato starch and mix on low speed until the dry ingredients are all mixed in.

3　Pour the batter into the prepared pan and spread with a silicone spatula. Bake for 12 minutes. Let cool for 45 minutes and then remove from the pan by turning the pan over and flipping the cake onto a rack.

4　Place the whipping cream and the remaining ½ teaspoon of vanilla in a mixing bowl and beat with an electric mixer on high speed until you have a thick whipped cream.

5　Peel the parchment circle off the cake and slice into 2 layers, following the instructions in "Slicing cake layers" (see Foolproof Tips and Techniques). Set the half that was covered with the parchment circle aside. It will be the top of the cake. Place the other half, top-side down, on a serving plate.

6　Wash and dry the strawberries, remove the stems, and cut into thin slices. Spread about 1 cup of the whipped cream evenly over the bottom layer. Cover with the strawberry slices. Place the other piece of cake on top, so the smooth bottom-side is facing up. Take the rest of the whipped cream and spread to cover the top and sides of the cake. You can smooth the top and sides by heating a long metal flat-blade spatula in hot water, drying it slightly, and then sliding it around the top and sides of the cake. Place in refrigerator at least 1 hour.

7　To decorate, just before serving, you can cover the top with thin, overlapping slices of strawberries. Place a circle of strawberry halves on the top rim of the cake or use concentric circles of different berries or fruit. You can also press some strawberry slices into the sides of the cake as well. Serve with strawberry sauce, if desired.

Lemon Layer Cake

MAKES ONE 9-INCH 3-LAYER CAKE, 12 SERVINGS

STORAGE

*Store in the refrigerator until serving and up to four days or freeze
up to three months.*

The basis for this layer cake is what my grandmother served as a giant sponge cake all
year round to the people of Sea Gate, Brooklyn, and the Fountains in West Palm Beach,
Florida. I am pretty sure my father-in-law only agreed to let me marry his son after he
ate the sponge cake. Here I have updated her recipe and made it into a layer cake with a
lemon cream filling.

SPONGE CAKE

Parve margarine, for greasing pan

4 large eggs, separated

3 tablespoons water

2 tablespoons fresh lemon juice

1 cup sugar

⅓ cup matzoh cake meal

⅓ cup potato starch

1¼ teaspoons lemon zest (grated outer peel)

Dash of salt

LEMON CREAM

3 large eggs plus 2 egg yolks

1 cup sugar

5 tablespoons fresh lemon juice (from 2 to 3 lemons)

Zest (grated outer peel) of 1 large lemon

5½ tablespoons parve margarine

———

1¼ cups parve whipping cream

Fresh raspberries, strawberry halves, or lemon slices, for decoration

1 Preheat the oven to 350°F. Trace the bottom of a 9-inch round baking pan onto a piece of parchment and cut out the circle. Grease the 9-inch round baking pan, place the parchment circle inside, and then grease again.

2 To make the sponge cake: In a bowl, beat the egg yolks, water, lemon juice, and sugar with a hand-held or stand electric mixer or by hand with a whisk. Add the cake meal, potato starch, and lemon zest and beat or whisk until combined.

3 In a separate bowl with a hand-held or stand electric mixer on high speed, beat the egg whites and salt until stiff. Gently fold the whites into the bowl with the egg-yolk mixture and then pour into the prepared pan.

4 Bake for 45 minutes. Let cool in the pan. Remove and wrap in plastic. Chill in freezer for 1 hour.

5 To make the lemon cream: Place the eggs, yolks, and sugar in a heatproof bowl and set over a medium saucepan with simmering water (or use a double boiler). Whisk in the lemon juice and zest. Cook the lemon curd, uncovered, whisking occasionally, until a thick mixture is formed. This takes approximately 25 minutes. Be patient and do not stir too much. Don't leave the whisk in the bowl with the lemon mixture while it cooks; it may get too hot to touch. If the water in the saucepan boils too fast, turn down the heat.

6 Remove the bowl from the heat and whisk in the margarine a tablespoon at a time. Cool for 10 minutes and then cover with plastic and refrigerate 4 hours or overnight. This can be made 3 days in advance. To use sooner, place the bowl of lemon cream over a larger bowl filled with ice and a little water (below the level of the cream bowl) for 15 to 20 minutes, or until the cream is chilled. Mix occasionally.

7 If necessary, trim the top of the cake to make it flat. For a more professional look, use a knife to trim the sides of the cake straight down, making them even. Following the instructions in "Slicing cake layers" (see Foolproof Tips and Techniques), slice the cake in thirds to create 3 layers.

8 Cut a circle of cardboard the size of the cake or place the cake directly on a platter. In a bowl, with an electric mixer on high speed, whip the whipping cream until stiff. Place a little lemon cream on the cardboard circle or platter and attach the top slice of cake, top-side down. Spread a third of the lemon cream on the cake. Add the second (center) piece of cake and add another third of the lemon cream. Place the cake bottom, bottom-side up, on top of the cream.

9 Mix the remainder of the lemon cream with the whipped cream. Spread the cream on the top and sides of the cake. Freeze 15 minutes. Spread some more cream to even out the sides and top and freeze another 5 minutes. Use a metal flat-blade spatula to smooth the cake by dipping the spatula in hot water, drying it, then sliding it all around the cake. Re-heat the spatula as necessary. Decorate with raspberries, strawberries, or lemon slices.

Flourless Chocolate Cake

MAKES ONE 10-INCH CAKE, 12 TO 16 SERVINGS
STORAGE
Store in the refrigerator for up to four days or freeze up to three months.

Slices of chocolate that melt in your mouth . . . what could be better?

16 ounces parve bittersweet or semisweet chocolate, roughly chopped

¾ cup (1½ sticks) parve margarine, plus extra for greasing pan

6 large eggs, separated

1 teaspoon parve unsweetened cocoa

½ cup sugar

1 recipe Strawberry, Raspberry, Blackberry, Mango or Kiwi Sauce (pages 293–94), to serve with cake

Fresh berries of your choice, to serve with cake

1 Preheat the oven to 350°F. Take a 10-inch springform pan, place a piece of parchment on the counter, and trace a circle around the bottom of the pan. Cut out the circle and set aside. Place a piece of foil on top of the bottom of the pan and fold the excess foil under the pan. Attach the sides of the pan, lock in place, and then wrap the foil that you folded under the pan up the exterior sides of the pan. Take another piece of foil and wrap around the bottom of the pan and up the sides; this prevents any water from leaking into the cake as it bakes in a water bath.

2 Grease the top of the foil in the bottom of the pan. Place the parchment circle on top of the foil. This step makes it easy to slide the finished cake onto your serving plate. Grease the parchment circle and the sides of the pan.

3 Place the chocolate and margarine in a heatproof bowl over a saucepan with simmering water and whisk often until melted. Remove the bowl from the heat and add the egg yolks and cocoa and whisk until thick.

4 In a separate bowl, beat the egg whites with an electric mixer on high speed until stiff. Turn the speed down to low, add the sugar slowly and, once all the sugar is added, turn the speed up to high for 1 minute.

5 Fold the egg whites into the chocolate mixture. Pour the batter into the prepared pan. Place the pan in a larger roasting pan and then add boiling water to reach halfway up the sides of the cake pan. The easiest way to do this is to place the roasting pan with the cake pan in the oven first, then bring the boiling water to the oven and pour into the roasting pan around the cake.

6 Bake for 40 minutes, or until set. Remove the cake from the water bath (leaving the roasting pan with the water in the oven to cool safely) and let cool. Place in the refrigerator a minimum of 4 hours or overnight.

7 Open the spring and remove the sides of the pan. Use a metal flat-blade spatula to separate the parchment circle from the foil and slide the parchment and cake onto a serving plate. Store the cake in the refrigerator and then place in the freezer 1 hour before serving to help you cut perfect slices.

8 Serve with a fruit sauce of your choice and some fresh berries.

Chocolate Mousse Meringue Layer Cake

MAKES ONE 8-INCH CAKE, 12 SERVINGS
STORAGE

Store in the freezer for up to three months.

This was one of my most popular cakes when I had a catering business in Switzerland. It is my favorite adult birthday cake though my kids love it, too. Although the recipe is long, it is really not that hard—I promise—and you and your guests will be impressed. People like the combination of creamy mousse and crunchy meringue. To make this cake you will need a dessert ring: a 2½-inch tall bottomless ring, 8 inches in diameter (see photo on page xxi).

MERINGUE

⅔ cup confectioners' sugar

2 tablespoons parve unsweetened cocoa

4 large egg whites

⅔ cup sugar

MOUSSE

8 ounces parve bittersweet chocolate, chopped or broken
   into 1-inch pieces

5 large egg yolks

2¼ cups parve whipping cream, divided

1 tablespoon sugar

_____

Parve bittersweet chocolate or chocolate chips, melted, to decorate
   top of cake (optional)

1 Preheat the oven to 230°F. Tear off a piece of parchment the size of your largest cookie sheet. Take an 8 x 2½-inch-high dessert ring and trace 3 circles on your parchment; the circles may touch each other or even overlap because the meringue circles will be smaller than the ring size. If necessary, use 2 cookie sheets. Turn the paper over and place on your cookie sheet.

2 To make the meringue: Sift the confectioners' sugar and cocoa together in a bowl.

3 In the bowl of a stand mixer, or in a mixing bowl with a hand-held mixer, beat the egg whites on medium-high speed until they start to stiffen. Turn the mixer to low and add the granulated sugar gradually, and then beat another minute on high speed until the whites are stiff. Sift the confectioners' sugar and cocoa a second time into the bowl with the egg whites. Turn your machine to low and beat until just combined.

4 Fill a pastry bag with a ¼-inch round tip with the meringue batter. Starting from the center of each circle drawn on the parchment, squeeze out spirals until your circles are about ½ inch smaller than the drawn circles. Do not worry if your circles are not perfect; you can use the back of a spoon to smooth over the "holes." If you do not have a pastry bag, use a silicone spatula to shape 3 circles of meringue batter, no higher than 1 inch.

5 Use any leftover batter to make any shapes you like to decorate the cake, such as kisses, letters, lines, or hearts. Place in the oven and bake for 2 hours. Turn off the oven and let the meringues remain in the oven another 2 hours so they can dry out. You can make the meringues up to 3 days in advance and store covered at room temperature.

6 To make the mousse: Melt the chocolate either on the stovetop or in the microwave, following the "Melting chocolate" instructions (see Foolproof Tips and Techniques). Heat ¼ cup of the whipping cream and the sugar in a small saucepan on medium heat, stirring often, until the sugar melts and the cream starts to boil. You can also heat the cream and sugar in the microwave in a glass measuring cup until the sugar is dissolved, about 1 minute. Don't worry if the cream starts to looks gloppy.

7 When the chocolate is melted, whisk in the cream and sugar mixture until smooth. Add the egg yolks one at a time and whisk well.

8 In a large bowl, with an electric mixer on high speed, beat the remaining 2 cups whipping cream until it is just whipped. Watch carefully and stop mixing when you see the top of the whipped cream forming ribbons or swirls. Add the whipped cream to the chocolate mixture and mix until well blended.

9   To assemble the cake, you will need an 8-inch cardboard circle, or you can cut one yourself. Take a piece of cardboard, trace the inside of your ring, and then cut out the circle. Line another cookie sheet with parchment, place the ring on top, and place the cardboard circle into the ring. Place a tablespoon of the mousse on the cardboard to help glue the meringue circle in place. Place one of the meringue circles in the center of the ring. Pour a third of the mouse into the ring to cover the meringue. Make sure you get some mousse between the meringue and the ring on the sides. Add the second meringue circle and another third of the mousse. Repeat with the last circle and more mousse and then use a flat-blade metal spatula to smooth the top, reserving any extra mousse in a small bowl stored in the refrigerator to decorate the top, if desired. Place into the freezer for 4 hours or overnight.

10 Remove from the freezer. To remove the ring, place the cake (with the cardboard bottom) on top of a large can (a can of tomatoes works well). Place boiling water in a small bowl. Take a towel or paper towel, dip it into the hot water, and then rub around the outside of the ring; this will help release the ring from the mousse. Go around the entire ring with the hot towel. Use your hands to gently slide the ring down off the cake. You can also use a blowtorch to heat the ring and then slide it off. Place the cake back on the parchment-lined cookie sheet.

11 To decorate the cake, you can use the extra meringues you made or you can melt some chocolate chips and drizzle the top of the cake in any design you like. You can also place any reserved mousse in a pastry bag with a decorative tip and decorate. I have also used a potato peeler to shave little chocolate pieces, then pressed those into the side of the cake. I like to store the cake in the freezer and then remove it 20 to 30 minutes before serving so I can cut perfect slices.

Mandelbread

MAKES ABOUT 30 COOKIES

STORAGE

> *Place in an airtight container or freezer bags and store at room temperature*
> *for up to five days or freeze up to three months.*

If a diabetic is coming to dinner and I am pressed for time, this is the recipe I always choose to make. I find these cookies very addicting even though they are sugar-free. My first version of these cookies arrived in Boca Raton, Florida, in crumbs. After some retooling, they taste better and can now survive a voyage.

---

3 cups all-purpose flour

2 teaspoons baking powder

Dash of salt

¾ cup granulated sugar substitute, such as Splenda

1 teaspoon sugar-free vanilla syrup

3 large eggs

½ cup canola or vegetable oil

¼ cup orange juice

⅓ cup sliced almonds

⅓ cup whole, unsalted, cashews, or shelled pistachio nuts
   (for pistachios, about ¼ pound of nuts in their shells)

⅓ cup dried cranberries (not the sweetened kind)

⅓ cup raisins

---

1 Preheat the oven to 350°F. Line a cookie sheet with parchment.

2 In a bowl, combine the flour, baking powder, salt, sugar substitute, vanilla syrup, eggs, oil, and orange juice. Set aside.

3 Place the sliced almonds and cashews or whole pistachio nuts in the bowl of a food processor fitted with a metal blade. Process for about 45 seconds, or until the nuts are in small pieces but not completely ground. You can also place the nuts in a bag and bang with a rolling pin until they are in small pieces. Add to the dough. Place the cranberries and raisins in the food processor and chop into small pieces, about 30 seconds. You can also chop by hand. Add to the dough and mix in.

4 Divide the dough in half and use your hands to shape into 2 loaves, 3 x 8 inches each. Place on the prepared cookie sheet about 4 inches apart.

5 Bake for 35 minutes. Slide the parchment off the cookie sheet. Use a sharp knife to slice each loaf into ¾- to 1-inch slices.

6 Place a new piece of parchment on the cookie sheet and place the slices cut-side down on the parchment. Bake for 5 minutes. Let cool on a rack.

For sugar-free flavored syrups, try the DaVinci Gourmet or Torani brands, which I have found wherever there is a good selection of sugar-free foods.

Chocolate Chunk Scones

MAKES 12 SCONES

STORAGE

*Place in an airtight container or freezer bags and store at
room temperature for up to five days or freeze up to three months.
Defrost 2 hours before serving.*

I knew I could make sugar-free scones after I was baking scones with a group of teenagers at Camp Ramah Palmer and we forgot to put sugar into one batch of scone dough. The kids thought they tasted fine, especially drowned with jam. Remember to serve with sugar-free jam.

¼ cup whole-wheat flour

1¾ cups plus 1 to 2 tablespoons all-purpose flour, divided

3 tablespoons granulated sugar substitute

1 tablespoon baking powder

½ teaspoon salt

6 tablespoons parve margarine, frozen for 15 minutes

2 large eggs, divided

½ cup parve plain soy milk

2 ounces sugar-free bittersweet parve chocolate (Elite brand), chopped

---

1 Preheat the oven to 425°F. Grease a 9-inch round baking pan and set aside. (*Note*: These do not bake as well in disposable aluminum pans.)

2 Place the whole-wheat flour and 1¾ cups of the all-purpose flour, the sugar substitute, baking powder, and salt in the bowl of a food processor fitted with a metal blade. Process for 10 seconds.

3 Cut the chilled margarine into small pieces and scatter over the dry ingredients. Process for about 10 seconds, or until mixture resembles sand. You can also mix by hand by cutting the margarine into the dry ingredients with two knives or a pastry cutter. Beat 1 of the eggs and add it and the soy milk to the flour mixture. Process or mix just until dough starts to come together, about 5 seconds.

4 Sprinkle 1 tablespoon of the flour on the counter. Remove the dough from the processor or bowl, place on top of the flour, and knead gently until the dough is soft. Add another tablespoon of the flour if the dough seems sticky. Add the chopped chocolate and knead into the dough.

5 Shape the dough into a ball and then flatten into a pancake the size of your baking pan. Place the dough in the pan. With a sharp knife dipped in flour, score (mark, but do not cut through) the top of the dough into 8 to 12 wedges. Beat the remaining egg and brush the top of the dough.

6 Bake 15 to 20 minutes, or until the top is brown. Let cool for 5 minutes and then remove from the pan. Cut on the scored lines into wedges. Serve warm or at room temperature.

Brownies

MAKES 16 BROWNIES

STORAGE

Place in an airtight container and store at room temperature for up to five days or freeze up to three months.

My diabetic father is still grieving his loss of Entenmann's cakes. I try to create something new for him each time he visits.

———

Parve margarine, for greasing pan

10 ounces sugar-free parve bittersweet chocolate, chopped or broken into 1-inch pieces

½ cup canola or vegetable oil

2 tablespoons parve unsweetened cocoa

4 large eggs

1½ cups ground almonds (see "Making ground almonds," page xxviii)

⅓ cup granulated sugar substitute

———

1 Preheat the oven to 350°F. Line an 8-inch square pan with foil, allowing some to overhang the sides, and grease well with margarine.

2 Place the chocolate, oil, and cocoa in a small saucepan and cook uncovered over low heat until melted, stirring frequently with a wooden spoon.

3 While the chocolate is melting, whisk the eggs in a bowl. When the chocolate is melted, pour into the bowl with the eggs and whisk well. Add the ground almonds and sugar substitute and mix again.

4 Pour the batter into the prepared pan and spread evenly with a silicone spatula. Bake for 25 to 28 minutes, or until a skewer inserted in the center comes out clean.

5 Let cool for 5 minutes in the pan and then use the foil to lift up and remove the brownie to a rack to cool completely. Cut into squares.

Apricot Bars

MAKES THIRTY-SIX 1½ X 3-INCH BARS OR TWENTY-FOUR SQUARES
STORAGE

Place in an airtight container or freezer bags and store at room temperature for up to five days or freeze up to three months.

The only sugar in this cookie is in the dried apricots. Each bar probably contains about six apricot halves.

2½ cups all-purpose flour, plus extra for dusting work surface
    and sprinkling
½ teaspoon salt
½ cup (1 stick) parve margarine, frozen for 15 minutes
½ cup solid vegetable shortening, frozen for 15 minutes
8 tablespoons cold water
1 pound dried apricots (2½ cups apricot halves)

---

1 Place the flour, salt, chilled margarine, and shortening into the bowl of a food processor fitted with a metal blade and pulse for 20 seconds, or until the mixture looks like sand. You can make the dough by hand by cutting the margarine and shortening into the dry ingredients. Add the cold water, 2 tablespoons at a time, and process or mix just until the mixture comes together.

2 Divide in half, wrap each piece in plastic, and flatten. Place in the freezer for 40 minutes, or overnight in the refrigerator.

3 About 20 minutes before you plan to roll out the dough, place the dried apricots in a bowl and cover with 2 cups boiling water. Let sit for 20 minutes. Drain the apricots and purée in a food processor or blender. Set aside.

4 Preheat the oven to 400°F. Cut out 2 pieces of parchment the size of a jelly roll pan. Set one piece of parchment on the counter, sprinkle it with some flour, and place

one of the dough halves on top. Sprinkle a little flour on the dough and then place the second piece of parchment on top. Roll on top of the parchment to roll the dough out to the size of the bottom parchment, rolling all the way to the edges. Peel back the top parchment a few times and sprinkle a little more flour on the dough.

5 Peel off the top parchment and slide the bottom parchment and dough onto the jelly roll pan. Use a silicone spatula to spread the apricot mixture onto the dough, leaving a ½-inch border of just dough on all sides. Repeat with the other half of dough, rolling it out to the size of the second parchment cut to the size of the jelly roll pan. Peel off the top parchment. Place your hand under the bottom piece of parchment and turn the dough over on top of the apricot mixture. Peel off the parchment and pinch all sides to seal tightly.

6 Bake for 35 minutes, or until the top dough starts to brown. Let cool. Trim off the sides (eat them) and then cut into 24 squares or 1½ x 3-inch bars.

Low-Sugar Apple Pear Pie

MAKES ONE 9-INCH PIE, 8 TO 12 SERVINGS
STORAGE
Store covered in plastic in the refrigerator for up to four days or freeze up to three months.

The ready-made pie shell has only 2 grams of sugar per serving.

———

1 frozen parve 9-inch pie shell

2 Granny Smith apples, peeled and cored

2 pears, peeled and cored

Juice of ½ lemon

2 teaspoons ground cinnamon, divided

¼ teaspoon ground nutmeg

¼ teaspoon ground ginger

1 tablespoon granulated sugar substitute

⅓ cup almond flour (see "Making almond flour," page xxviii)

2 tablespoons flour, divided

⅔ cup pecan halves

1 tablespoon parve margarine

1 Preheat the oven to 350°F. Place the pie shell on a cookie sheet. Cut the apples and pears into ¼- to ½-inch pieces and place in a large bowl. Add the lemon juice and toss gently. Add 1 teaspoon of the cinnamon, the nutmeg, ginger, sugar substitute, almond flour, and 1 tablespoon of the flour and toss to coat all the apple and pear pieces. Place in the pie shell.

2 Place the pecan halves in a freezer bag and crush with a rolling pin until the pieces are about ¼-inch long. Add the remaining teaspoon of cinnamon and remaining tablespoon of flour to the bag and shake to mix. Add the margarine and work with your fingers to mix together. Sprinkle clumps of the nut mixture on top of the apple and pear mixture. Bake for 45 minutes, or until the edges are brown and the apples are bubbly.

Peach-Blueberry Galette

SERVES 8

STORAGE

Store covered in plastic in the refrigerator for up to four days.

A galette is a free-form pie easily made by rolling out a circle of dough, adding filling, and folding the dough over the filling.

1¼ cups all-purpose flour, plus extra for sprinkling

¼ teaspoon salt

6 tablespoons parve margarine, frozen for 30 minutes and
    cut into 6 pieces

1 large egg, separated

3 tablespoons ice water

1 cup fresh blueberries

2 cups fresh peach slices, about 2 to 3 peaches peeled and cut
    into ½-inch slices

¼ teaspoon ground cinnamon

2 teaspoons cornstarch

1 tablespoon granulated sugar substitute

1 To make the dough: Place the flour, salt, and margarine into the bowl of a food processor fitted with a metal blade. Pulse 10 times or cut the margarine into the flour and salt by hand with two knives or a pastry cutter. Add the egg yolk (reserve the white) and 1 tablespoon of the ice water. Pulse 5 times or mix gently by hand. Add another tablespoon of the ice water and pulse another 5 times or mix again. Add the last tablespoon of water, a little at a time, pulsing or lightly mixing the dough for 10 to 15 seconds until it looks like clumps of couscous; the dough does not have to come completely together. Gather the dough into a ball.

2 Take a large piece of plastic and sprinkle some flour on it. Place the dough on top and wrap and flatten. Place in the freezer for 20 minutes.

3 Meanwhile, preheat the oven to 425°F. Place a rack on the lowest shelf of the oven. Place another rack in the middle of the oven.

4 Take a large piece of parchment and sprinkle with some flour. Place the dough on top, sprinkle with more flour, and place a second piece of parchment on top of the dough. Roll on top of the parchment to roll out the dough until it is about 12 to 13 inches in diameter, trying your best to keep the shape round. Peel back the top parchment and sprinkle a little more flour once or twice while you are rolling.

5 Place the fruit in a medium bowl. In a separate small bowl, mix together the cinnamon and cornstarch. Sprinkle on top of the fruit and mix gently until the cornstarch disappears.

6 Place the fruit in the center of the dough and spread a little, leaving a 2- to 3-inch border on the outside. Take one small section of the dough border, about 2 inches, and fold it over the fruit, leaving the fruit-filled center open. Pick up another 2-inch section of the border and repeat, pressing one section into the next to seal it, so you end up with dough pleats.

7 Beat the reserved egg white and brush all over the dough. Sprinkle the dough and fruit with the sugar substitute. Bake for 30 minutes. Move to the middle rack of the oven and bake another 10 minutes. Let cool for 20 minutes.

Low-Sugar Pear Strudel

MAKES 4 ROLLS, 20 SERVINGS

STORAGE

Store in the refrigerator for up to three days.

The only sugar in this recipe is the small amount in the challah bread crumbs.

———

Juice of 1 lemon

7 pears

1 tablespoon granulated sugar substitute

2 teaspoons ground cinnamon

⅓ cup challah bread crumbs (see tip, page 222), plain bread crumbs, or ground almonds

1 package filo dough, thawed according to package directions

½ cup (1 stick) parve margarine, melted

⅓ cup chopped nuts (optional)

———

1 Preheat the oven to 350°F. Line a large cookie sheet or jelly roll pan with parchment.

2 Place the lemon juice in a bowl. Peel and core the pears, chop into 1-inch pieces and add to lemon juice. Add the sugar substitute, cinnamon, and bread crumbs and toss lightly.

3 To make the strudel: Have ready a clean, damp (not dripping) kitchen towel. Cover the counter with a piece of parchment the size of your baking pan. Take the filo out of its package and unroll. Separate one sheet and place it on top of the parchment. Use a pastry brush to brush the filo sheet with the margarine. Place a second sheet on top and brush with more margarine. Repeat with two more sheets. Cover the remaining filo with the damp towel.

4 Place one-quarter of the pear filling along one long end of the filo, 2 inches from the edge. Fold the right and left sides (the short sides) in 1 inch. Starting from the side with the filling, roll up tightly until you have a long log. Place on the baking sheet. Repeat with additional filo and the rest of the filling to make three more logs.

5 Place the logs on the prepared baking sheet and bake for 40 minutes, or until lightly browned. The strudel is best served warm. You can refrigerate overnight and warm in a low oven for 15 to 30 minutes.

Cinnamon Pecan Babka

MAKES 1 LOAF, 12 SERVINGS

STORAGE

Store wrapped in foil at room temperature. If you will not eat it within
24 hours, freeze it for up to three months. Thaw at room temperature for
4 hours before serving.

As my chocolate babka is my most popular dessert, I felt that it was only fair to develop a sugar-free version.

DOUGH

¼ cup warm water

¼ ounce (1 envelope) active dry yeast

¼ cup granulated sugar substitute

2½ cups all-purpose flour

½ cup (1 stick) parve margarine, at room temperature

1 large egg plus 1 white (reserve yolk in a covered bowl in
   the refrigerator for glazing)

———————

Spray oil, for greasing pan

FILLING

1 cup granulated sugar substitute

1 cup (2 sticks) parve margarine, at room temperature

2 tablespoons ground cinnamon, divided

6 tablespoons chopped pecans, divided

½ cup raisins, chopped into small pieces, divided

———————

1 tablespoon water

———————

1 To make the dough: Place the warm water and yeast in a large bowl and let sit 5 minutes. Add the sugar substitute, flour, margarine, egg, and egg white. Combine using a dough hook in a stand mixer or mix by hand until the dough is smooth. Cover the bowl with plastic and let rise 2 to 4 hours, until the dough has increased in size.

2 Preheat the oven to 375°F. Grease a 12-inch loaf pan with spray oil.

3 To make the filling: In a bowl, beat together the sugar substitute, margarine, and 5 teaspoons of the cinnamon by hand or with a hand-held or stand electric mixer on medium-high speed.

4 Divide the dough into 2 pieces. Roll each piece into a 10 x 7-inch rectangle. Spread half of the filling on one piece of dough and sprinkle with 3 tablespoons of the chopped pecans and ¼ cup of the raisins. Starting with a long side, roll the dough up to create a long roll. Set aside and repeat with the other half of the dough.

5 When you have two rolls, twist them together, keeping the seams on the bottom. Tuck the ends under and place in the prepared loaf plan.

6 To the reserved egg yolk, add the tablespoon of water and the remaining 1 teaspoon of cinnamon and mix. Brush the egg white on top of the loaf. Bake for 45 minutes, or until browned. Cool for 10 minutes and then run a knife around the sides and remove from pan.

Profiteroles with Compote

MAKES 16 PROFITEROLES, 8 SERVINGS

STORAGE

Store the compote covered in the refrigerator for up to four days and store the puffs in an airtight container at room temperature or freeze up to three months.

You can make the compote with any fruit you like. The total amount of cut fruit should equal 5 cups. You can also fill the puffs with sugar-free sorbet.

CHOUX PASTRY

¼ cup parve plain soy milk

¼ cup water

4 tablespoons parve margarine, cut into small pieces

Dash of salt

½ cup all-purpose flour, sifted after measuring

3 large eggs, divided

      4 plums, cut into ½-inch slices

      2 apricots, cut into ½-inch slices

      2 apples, peeled and cut into ½-inch cubes

      ¼ teaspoon ground cinnamon

      1 teaspoon sugar-free vanilla syrup

1. Preheat the oven to 475°F. Line a cookie sheet with parchment.

2. Bring the soy milk, water, margarine, and salt to a boil in a small saucepan over medium-low heat. Remove from the heat and, with a wooden spoon, mix in the sifted flour. Place the saucepan back over low heat and cook 1 minute more, stirring constantly to dry out the dough. Remove from the heat.

3. Place the dough in a bowl and add 2 of the eggs, one at a time, mixing thoroughly after the addition of each egg. You will need to mix vigorously to completely incorporate the egg into the dough.

4. Place the dough in a pastry bag with a ½-inch round tip and pipe out circles of dough, about 2 inches in diameter, onto the parchment-lined cookie sheet, leaving an inch between each one. It's easiest to hold the pastry bag vertically, tip down, squeezing slowly until you have the size you want, then lifting up the tip.

5. Beat the remaining egg in a small bowl and brush the top of each circle to smooth out the little tip on the top.

6. Place the cookie sheet in the oven and immediately turn off the oven. After 15 minutes, turn the oven on again to 350°F. Bake the pastries another 30 to 40 minutes, or until the cracks on the top are the same color as the rest of the pastry. Remove to rack and let cool. Store in an airtight container if not using immediately.

7. To make the compote: Place the cut plums, apricots, and apples in a medium saucepan over medium heat. When the fruit starts to sizzle, add the cinnamon and vanilla syrup and stir. Turn the heat to low and cook uncovered for 5 minutes, stirring once or twice. The fruit should not have fallen apart; you want to see some large fruit pieces. Let cool.

8. To serve, use your fingers to partially open up a puff from the side, taking care not to lift off the top. Scoop up about ¼ cup of the compote and place into the open puff. Repeat with rest of the puffs and compote. Serve 2 per person.

Low-Sugar Chocolate Mousse

SERVES 6 TO 8

STORAGE

Store covered in plastic in the refrigerator for up to three days.

I served this at a party for my neighbors after one of the photo shoots we did for the book, and I forgot to tell anyone that the mousse was sugar free. They didn't even notice. The parve whipping cream has a very small amount of sugar in it.

————

6 ounces parve sugar-free bittersweet chocolate, chopped or broken into 1-inch pieces

4 large egg yolks

1½ cups parve whipping cream

1　Melt the chocolate either on the stovetop or in the microwave, following the "Melting chocolate" instructions (see Foolproof Tips and Techniques).

2　When the chocolate is melted, whisk in the egg yolks, beating vigorously. The mixture will be thick and seem pasty.

3　In a bowl, whip the cream with an electric mixer on high speed. Watch carefully and stop mixing when you see the top of the whipped cream form ribbons or swirls. Add one-third of the whipped cream to the chocolate and whisk until well blended. Slowly mix another third of the whipped cream into the chocolate mixture. Add the rest of the whipped cream and mix well.

4　Spoon the chocolate mixture into a serving bowl or into 6 to 8 individual glasses or cups. Smooth the top with the back of a spoon. Cover with plastic and chill 8 hours or overnight.

Appendix
Sauces and Frostings

This section allows you to be more creative with your desserts. You can serve any simple cake with a fruit sauce. I have also served different-color fruit sauces along with a simple fruit salad—the sauces can serve as "dressing" for the fruit. You can pour the fruit, caramel, or chocolate sauces over parve ice cream or any of the mousses in the book. And there are several options for icings and frostings that you can mix and match with different cakes or cupcakes.

Mango Sauce
STORAGE

Store fruit sauces covered in the refrigerator for up to four days.

2 cups mango cubes
¼ to ½ cup hot water (depends on
    ripeness of fruit—softer fruit needs
    less water)
1 teaspoon confectioners' sugar, or more
    to taste

Place the mango cubes, hot water, and confectioners' sugar in a blender or food processor and process until completely puréed. Add more water as necessary to get a smooth consistency.

Strawberry, Raspberry, or Blackberry Sauce

2 cups halved strawberries, whole raspberries, or whole blackberries
¼ cup hot water
1 teaspoon confectioners' sugar, or more to taste

Place the fruit, hot water, and confectioners' sugar in a blender or food processor and process until completely puréed. Strain if desired.

Kiwi Sauce

4 kiwis, peeled and cut into quarters
1 tablespoon hot water (or more if needed to make a pourable sauce)
2 teaspoons confectioners' sugar

Place the kiwi pieces, hot water, and confectioners' sugar in a blender or food processor and process until completely puréed.

Basic Sugar Syrup

½ cup water
⅔ cup sugar

Place the water and sugar in a small saucepan over medium-high heat. Bring to a rolling boil, stirring to dissolve the sugar, and then remove from the heat. Store at room temperature for five days.

FLAVORED SUGAR SYRUP

Add 1 tablespoon of any flavor extract or liqueur to the recipe for Basic Sugar Syrup to create a flavored syrup.

Shiny Chocolate Sauce

1 cup water

1⅓ cups sugar

6 ounces parve semisweet or bittersweet chocolate, chopped or broken
    into 1-inch pieces

1 To make this sauce, you will first make a simple sugar syrup. Place the water and
   sugar in a small heavy saucepan over medium heat. Stir to dissolve the sugar and
   bring to a rolling boil. Remove from the heat. This can be made 2 to 3 days in
   advance and stored at room temperature.

2 Melt the chocolate either on the stovetop or in the microwave, following the
   "Melting chocolate" instructions (see Foolproof Tips and Techniques). Whisk
   until smooth. Add the sugar syrup a tablespoon at a time and whisk until you get
   a consistency you can drizzle. If the sauce starts to harden, just add a little more
   sugar syrup and whisk until you get a thick, pourable consistency. Store covered
   at room temperature and reheat in a microwave and whisk until smooth.

Caramel Sauce

1 cup sugar

1 cup boiling water

Place the sugar in a heavy-bottomed saucepan over medium heat and cook,
stirring often, until all of the sugar has melted and you have a deep amber-colored
syrup. Remove from the heat and carefully add the boiling water. The mixture
will boil up and you will see some balls of caramel in the pot. Return the pan to
medium heat and cook at a rolling boil for 10 minutes. Stir often until all of the
caramel pieces have melted and you have a smooth syrup. Let cool, cover with
plastic, and store at room temperature. This can be made 3 days in advance.

Cinnamon Crème Anglaise Sauce

1½ cups parve plain soy milk

¼ cup parve whipping cream

1 vanilla bean, split lengthwise and scraped (reserve seeds)

4 large egg yolks

½ cup sugar

½ teaspoon ground cinnamon

1 In a small saucepan, bring the soy milk, whipping cream, vanilla bean and scraped seeds to a boil.

2 Meanwhile, in a large bowl, whisk together the egg yolks, sugar, and cinnamon. When the soy milk and cream boil, strain some of the liquid into the bowl with the egg mixture and whisk well. Strain the rest of the soy milk and cream into the egg mixture and whisk well. Discard the vanilla bean. Pour back into the pan and cook on low heat, stirring constantly, for 2 minutes, or until the sauce starts to thicken slightly. Serve warm or cold. Store in the refrigerator for up to four days.

VANILLA CRÈME ANGLAISE SAUCE

To make a vanilla crème anglaise, simply omit the cinnamon.

Quick Buttercream Icing

½ cup solid vegetable shortening

½ cup (1 stick) parve margarine

1 teaspoon pure vanilla extract

1 pound confectioners' sugar, sifted

2 tablespoons parve plain soy milk

Food coloring of your choice (optional)

In a bowl, with a hand-held or stand electric mixer on medium-high speed, beat the shortening and margarine until creamy. Add the vanilla and beat again. Add the confectioners' sugar to the bowl in three parts, mixing well after each addition. Scrape the bowl down after each addition of sugar. When I use a stand mixer, I usually cover the top of the bowl with plastic wrap so the sugar does not fly out of the bowl. Add the soy milk and beat on medium speed for 2 minutes. You can now add food coloring to the icing, if desired. Store in the refrigerator covered with plastic wrap for up to five days. Before using, let the icing soften at room temperature or microwave for 4 seconds so it can be spread.

Traditional Buttercream Icing (Vanilla, Almond, or Coffee)

1½ cups sugar

¼ cup water

3 large eggs

2½ sticks (1¼ cups) parve margarine, at room temperature
   (set out for at least 1 hour)

For vanilla-flavored icing: 1 tablespoon pure vanilla extract

For almond-flavored icing: 4 teaspoons almond extract

For coffee-flavored icing: 1 tablespoon coffee extract or dissolve
   1 tablespoon coffee granules into 2 tablespoons boiling water

1 Place the sugar and water in a small heavy saucepan over high heat, stirring to dissolve the sugar. Meanwhile, place the eggs in the bowl of a stand mixer fitted with the wire whisk. If using a hand-held mixer, place the eggs into a medium bowl. Insert a candy thermometer into the saucepan. Dip a pastry brush in cold water and brush the sides of the saucepan to dissolve any sugar crystals that form above the sugar mixture. Watch the thermometer closely. When it reaches 230°F, turn the stand mixer on to medium speed to beat the eggs. When the thermometer goes up another 5 degrees to 235°F, turn off the heat and bring the saucepan over to the mixer. If using a hand-held mixer, when the sugar reaches 230°F, beat the eggs for 1 minute, turn off the mixer, and then bring the sugar over to your bowl when it reaches 235°F and pour in as explained below.

2 Turn the speed of the mixer down to low and then slowly pour the cooked sugar into the bowl, down the side of the bowl, not directly onto the wire whisk. When all of the syrup has been poured in, turn the mixer up to high speed and beat for a full 10 minutes, or until the bowl is completely cool to the touch. The mixture will start out very yellow, but over time will turn a light yellow to beige color. Do not rush the mixing; it is very important to make sure the mixture is completely cool before adding the margarine to the cream.

3 Turn the speed to low and use a dull knife or spoon to add the very soft margarine in clumps into the bowl. When all the margarine has been added, turn up the mixer speed to medium-high and beat for 2 minutes more, or until the mixture is

light and creamy. Add the desired flavoring and beat on high speed for 20 seconds. Place the cream in the refrigerator until you're ready to use it. This can be made up to 3 days in advance.

Vanilla Cream Cheese Frosting

8 ounces parve cream cheese
4 tablespoons parve margarine
1 teaspoon pure vanilla extract
4 cups confectioners' sugar
1 tablespoon parve plain soy milk

Place the cream cheese and margarine in a bowl and beat with a hand-held or stand electric mixer on medium-high speed, or by hand with a whisk, until creamy. Add the vanilla and mix again. Add the confectioners' sugar, 1 cup at a time, and mix in with the mixer at medium speed or with a whisk. When the sugar is all mixed in, add the soy milk and beat or whisk for 1 minute. Store covered in the refrigerator for up to 5 days.

Cinnamon Honey Cream Cheese Frosting

12 ounces parve cream cheese
1½ teaspoons pure vanilla extract
2¼ teaspoons ground cinnamon
3 tablespoons honey
7 cups confectioners' sugar
1½ tablespoons parve plain soy milk

Place the cream cheese, vanilla, cinnamon, and honey in a large bowl and beat with a hand-held or stand electric mixer at high speed or by hand with a whisk to combine. Add the confectioners' sugar in three parts, mixing in each addition completely on medium speed or vigorously with a whisk before adding the next one. When using a stand mixer, I wrap plastic wrap all around the top of the mixer and around the bowl after the second and third additions of sugar so that my hair and all kitchen surfaces are not covered in white. Add the soy milk and beat for 30 seconds until the frosting looks creamy. Store covered in the refrigerator for up to 5 days.

Seven-Minute Frosting

1½ cups sugar

⅓ cup warm water

3 large egg whites, at room temperature

1 tablespoon light corn syrup

Dash of salt

1 teaspoon pure vanilla extract

Pour a few inches of water into the bottom of a double boiler or a medium saucepan and bring to a boil, then reduce the heat to medium. Off heat, place the sugar and ⅓ cup warm water in the top of the double boiler or in a metal or other heatproof bowl that can sit on top of the saucepan without falling in. Whisk to dissolve the sugar. Add the egg whites, corn syrup, and salt and beat for 1 minute with an electric mixer on medium-high speed. Place over the gently boiling water and beat with an electric mixer on high speed for a full 7 minutes. If the water starts to bubble too much, turn the heat down. Remove from heat, add vanilla and beat until the frosting is thick and has soft peaks, another 30 seconds.

Poured Fondant Icing

6 cups confectioners' sugar

½ cup water

2 tablespoons light corn syrup

1 teaspoon almond extract

Food coloring of your choice

Place the confectioners' sugar, water, and corn syrup in a saucepan. Cook over low heat, whisking constantly, until the sugar has melted and the mixture is smooth, about 4 minutes. Remove from heat and whisk in the almond extract. Whisk in the food coloring, 1 drop at a time, until the desired color is achieved.

Resources

The following are some online and retail sources for finding kosher ingredients and baking equipment.

Kosher.com
www.kosher.com
General kosher baking ingredients

My Kosher Market
www.mykoshermarket.com
Alprose parve chocolate and other
   baking ingredients

The Peppermill
www.thepeppermillinc.com
Baking ingredients and baking
   equipment

King Arthur Flour Company
www.kingarthurflour.com
Flour, baking equipment, and baking
   ingredients

Sur La Table
www.surlatable.com
General and specialty baking
   ingredients

Bridge Kitchenware
www.bridgekitchenware.com
Baking equipment

Wilton
www.wilton.com
Baking pans, cake decorating supplies,
   pastry bags, and icing colors

Beryl's Cake Decorating and
   Pastry Supplies
www.beryls.com
Baking pans, specialty cake decorating
   supplies, and cardboard circles

Pastry Chef Central
www.pastrychef.com
Baking equipment, pastry tools, and
   some kosher ingredients

Metric Conversions

American bakers use standard containers for measurements: glass or plastic measuring cups with spouts for liquids, scooping cups that can be leveled for dry ingredients. The American method makes it difficult to provide equivalents for those using metric measurements. The chart below has the best approximations of the liquid and dry measures converted into volume and weight measurements. You can go on-line and find websites that will do the conversions for you as well as sites that have more precise charts for individual baking items.

LIQUID MEASUREMENTS

Fluid ounces	U.S.	Milliliters
	1 teaspoon	5
¼	2 teaspoons	10
½	1 tablespoon	14
1	2 tablespoons	28
2	¼ cup	56
4	½ cup	110
6	¾ cup	170
8	1 cup	225
10	1¼ cups	280
12	1½ cups	340
16	2 cups	450
18	2¼ cups	500 (½ liter)
20	2½ cups	560
24	3 cups	675
28	3½ cups	750
30	3¾ cups	840
32	4 cups (1 quart)	900
36	4½ cups	1,000 (1 liter)
40	5 cups	1,120

SOLID MEASURES

Ounces	Pounds	Grams	Kilos
1		28	
2		56	
3½		100	
4	¼	112	
5		140	
6		168	
8	½	225	
9		250	¼
12	¾	340	
16	1	450	
18		500	½
20	1¼	560	
24	1½	675	
27		750	¾
28	1¾	780	
32	2	900	
36	2¼	1,000	1
40	2½	1,100	
48	3	1,350	
54		1,500	1½

OVEN TEMPERATURE EQUIVALENTS

Fahrenheit	Celsius
250	130
275	140
300	150
325	170
350	180
375	190
400	200
425	220
450	230
475	240
500	250

Index